Communications in Computer and Information Science   1668

More information about this series at https://link.springer.com/bookseries/7899

Giuseppe Agapito · Anna Bernasconi ·
Cinzia Cappiello · Hasan Ali Khattak ·
InYoung Ko · Giuseppe Loseto · Michael Mrissa ·
Luca Nanni · Pietro Pinoli · Azzurra Ragone ·
Michele Ruta · Floriano Scioscia ·
Abhishek Srivastava (Eds.)

Current Trends in Web Engineering

ICWE 2022 International Workshops,
BECS, SWEET and WALS, Bari, Italy, July 5–8, 2022
Revised Selected Papers

 Springer

Editors
Giuseppe Agapito ⓘ
Magna Graecia University
Catanzaro, Italy

Anna Bernasconi ⓘ
Politecnico di Milano
Milano, Italy

Cinzia Cappiello ⓘ
Politecnico di Milano
Milano, Italy

Hasan Ali Khattak ⓘ
National University of Sciences
and Technology
Islamabad, Pakistan

InYoung Ko ⓘ
Korea Institute of Science and Technology
Daejeon, Korea (Republic of)

Giuseppe Loseto ⓘ
LUM University
Casamassima, Italy

Michael Mrissa ⓘ
University of Primorska
koper, Slovenia

Luca Nanni ⓘ
University of Lausanne
Lausanne, Switzerland

Pietro Pinoli ⓘ
Politecnico di Milano
Milano, Italy

Azzurra Ragone ⓘ
University of Bari Aldo Moro
Bari, Italy

Michele Ruta ⓘ
Polytechnic University of Bari
Bari, Italy

Floriano Scioscia ⓘ
Polytechnic University of Bari
Bari, Italy

Abhishek Srivastava ⓘ
Indian Institute of Technology Indore
Indore, India

ISSN 1865-0929　　　　　　ISSN 1865-0937 (electronic)
Communications in Computer and Information Science
ISBN 978-3-031-25379-9　　　ISBN 978-3-031-25380-5 (eBook)
https://doi.org/10.1007/978-3-031-25380-5

This Springer imprint is published by the registered company Springer Nature Switzerland AG
The registered company address is: Gewerbestrasse 11, 6330 Cham, Switzerland

Preface

This volume collects the papers presented at the workshops co-located with the 22nd International Conference on Web Engineering (ICWE 2022), held on July 5 in Bari, Italy. The objective of the conference is to bring together researchers and practitioners from various disciplines in academia and industry to address and discuss the emerging challenges in the engineering of Web applications and associated technologies, as well as to assess the impact of these technologies on society, media, and culture.

As in previous years, the main conference program was complemented by a number of co-located workshops that provided a forum for participants to discuss novel and cutting-edge topics, both within the Web engineering community and at the crossroads with other communities. We accepted the following three workshops, whose papers are included in this volume after they underwent a rigorous peer-review process and were presented during the workshops on July 5, 2022:

- Second International Workshop on Big Data driven Edge Cloud Services (BECS 2022)
- First International Workshop on the Semantic WEb of Everything (SWEET 2022)
- First International Workshop on Web Applications for Life Sciences (WALS 2022)

The BECS workshop aims to provide a venue to discuss ongoing work on providing value-added Web services for users by utilizing big data in edge cloud environments. This year's workshop included five papers and two keynotes for which we report the abstract.

The SWEET workshop focused on the diffusion of AI techniques and technologies in the Web of Things with particular attention to innovative models, architectures, algorithms and applications. Seven papers were presented.

The WALS workshop provided an open discussion space, starting from the three accepted papers related to new approaches to support search, knowledge extraction, and data science on the Web, thereby achieving significant results for healthcare, precision medicine, biology, genomics, and virology.

We would like to thank everyone who contributed to ICWE 2022 Workshops. First, wethanktheworkshoporganizersfortheirexcellentworkinidentifyingcutting-edgeand cross-disciplinary topics in the rapidly moving field of Web engineering and organizing inspiring workshops around them. Secondly, we thank the conference organizers and hosts.

In each workshop, the papers were selected using a single blind review process and were reviewed by at least three members of the Technical Program Committee.

A word of thanks goes to the reviewers who provided thorough evaluations of the papers and contributed to the promotion of the workshops. Last but not least, we thank all the authors who submitted and presented papers at the workshops for having shared their work with the community and contributing to the success of these events.

July 2022   Cinzia Cappiello
                                                                                                  Azzurra Ragone

Organization

ICWE 2022 Workshop Co-chairs

Cinzia Cappiello   Politecnico di Milano, Italy
Azzurra Ragone   University of Bari "Aldo Moro", Italy

BECS 2022 Workshop Co-chairs

In-Young Ko   Korea Institute of Science and Technology, Korea
               (Republic of)
Abhishek Srivastava   Indian Institute of Technology Indore, India
Michael Mrissa   InnoRenew CoE and University of Primorska,
               Slovenia

SWEET 2022 Workshop Co-chairs

Giuseppe Loseto   LUM University, Italy
Hasan Ali Khatthak   National University of Sciences and Technology,
               Islamabad, Pakistan
Michele Ruta   Polytechnic University of Bari, Italy
Floriano Scioscia   Polytechnic University of Bari, Italy

WALS 2022 Workshop Co-chairs

Anna Bernasconi   Politecnico di Milano, Italy
Giuseppe Agapito   "Magna Graecia" University, Italy
Luca Nanni   University of Lausanne, Switzerland
Pietro Pinoli   Politecnico di Milano, Italy

Technical Program Committee

Doo-Hwan Bae   Korea Advanced Institute of Science and
               Technology, South Korea
Jongmoon Baik   Korea Advanced Institute of Science and
               Technology, South Korea
Ben Njima Cheyma   MARS Lab, Tunisia
Eunkyoung Jee   Korea Advanced Institute of Science and
               Technology, South Korea

Minsoo Kim	Korea Advanced Institute of Science and Technology, South Korea
Jemin Lee	Sungkyunkwan University, South Korea
Faïza Loukil	Université Polytechnique Hauts-de-France, France
Martin Musicante	UFRN, Brazil
Jongse Park	Korea Advanced Institute of Science and Technology, South Korea
Placido Souza Neto	IFRN, Brazil
Prabhat K. Upadhyay	Indian Institute of Technology Indore, India
Seongwook Youn	Korea National University of Transportation, South Korea
Giuseppe Anastasi	University of Pisa, Italy
Fernando Bobillo	University of Zaragoza, Spain
Antonio Caruso	University of Salento, Italy
Luca De Cicco	Polytechnic University of Bari, Italy
Daniela De Venuto	Polytechnic University of Bari, Italy
Pasquale Del Vecchio	LUM University "Giuseppe Degennaro", Italy
Eugenio Di Sciascio	Polytechnic University of Bari, Italy
Francesco M. Donini	University of Tuscia, Italy
Giancarlo Fortino	University of Calabria, Italy
Nicola Magaletti	LUM Enterprise, Italy
Agostino Marcello Mangini	Polytechnic University of Bari, Italy
Andrea Omicini	University of Bologna, Italy
Evan Patton	Massachusetts Institute of Technology, USA
Giovanni Schiuma	LUM University "Giuseppe Degennaro", Italy
Giustina Secundo	LUM University "Giuseppe Degennaro", Italy
Oshani Seneviratne	Rensselaer Polytechnic Institute, USA
Quan Z. Sheng	Macquarie University, Australia
William Van Woensel	Dalhousie University, Canada
Felice Vitulano	Exprivia S.p.A., Italy
Sherali Zeadally	University of Kentucky, USA
Arif Canakoglu	Policlinico di Milano Ospedale Maggiore - Fondazione IRCCS Ca' Granda, Italy
Mario Cannataro	"Magna Graecia" University of Catanzaro, Italy
Stefano Ceri	Polytechnic University of Milan, Italy
Carlo D'Eramo	Technical University of Darmstadt, Germany
Jose Luis Garrido	University of Granada, Spain
Giancarlo Guizzardi	University of Twente, Netherlands
Ana Léon Palacio	Universitat Politècnica de València, Spain
Sergio Lifschitz	Pontifical Catholic University of Rio de Janeiro, Brazil

Oscar Pastor	Universitat Politècnica de València, Spain
Rosario Michael Piro	Polytechnic University of Milan, Italy
José Fabián Reyes Román	Universitat Politècnica de València, Spain
Pasquale Stano	University of Salento, Italy
Emanuel Weitschek	UniNettuno University, Italy

Contents

Second International Workshop on Big Data Driven Edge Cloud Services (BECS 2022)

Reliable and Data-driven AI Applications in Edge-Cloud Environments

In-Young Ko[1] , Michael Mrissa[2] , and Abhishek Srivastava[3]

[1] School of Computing, Korea Advanced Institute of Science
and Technology, Korea
iko@kaist.ac.kr

[2] InnoRenew CoE, and Faculty of Mathematics, Natural Sciences and Information Technologies, University of Primorska, Slovenia
michael.mrissa@innorenew.eu

[3] Department of Computer Science and Engineering, Indian Institute of Technology Indore, India
asrivastava@iiti.ac.in

Abstract. To maximize the benefit of using edge-cloud environments, it is necessary to define new Web engineering paradigms and practices to make data-driven edge-cloud AI applications more efficient and reliable. The second international workshop on Big data-driven Edge Cloud Services (BECS 2022) was held to provide a venue in which scholars and practitioners can share their experiences and present ongoing work on providing reliable and efficient Web services for users by utilizing big data in edge cloud environments.

Keywords: Edge cloud · Big data · Machine learning · AI applications

1 Introduction

Distributed clouds called edge clouds are becoming a new computing infrastructure for improving the efficiency, scalability, and privacy of providing data-driven AI services. An *edge cloud* is a localized cloud computing environment in which the Web of Things (WoT) devices can be connected and utilized locally via low-latency and reliable communication technologies such as 5G. To maximize the benefit of using these edge-cloud environments, it is necessary to define new Web engineering paradigms and practices to make data-driven edge-cloud AI applications more efficient and reliable.

The second international workshop on Big data-driven Edge Cloud Services (BECS 2022) was held to provide a venue in which scholars and practitioners can share their experiences and present ongoing work on providing reliable and efficient Web services for users by utilizing big data in edge cloud environments. The workshop was held in conjunction with the 22nd International Conference on Web Engineering (ICWE 2022), which was held in Bari, Italy on July 5–8, 2022.

The second edition of the BECS workshop was especially focused on the following topics: Web services in edge clouds; Web of Things in edge clouds; AI in edge computing (Edge AI); dependable and highly usable big data platforms; distributed data collection, analysis, and prediction; stream data processing in edge clouds; big knowledge graphs for distributed edge cloud environments; modeling and mashup of edge cloud services; micro-service architecture for edge cloud environments; and edge-cloud interaction and collaboration.

2   Keynotes

The BECS 2022 workshop started with two keynote talks.

The first keynote talk titled Autonomic Edge Computing for Air Quality Monitoring was given by Prof. Michael Mrissa from InnoRenew CoE, and the University of Primorska, Slovenia. In his talk, Prof. Mrissa presented the J2-2504 project funded by the Slovenian Research Agency that features several contributions for decentralized indoor air quality monitoring. In this work, sensors contribute to implementing data analysis algorithms in a decentralized fashion, to avoid the problems that typical centralized architecture face due to the presence of a single point of failure. The solution developed in the project relies on blockchain to guarantee decentralized trust, distributed hash table for data storage, onion routing, and encryption to enable the decentralized execution of data analysis tasks and prevent monitoring attacks. Incremental solutions based on Hoeffding trees have been explored to realize the decentralized data mining tasks. Hoeffding trees have proven to asymptotically come very close to non-incremental learners. The constraint to comply with, for this category of solutions to be relevant, is that the data distribution is known.

The title of the second keynote talk is Fire management at the Melghat Tiger Reserve through Edge Computing, and Abhishek Srivastava at the Indian Institute of Technology Indore in India gave the talk. The talk was largely about the unique set of challenges that forest fire detection and management face in a warm country like India. With temperatures soaring to the late forties (in degrees Celsius), temperature and humidity sensors that are normally deployed for fire detection fall prey to false positives. This leads to large losses in terms of human and material resources to localize and control the fires. The approach taken by the research group of Prof. Srivastava at IIT Indore is to implement AI algorithms in a manner that they are accommodated and executable within the resource-constrained edge environments. The AI-enabled edge nodes are efficacious in minimizing false positives in fire detection and do so with minimum temporal latency and energy overhead. The talk also featured short discussions on an anomaly detection algorithm and a classification algorithm for resource-constrained environments that have successfully been implemented for fire detection.

3   Presentations

In the BECS 2022 workshop, five papers were selected for presentation. All five papers were selected as full papers.

The first paper, "CodeBERT Based Software Defect Prediction for Edge-Cloud Systems" written by Sunjae Kwon, Jong-In Jang, Sungu Lee, Duksan Ryu, and Jongmoon Baik, proposes a just-in-time software defect prediction model that can be applied to edge-cloud systems. They especially investigate the effectiveness of using the CodeBERT model for efficient allocation of limited resources for testing edge-cloud software systems.

The second paper, "A Novel Hybrid Approach for Localization in Wireless Sensor Networks" written by Uttkarsh Agrawal and Abhishek Srivastava, proposes a hybrid technique for node localization in large wireless sensor network deployments. The hybrid technique is developed by combining a machine-learning-based approach for localization with a multilateration approach.

The third paper, "An Empirical Analysis on Just-In-Time Defect Prediction Models for Self-driving Software Systems," is written by Jiwon Choi, Saranya Manikandan, Duksan Ryu, and Jongmoon Baik. In this paper, the authors present the results of an empirical study done for analyzing the effectiveness of applying just-in-time defect prediction models to AI-enabled self-driving systems. They found specific factors and features that affect the performance of the defect prediction models for self-driving systems.

The fourth paper, "Knowledge Sharing in Proactive WoT Multi-Environment Models" written by Rubén Rentero-Trejo, Jaime Galán-Jiménez, José García-Alonso, Javier Berrocal, and Juan Manuel Murillo Rodríguez, presents an approach to effectively sharing knowledge across different Internet of Things (IoT) environments. In this work, the authors focus on knowledge distillation and teacher-student relationships to transfer knowledge between IoT environments in a model agnostic fashion.

Finally, the paper written by Jungmo Kang and Myoungho Kim, Multivariate Time Series Anomaly Detection Based on Reconstructed Differences Using Graph Attention Networks, proposes a new multivariate time series anomaly detection method using series differences between adjacent timestamps. The proposed approach utilizes both graph attention networks and spatio-temporal connections to improve the accuracy and efficiency of detecting anomalies from time series data under restricted computing resources in edge computing environments.

Organization

Workshop Co-chairs

In-Young Ko   Korea Advanced Institute of Science and
                           Technology (KAIST), South Korea
Abhishek Srivastava   Indian Institute of Technology Indore, India
Michael Mrissa   InnoRenew CoE & University of Primorska,
                           Slovenia

Technical Program Committee

Doo-Hwan Bae   KAIST, South Korea
Jongmoon Baik   KAIST, South Korea
Ben Njima Cheyma   MARS Lab, Tunisia
Eunkyoung Jee   KAIST, South Korea
Minsoo Kim   KAIST, South Korea
Jemin Lee   Sungkyunkwan University, South Korea
Faïza Loukil   Université Polytechnique Hauts-de-France,
                           France
Martin Musicante   UFRN, Brazil
Jongse Park   KAIST, South Korea
Placido Souza Neto   IFRN, Brazil
Prabhat K. Upadhyay   Indian Institute of Technology Indore, India
Seongwook Youn   Korea National University of Transportation,
                           South Korea

Acknowledgment. We would like to thank all the program committee members and reviewers for their efforts in providing high-quality reviews and constructive comments. The BECS 2022 workshop was supported by the Ministry of Science and ICT (MSIT), Korea, under the Information Technology Research Center (ITRC) support program (IITP-2022-2020-0-01795) supervised by the Institute of Information & Communications Technology Planning Evaluation (IITP). We would like to thank their support. Last, but not least, we would like to thank the authors who submitted and presented their research work for the workshop and all the participants who contributed to making the workshop successful.

Keynote Abstracts

Autonomic Edge Computing for Air Quality Monitoring

Michael Mrissa[1,2]

[1] Faculty of Mathematics, Natural Sciences and Information Technologies
University of Primorska, 6000 Koper, Slovenia
[2] InnoRenew CoE, Livade 6, 6310 Izola, Slovenia
michael.mrissa@innorenew.eu

Abstract. Buildings are the main source of CO_2 emissions on the planet, thus making their monitoring and the optimization of their life cycle a major objective to mitigate climate change and improve our daily life. This keynote shows the potential for decentralized sensor networks to address this issue with a combination of technological solutions that can be integrated into a single framework to realize the vision of building communities that exchange information about their conditions and performance in order to optimize energy consumption, maintenance, and inform future building design.

Keywords: Blockchain · Privacy · Security · WSN

Summary

As shown in the latest reports from the International Energy Agency[1], buildings and their lifecycle are responsible for more than 35% of the global CO_2 emissions on the planet. As part of the effort to reduce CO_2 emissions, indoor air quality (IAQ) monitoring is crucial as it enables optimizing building performance and operation, while improving the well-being of building occupants. In the project J2-2504 entitled "œAutonomic edge computing for air quality monitoring", funded by the Slovenian Research agency, we are exploring the development of decentralized architectures to support IAQ monitoring. Our vision promotes communities of buildings equipped with wireless sensor networks that exchange information about IAQ and about the performance status of their elements to help optimize energy consumption, maintenance, and inform future building design.

Our approach aims at combining onion routing, blockchain and smart contracts to guarantee the decentralized execution of data mining tasks over the sets of nodes that monitor a building [1]. The actual data mining task is realized using Hoeffding trees, an incremental learning algorithm that delivers results asymptotically close to non-incremental learners when the distribution of the data is stable over time [2]. We are also developing optimization algorithms that allow us to optimize data exchange over

---

[1] https://www.iea.org/.

the sensor nodes, based on the identification of the most influential nodes in the network that are particularly interesting for data sharing and can be utilized as gateways to enable communication between buildings [3]. Our solution optimizes network usage, supports dynamic network configuration and data management, and enables distributed on-site data processing, low latency response to network changes, and independence from cloud providers. We are currently deploying our sensors to demonstrate our work with 4 pilots in Slovenia, France, Hungary, and Oregon (USA).

Acknowledgments. The authors gratefully acknowledge the European Commission for funding the InnoRenew project (Grant Agreement #739574) under the Horizon2020 Widespread-Teaming program, the Republic of Slovenia (Investment funding of the Republic of Slovenia and the European Regional Development Fund) and the Slovenian Research Agency ARRS for funding the project J2-2504.

References

1. Mrissa, M., et al.: Privacy-aware and secure decentralized air quality monitoring. Appl. Sci. **12**(4) (2022)
2. Hrovatin, N., Tošić, A., Mrissa, M., Kavšek, B.: Privacy-preserving data mining on blockchain-based wsns. Appl. Sci. **12**(11) (2022)
3. Hajdu, L., Baíazs Dávid, B., Krész, M.: Gateway placement and traffic load simulation in sensor networks. Pollack Periodica **16**(1), 102–108 (2021)

Fire Management at the Melghat Tiger Reserve Through Edge Computing

Abhishek Srivastava ⓘ

Department of Computer Science and Engineering, Indian Institute of
Technology Indore, India
asrivastava@iiti.ac.in

Abstract. The use of Wireless Sensor Networks for early detection of forest fires is impeded by false positives in regions of with hot climates. False positives can be eliminated through the use of learning algorithms deployed over the cloud. While this is effective, the overhead imposed due to frequent communication with the cloud is undesirable. In this work we explore the possibility of deployed simple machine learning algorithms on the edge to eliminate false positives at the WSN node itself.

Keywords. WSN · Anomaly detection · Classification

Summary

Forest fires are a scourge that has afflicted countries across the world. In addition to the immediate large-scale destruction of flora and displacement of fauna, forest fires contribute to pernicious developments like global warming, soil erosion, loss of biodiversity, and ozone layer depletion. Some of these factors, like global warming and ozone layer depletion [1], in their own way, contribute to more frequent and larger forest fires, thus feeding into a vicious cycle. India, for example, has seen a 158% increase in the number of reported forest fires in the six-year period between 2011 and 2017 [2], largely attributed to global warming and compromised biodiversity. There has been a decrease of roughly 80 million hectares of forest cover around the world between 1990 and 2020 [3] and 38–45% of this is owing to forest fires [4].

Early detection of forest fires is an effective means to minimize damage caused by them. Several approaches for fire detection are harnessed across the world but most of these are able to detect the fire only after it has taken on large proportions and is difficult to control. An approach that is finding traction is the use of Wireless Sensor Network (WSN) deployments for early fire detection. The use of WSN for early fire detection is most effective but for an important limitation of false positives in a hot country in India. It is not uncommon for temperatures in Indian summers to almost touch 50 degrees Celsius and sensors on WSN nodes are falsely triggered to indicate a fire. The approach discussed in this talk involves addressing this limitation of false positives through the implementation of AI algorithms in a manner that they are accommodated and executable within the resource-constrained edge environments of a WSN node. The AI-enabled edge nodes are efficacious in minimizing false positives in fire detection and do so with minimum temporal latency and energy overhead. The talk includes short discussions on an anomaly detection algorithm [5] and a classification algorithm [6] for resource-constrained environments that have successfully been implemented for fire detection.

Acknowledgements. The authors gratefully acknowledge the support provided by the DeFries-Bajpai Foundation, USA, through its scheme of grants for conserving Central India for supporting this work.

References

1. Bahuguna, V. K., and Upadhay, A. "Forest fires in India: policy initiatives for community participation." Int. Forest. Rev. **4**(2), 122–127 (2002)
2. Paliath, S. 2018. "Forest Fires Increased 158% In 6 Years, Warming A Factor: Experts." IndiaSpend. Available: {https://www.indiaspend.com/forest-fires-increased-158-in-6-years-warming-a-factor-experts-53125}
3. FAO and UNEP. 2020. The State of the World's Forests 2020. Forests, biodiversity and people. Rome. Available: {https://doi.org/10.4060/ca8642en}
4. van Wees, D., van Der Werf, G. R., Randerson, J. T., Andela, N., Chen, Y., and Morton, D. C. "The role of fire in global forest loss dynamics." Global Change Biology, **27**(11), 2377–2391, 2021.
5. Jain, P., Jain, S., Zaiane, O., Srivastava, A. "Anomaly Detection in Resource Constrained Environments with Streaming Data", In: IEEE Transactions on Emerging Topics in Computational Intelligence (2021)
6. Kumar, A., Wang, Z., Srivastava, A.: A Novel Approach for Classification in Resource Constrained Environments, ACM Transactions on Internet of Things (2022)

CodeBERT Based Software Defect Prediction for Edge-Cloud Systems

Sunjae Kwon[1], Jong-In Jang[1], Sungu Lee[1], Duksan Ryu[2],
and Jongmoon Baik[1(✉)]

[1] Korea Advanced Institute of Science and Technology, Daejeon, Republic of Korea
jbaik@kaist.ac.kr
[2] Jeonbuk National University, Jeonju, Republic of Korea

Abstract. Edge-cloud system is a crucial computing infrastructure for the innovations of modern society. In addition, the high interest in the edge-cloud system leads to various studies for testing to ensure the reliability of the system. However, like traditional software systems, the amount of resources for testing is always limited. Thus, we suggest CodeBERT Based Just-In-Time (JIT) Software Defect Prediction (SDP) model to address the limitation. This method helps practitioners prioritize the limited testing resources for the defect-prone functions in commits and improves the system's reliability. We generate GitHub Pull-Request (GHPR) datasets on two open-source framework projects for edge-cloud system in GitHub. After that, we evaluate the performance of the proposed model on the GHPR datasets in within-project environment and cross-project environment. To the best of our knowledge, it is the first attempt to apply SDP to edge-cloud systems, and as a result of the evaluation, we can confirm the applicability of JIT SDP in edge-cloud project. In addition, we expect the proposed method would be helpful for the effective allocation of limited resources when developing edge-cloud systems.

Keywords: Edge-cloud system · Just-in-time software defect prediction · CodeBERT

1 Introduction

Edge-cloud system is an important computing infrastructure for collecting and processing big data with low latency, which is essential for the innovations of modern society. As interest in the edge-cloud system increased, research on the testing edge-cloud system to ensure reliability also has been actively studied [10]. However, edge-cloud system has a complex structure and a massive volume of source code to work in geographically and conceptually distributed environments. So, the amount of resources that can be invested in the testing of edge-cloud systems is always limited. Thus, we suggest Software Defect Prediction (SDP) to address the limitation.

G. Agapito et al. (Eds.): ICWE 2022 Workshops, CCIS 1668, pp. 11–21, 2023.
https://doi.org/10.1007/978-3-031-25380-5_1

SDP is a technique that predicts defect-prone modules through intelligent predictive models to prioritize the limited resources to the defect-prone modules [21]. Though it has been one of the actively studied subjects in Software Engineering (SE), it has been mostly focused on legacy projects written in C and JAVA language [18]. In addition, to the best of our knowledge, there has never been a research to utilize SDP in edge-cloud projects. Thus, we focus on edge-cloud projects written in Go language, one of the most popular programming languages in the edge-cloud system.

We implement CodeBERT based Just-In-Time (JIT) SDP model. First, CodeBERT is a powerful deep learning bi-language model pre-trained on large number of pairs of Programming Language (PL) and Natural Language (NL) [12], so it is suitable for directly applying the projects written in Go language, which has not been studied in SDP literature. Second, JIT SDP is one type of SDP and predicts defect-prone commits based on historical commits data. It is suitable for CodeBERT, because each commit has a commit message in NL and source code in PL, and CodeBERT can generate an embedding vector having compressed the information of a commit. Using the embedding vector, CodeBERT can be fine-tuned for predicting defect-prone commits.

In summary, we suggest CodeBERT-based JIT SDP model for edge-cloud project written in Go language, and, to the best of our knowledge, it is the first attempt to apply SDP in edge-cloud system, also in projects written in Go language. To evaluate the performance of the model, we select two open-source framework projects for edge-cloud system in Go language, and generate GitHub Pull-Request (GHPR) datasets through a novel approach to collecting and labeling defect data from GitHub platform [23]. After that, we evaluate the performance of the model on the GHPR datasets in within-project and cross-project environments. Experiment results show that SDP can be applied effectively in edge-cloud project. In addition, we expect the proposed method would help deal with the resource limitation when testing edge-cloud systems.

2   Background and Related Work

2.1   Edge-Cloud System and Software Defect Prediction (SDP)

Smart factory, smart health care systems, and smart transportation systems, which are significant technical innovations of modern society achieved through edge-cloud computing, have shed light on studies about testing edge-cloud systems [10]. However, like traditional software systems, the amount of resources that can be invested in the testing of edge-cloud systems is limited. Thus, we suggest SDP as an alternative solution.

SDP is a technique that predicts defect-prone modules through intelligent predictive models to prioritize the limited resources to the defect-prone modules and finally improve the system's quality [21]. Moreover, SDP is highly suitable for edge-cloud systems' geographically and conceptually distributed environments because it can prevent defect-prone modules from spreading into the distributed environment by predicting them before deployment of the module.

SDP can be divided into two categories by the features it use: handcrafted features and automatically learned features [19]. The handcrafted features are defined and calculated by expert from source code or development process, and the automatically learned features are directly extracted by deep neural network (DNN) from the source code and other additional information. Due to advances in DNN, various SE fields including SDP actively apply automatically learned features, showing remarkable results over traditional handcrafted features [11, 15,19,24]. This study also utilizes automatically learned features extracted from CodeBERT, i.e., transformer-based DNN model pre-trained on a large corpus of source code.

2.2   Edge-Cloud System and Go Language

Go language is a relatively new language with its first release in 2012. With its recent development, Go language has lots of advantages over other PLs in edge-cloud systems. First, Go language is type-safe and providing memory safety [9]. This characteristic makes up for the possible vulnerability, which is especially important in edge-cloud systems, where geographically and conceptually distributed edges work in different environments. Also, the concurrent primitives of Go language allow us to add concurrency to programs easily. This makes Go language more expressive than other high performance PLs in edge-cloud systems [9], where continuous communication between edges and cloud happens.

Due to the advantages, the usefulness of Go language in the mobile-cloud-computing environments is raised [8,16]. In addition, Google, Meta, and Microsoft adopted Go language as the key language for some projects (e.g., Docker and kubernetes). Moreover, open-source framework projects for edge-cloud system on GitHub (e.g., EdgeX Foundry [3], KubeEdge [6], Baetyl [1], and Simpleiot [7]) also use Go language as the main language. Thus, we focus on edge-cloud projects written in Go language in this study.

2.3   CodeBERT and Just-In-Time (JIT) SDP

CodeBERT is a pre-trained model on the CodeSearch dataset [13] containing 2.1 million bi-model code-documentation pairs and 6.4 million uni-model code snippets written in six PLs including Go language. Like BERT, it is well-trained encoder that encodes pair of NL and PL into single vector containing their semantic meaning [12], so various SE fields, including SDP, utilize the single vector for their tasks [17,24]. Moreover, it is suitable for directly applying the projects written in Go language, which has not been studied in SDP literature, because CodeBERT has already been pre-trained on a large corpus of codes written in Go language.

JIT SDP model is an actively studied type of SDP and predicts defect-prone commits based on historical commits data. It is considered a practical version of SDP because it provides earlier feedback for developers while design decisions are still fresh in their minds [14]. Most of all, it is suitable for CodeBERT, because each commit, the prediction granularity of JIT SDP, has a commit message in

NL and source code in PL, and CodeBERT can generate an embedding vector having compressed the information of the commit. Using the embedding vector, we can fine-tune CodeBERT for predicting defect-prone commits. Thus, due to the promising performance of CodeBERT and the suitability of JIT SDP in CodeBERT, we propose CodeBERT-based JIT SDP model.

3   Approach

3.1   GHPR Crawler and GitHub Pull-Request (GHPR) Dataset

GHPR is a novel approach to automatically collecting and labeling defect data from GitHub platform through defect-related pull-request (PR), which is a message from a developer to repository maintainers to review of changes for solving a defect [23]. Most of all, it can solve the shortage of software defect data and class imbalance problems that most datasets for SDP studies have.

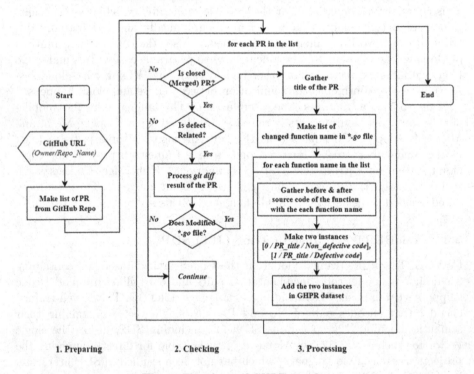

Fig. 1. Flowchart of GHPR crawler

We implement a python script for GHPR (i.e. GHPR crawler) based on *ghpr-tools* [4]. The *ghpr-tools* only gathers meta-information of PR, so we enhance it to collect pairs of defective and clean source code using RESTful GitHub API provided by the GitHub platform [5]. The flowchart of the GHPR crawler is shown in Fig. 1. The GHPR crawler consists of 3 stages and, as a result, generates a GHPR dataset which is composed of instance with a PR title in NL, a short description of the PR, and clean or defective source codes by function level. The details of each stage of the script for GHPR are as follows.

1) In the preparing stage, it requires the URL of the GitHub repository. Using the RESTful GitHub API with the repository URL, it makes a list of PRs enrolled in the repository.
2) In the checking stage, it checks if each PR has an association with defect and Go language. First, it checks if each PR is merged into the main branch; in other words, it checks if the PR is closed state. Second, it checks if the closed PR is related to a defect. To check this, we confirm that the PR is labeled with *bug* or the PR title has keywords (e.g., fix, solve, resolve). After that, it processes the *git diff* result of the PR and checks if the PR modifies *.go* files because we only focus on Go language.
3) In the processing stage, it gathers the title of the PR and makes a list of changed function names using the *git diff* result acquired at the checking stage. Then, it gathers each source code of function in the list before and after the change. After that, it makes two instances per changed function with a class label (i.e., 0 or 1), the PR title in NL, and defective or non-defective source code written in Go language. Finally, the two instances are added to the GHPR dataset.

The GHPR crawler generates GHPR dataset at the function level. Because the CodeBERT, which is the base model of our work, is trained on function-level data. In addition, it is possible to prevent the case where the code is cut by the maximum length of input tokens of CodeBERT. The detailed analysis of the GHPR dataset will be covered in the result of RQ2 (i.e., Sect. 4.4).

3.2 CodeBERT Based JIT SDP

We implement JIT SDP model using a pre-trained tokenizer and CodeBERT model for a classification (i.e., Code Search) task, which is available on the HuggingFace website [2], and the overall workflow of JIT using CodeBERT is shown in Fig. 2.

1) In the preparing dataset stage, GHPR dataset is randomly divided into training, validation, and test datasets with the ratio of 8:1:1.
2) In the fine-turning CodeBERT stage, the pre-trained tokenizer tokenizes each instance of the training set, and the tokenized instance is fed into the pre-trained CodeBERT model for fine-tuning. The format of each instance fed into the CodeBERT is as Fig. 2, and it is the same as the CodeBERT model for a classification (i.e.,. Code Search) task in the original paper. It starts from *CLS* token, and tokenized PR title in NL and source code in PL are separated by *SEP*. In addition, the entire fine-tuning process is also the same as the Code Search task.

3) In the prediction stage, each instance of the testing dataset is also tokenized and fed into the fine-tuned model, and then the model predicts the proneness of the instance.

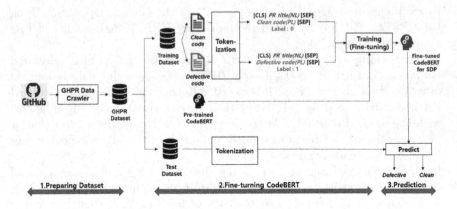

Fig. 2. Overall workflow of CodeBERT based JIT SDP

This model which predicts defect-prone function is more fine-grained than the traditional JIT SDP, which predicts defect-prone commit; a commit has consist of more than one changed function. The reasons are that, first, CodeBERT has been pre-trained on function-level pairs of NL and PL. Second, the sequence length that can be put into the CodeBERT is limited, so we train the model in the unit of function that does not exceed the sequence length. Third, it can help practitioners allocate testing resources to smaller parts more efficiently than traditional JIT SDP.

4   Experimental Setup

4.1   Research Questions

This study establishes two research questions for the following reasons. First, it is the first attempt to generate GHPR datasets on edge-cloud projects. Thus, the suitability of the implemented GHPR crawler and the applicability of the generated GHPR dataset to the proposed method are needed to study. Second, it is the first attempt to apply SDP to edge-cloud system. So, to confirm the applicability of the proposed model, we evaluate it in two different environments; within-project environment where training and test datasets are included in a GHPR dataset and cross-project environment where training and test datasets come from different GHPR datasets. The two research questions are as follows.

1. **RQ1:** Is the proposed method applicable to edge-cloud system?
2. **RQ2:** Are the generated GHPR datasets suitable for the proposed method?

4.2   Subject Projects

We search projects on GitHub with keywords (e.g., edge, cloud, and IoT). Among 131 results, we remove non-serious projects (e.g., homework assignments) with less than 500 stars and 300 forks, After that, we select two subject projects implemented in Go language over 90% with more than 1000 closed PRs, because we only focus on Go language and extract enough GHPR data from the closed PRs to fine-tune CodeBERT for SDP. The characteristics and short descriptions of the projects are described in Table 1.

Table 1. Characteristics of subject projects

Name	Stars	Forks	Closed PR	Short description
EdgeX Foundry (EdgeX) [3]	994	410	1,770	Open source project building a common open framework for IoT edge computing
KubeEdge (Kube) [6]	4.9K	1.3K	2,336	Open source system for extending native containerized application to hosts at Edge

4.3   Experimental Design

In the fine-tuning step for SDP, we use the same fine-tuning settings as the settings of the CodeBERT original paper for the classification task (i.e., Code-Search) [12], except for the batch size due to the memory limitation. We set the learning rate as $1e^{-5}$, max sequence length as 200, batch size as 16, and epoch as 8. We use the Adam optimizer to update the parameters. For testing, we feed all test datasets to the best-performing model on the validation dataset among 8 epoch.

The performance of the model is evaluated on two metrics; Area Under the Receiver Operating Characteristic curve (AUC) and F-measure. AUC is area under the curve between the true positive rate and false-positive rate, and it is independent of the cut-off value. The performance of the model is categorized into 5 classes according to the AUC; Excellent (0.9–1.0), Good (0.8–0.9), Normal (0.7–0.8), Poor (0.6–0.7) and Fail (0.5–0.6). F-measure is harmonic mean of Precision and Recall. Precision focuses on where actual defective instances are predicted as defective instances, and Recall focuses on where actual defective instances are predicted as non-defective instances. F-measure seeks a balance of Precision and Recall. Precision and Recall can be calculated based on Table 2, and the equations for each metric are as follows.

Table 2. Confusion matrix

	Predict as defective	Predict as clean
Actually defective	TP	FN
Actually clean	FP	TN

$$Precision(= Prec) = \frac{TP}{TP + FP} , \quad Recall = \frac{TP}{TP + FN} \tag{1}$$

$$F - measure = \frac{2 * Recall * Prec}{Prec + Recall} \tag{2}$$

4.4 Experimental Result

RQ1: Is the Proposed Method Applicable to Edge-Cloud System?
Table 3 presents the performance of the model in within-project and cross-project environments. In the case of within-project environment, the proposed model achieves almost good performance (i.e., 0.8–0.9) on the two projects according to AUC score. In addition, it achieves above 0.75 F-measure scores on both projects. Though F-measure does not have a performance criterion like AUC, it is relatively acceptable performance. Moreover, as mentioned in Sect. 3.2, our model is more fine-grained than the original JIT SDP. In order words, our model makes a fine-grained prediction with less information than the original JIT SDP, making the prediction process more difficult. Given the difficulty, we can confirm the applicability of the model in within-project environment.

However, in the case of cross-project environment, the model's performance drastically decreases in contrast to the within-project environment. We assume the performance degradation comes from the differences in the styles and details of the source code between training and test projects, though the training and test projects are both related to edge-cloud system. In addition, the differences would drive fine-tuned CodeBERT on a project not to work well on other projects. Thus, we confirm the necessity of additional information other than a sequence of tokens from the source code for the cross-project environment.

In conclusion, we can confirm the applicability of the proposed model in within-project environment; however, we can also confirm that additional research is needed to apply our model in cross-project environment.

RQ2: Are the Generated GHPR Datasets Suitable for the Proposed Method?
Table 4 shows the characteristics of the generated two GHPR datasets. The first column shows the name of the subject projects, the second column indicates the number of the closed PR, the third column shows the number of PRs that are related to defects and PRs that modify more than one '.go' file, and the fourth column shows the number of changed '.go' files and functions per a PR that modifies '.go' file.

Table 3. Performance of the proposed model in two environments

	Within project env		Cross project env	
Train → Test	EdgeX → EdgeX	Kube → Kube	EdgeX → Kube	Kube → EdgeX
AUC	0.798	0.805	0.686	0.664
F-measure	0.752	0.750	0.583	0.522

First, both subject projects in common, approximately 60–70% of the closed PRs are related to a defect, and 40% of the closed PRs fix the defect by modifying the '.go' files. In other words, though more than 90% of the files of a subject project are written in Go language, only 40% of the PRs fix the defect by modifying the file written in Go language. Thus, it is essential to check whether a PR modifies a file written in Go language when creating the GHPR dataset for SDP.

Second, per a PR that modifies '.go' file, approximately 8–23 files written in Go language, and 16–34 functions in the files are modified. Though the number of files and functions modified in a PR is different for each project, a PR (i.e., a commit) and a file have many functions, and it makes the CodeBERT poorly work for embedding due to too long sequence of source code. Thus, it is suitable to fine-tune CodeBERT with a function-level instance that does not exceed the max sequence length for the model.

Third, the number of instances in a dataset is over 10,000, and it is not too small to fine-tune the CodeBERT. In addition, due to the characteristic of the GHPR as mentioned in Sect. 3.1, the dataset is always class-balanced, which is essential to reduce the model's prediction bias.

In conclusion, the script that we implement effectively makes GHPR dataset focused on Go language, and the generated datasets are suitable for fine-tuning the CodeBERT.

Table 4. Characteristics of GHPR datasets

Name	Total closed PR	# of PR related with		Per a '.go' related PR, # of	
		Defect (%)	'.go' file (%)	'.go' file (Total)	Function (Total)
EdgeX foundry (EdgeX)	1,770	1,253 (70.7%)	712 (40.2%)	8.64 (6,144)	16.74 (11,906)
KubeEdge (Kube)	2,336	1,475 (63.1%)	952 (40.7%)	23.96 (22,819)	34.06 (32,432)

5   Threats to Validity

5.1   Internal Validity

We generate GHPR datasets under active development, so the instances of the datasets can be changed depending on the execution time of crawling for the GitHub repository. In addition, we use the same fine-tuning parameter in [12], so the performance can be changed depending on the parameter settings.

5.2   External Validity

This study uses two subject projects that are publicly available in GitHub. Generally speaking, only two projects are not enough to show the generalizability of our findings. However, we can not find additional projects that meet the conditions mentioned in Sect. 4.2. In future work, we will generate more datasets with lower conditions and apply them to our model to alleviate this validity.

5.3   Construct Validity

This study applies AUC and F-measure as performance metrics. They are widely applied for CodeBERT-based SDP studies [17,22,24], and especially AUC is recommended for assessing the discriminatory power of SDP model [20].

6   Conclusion

As interest in the edge-cloud system increase, testing for the system has been actively studied. However, the amount of resources for testing is always limited, thus we propose CodeBERT-based JIT SDP model for edge-cloud project. To evaluate the performance of our model, we generate GHPR datasets on two open-source framework projects for edge-cloud. After that, we evaluate the performance of the model on the GHPR datasets in within-project and cross-project environments. As a result, although additional research is needed, we can confirm the applicability of SDP in edge-cloud project.

In the future work, we will improve the performance of the proposed model in within-project environment and investigate how to alleviate performance degradation in Cross-project environment.

Acknowledgment. This research was supported by the National Research Foundation of Korea (NRF-2020R1F1A1071888), the Ministry of Science and ICT (MSIT), Korea, under the Information Technology Research Center (ITRC) support program supervised by the Institute of Information & Communications Technology Planning & Evaluation (IITP-2022-2020-0-01795), and the Basic Science Research Program through the National Research Foundation of Korea (NRF) funded by the Ministry of Education (NRF- 2022R1I1A3069233).

References

1. baetyl. https://github.com/baetyl/baetyl
2. Codebert on huggingface. https://huggingface.co/microsoft/codebert-base
3. Edgex foundry. https://github.com/edgexfoundry/edgex-go
4. ghpr-tools. https://github.com/soroushj/ghpr-tools
5. Github restful API. https://docs.github.com/en/rest
6. Kubeedge. https://github.com/kubeedge/kubeedge
7. Simpleilot. https://github.com/simpleiot/simpleiot
8. Blondet, M.V.R., Badarinath, A., Khanna, C., Jin, Z.: A wearable real-time BCI system based on mobile cloud computing. In: 2013 6th International IEEE/EMBS Conference on Neural Engineering (NER), pp. 739–742. IEEE (2013)
9. Butterfield, E.H.: Fog computing with go: a comparative study (2016)
10. Buyya, R., Srirama, S.N.: Fog and Edge Computing: Principles and Paradigms. Wiley, Hoboken (2019)
11. Deng, J., Lu, L., Qiu, S.: Software defect prediction via LSTM. IET Softw. **14**(4), 443–450 (2020)
12. Feng, Z., et al.: Codebert: A pre-trained model for programming and natural languages. arXiv preprint arXiv:2002.08155 (2020)
13. Husain, H., Wu, H.H., Gazit, T., Allamanis, M., Brockschmidt, M.: CodeSearch-Net challenge: evaluating the state of semantic code search. arXiv preprint arXiv:1909.09436 (2019)
14. Khanan, C., et al.: JITBot: an explainable just-in-time defect prediction bot. In: Proceedings of the 35th IEEE/ACM International Conference on Automated Software Engineering, pp. 1336–1339 (2020)
15. Li, J., He, P., Zhu, J., Lyu, M.R.: Software defect prediction via convolutional neural network. In: 2017 IEEE International Conference on Software Quality, Reliability and Security (QRS), pp. 318–328. IEEE (2017)
16. de Matos, F.F.S., Rego, P.A., Trinta, F.A.M.: An empirical study about the adoption of multi-language technique in computation offloading in a mobile cloud computing scenario. In: CLOSER, pp. 207–214 (2021)
17. Pan, C., Lu, M., Xu, B.: An empirical study on software defect prediction using CodeBERT model. Appl. Sci. **11**(11), 4793 (2021)
18. Pandey, S.K., Mishra, R.B., Tripathi, A.K.: Machine learning based methods for software fault prediction: a survey. Expert Syst. Appl. **172**, 114595 (2021)
19. Shi, K., Lu, Y., Chang, J., Wei, Z.: Pathpair2vec: an AST path pair-based code representation method for defect prediction. J. Comput. Lang. **59**, 100979 (2020)
20. Tantithamthavorn, C., Hassan, A.E., Matsumoto, K.: The impact of class rebalancing techniques on the performance and interpretation of defect prediction models. IEEE Trans. Softw. Eng. **46**(11), 1200–1219 (2018)
21. Wahono, R.S.: A systematic literature review of software defect prediction. J. Softw. Eng. **1**(1), 1–16 (2015)
22. Xu, J., Wang, F., Ai, J.: Defect prediction with semantics and context features of codes based on graph representation learning. IEEE Trans. Reliab. **70**(2), 613–625 (2020)
23. Xu, J., Yan, L., Wang, F., Ai, J.: A GitHub-based data collection method for software defect prediction. In: 2019 6th International Conference on Dependable Systems and Their Applications (DSA), pp. 100–108. IEEE (2020)
24. Zhou, X., Han, D., Lo, D.: Assessing generalizability of CodeBERT. In: 2021 IEEE International Conference on Software Maintenance and Evolution (ICSME), pp. 425–436. IEEE (2021)

A Novel Hybrid Approach for Localization in Wireless Sensor Networks

Uttkarsh Agrawal and Abhishek Srivastava(✉) ⓘ

Indian Institute of Technology Indore, Indore 452020, MP, India
asrivastava@iiti.ac.in

Abstract. Accurate localization of nodes in a Wireless Sensor Network (WSN) is imperative for several important applications. The use of Global Positioning Systems (GPS) for localization is the natural approach in most domains. In WSN, however, the use of GPS is challenging because of the constrained nature of deployed nodes as well as the often inaccessible sites of WSN nodes' deployment. Several approaches for localization without the use of GPS and harnessing the capabilities of Received Signal Strength Indicator (RSSI) exist in literature but each of these makes the simplifying assumption that all the WSN nodes are within the communication range of every other node. In this paper, we go beyond this assumption and propose a hybrid technique for node localization in large WSN deployments. The hybrid technique comprises a loose combination of a Machine Learning (ML) based approach for localization involving random forest and a multilateration approach. This hybrid approach takes advantage of the accuracy of ML localization and the iterative capabilities of multilateration. We demonstrate the efficacy of the proposed approach through experiments on a simulated set-up.

Keywords: Localization · Multilateration · Random forest · RSSI · WSN

1 Introduction

Wireless Sensor Network (WSN) is an infrastructure-less, self-configured network of sensor nodes that communicate with each other via radio signals. Each node in a WSN is laden with sensors of various kinds and these are often deployed in terrains that are dangerous and inaccessible for humans. The sensors on these nodes send back relevant sensed data via an ad-hoc network of nodes, that constitutes a WSN, to a back end cloud for analysis. A sensor node once deployed in such terrains is on its own with limited energy and computational resources with no means of replenishing these. The aim, therefore, is to minimise energy expenditure and prolong the useful life of nodes. In such circumstances, localization of

This work was supported in part by the Ministry of Education, Government of India and the DeFries-Bajpai Foundation.

sensor nodes in WSN is an important issue. This is because the usual localization approach in outdoor locations using Global Positioning Systems (GPS) is infeasible. GPS comprises modules that are resource intensive and deploying these over WSN nodes shortens the latter's life significantly. In addition to this, the geographical locations in which such nodes are deployed often do not facilitate the proper functioning of GPS modules.

Outdoor localization without the use of GPS is broadly classified into *range-free* [1], and *range-based* [2] localization. In range-free localization, the approach is to utilise simple data like the 'number of hops' between the anchor nodes and the node being localized, to get a rough idea on the location of the node. Range-based localization on the other hand requires additional hardware for transmission and reception of signals at each node.

In this paper, we utilise a range-based technique, more specifically the Received Signal Strength Indicator (RSSI) technique for localization. Anchor nodes whose locations are known in advance transmit signals that are received by the node to be localized. The strength of the received signals from different anchor nodes are analysed using various algorithms. Based on this, the position of the node is determined. The algorithms used to analyse RSSI values and localize nodes are broadly classified into those employing Machine Learning (ML) techniques and those based on more conventional techniques like multilateration [3].

In a realistic scenario, where anchor nodes are few and there are a large number of unknown nodes far away (not within communication range) from the anchor node, Machine Learning techniques are not effective for localisation. Algorithms based on multilateration techniques are more useful in this regard and can be used for localizations that require multiple iterations. Here, one set of unknown nodes are localized first and these 'newly' localized unknown nodes are subsequently used to localize further nodes. While multilateration enables localization of nodes far away from anchor nodes through multiple iterations, its major drawback is lack of accuracy.

In this paper, we overcome the issues of both ML based localization techniques and multilateration based techniques by adopting a 'hybrid' approach wherein the ML and multilateration techniques are combined. The remainder of this paper is organized as follows: Sect. 2 is a detailed discussion of the method proposed in this paper; the proposed method is validated through experiments in Sect. 3; and finally Sect. 4 concludes the paper with pointers to future work.

2   Proposed Method

The method proposed in this paper is meant for localization of unknown nodes, without the use of a GPS device, in a WSN that is spread over a large area. 'Large area' here implies that most nodes in the WSN are not within the communication range of most other nodes owing to the large size of the area of interest. It is important to specify this as most existing localization techniques work on the assumption that each node in the WSN is within the communication range of every other node.

In this large area, we start with the assumption that the locations of a few sensor nodes, called *anchor nodes*, are known in advance. These anchor nodes are located at the periphery of the area of interest. This is a realistic assumption as the sensor nodes at the periphery of the WSN are usually accessible and within the reach and range of a GPS device. The sensor nodes located deep within the area of interest are usually not accessible by a GPS device because of a hostile geographical terrain and/or the presence of disrupting structures like trees, and tall buildings. It is these nodes that need to be localized.

This paper proposes a hybrid approach to localize such sensor nodes that comprises a Machine Learning (ML) approach combined with a more conventional multilateration approach. The ML algorithm harnessed here is random forest and it localizes a large number of unknown nodes by analysing the RSSI values of communication signals received at the unknown nodes from one or more anchor nodes. Subsequently, these newly localized unknown nodes now serve as the 'new' anchor nodes and are used to localize nodes deeper inside the area using multilateration. The multilateration approach is usually harnessed for more than one iteration until all unknown nodes are localized. Figure 1 is a high-level depiction of the steps followed for localization.

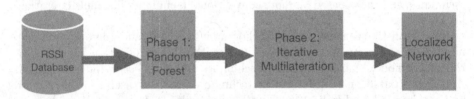

Fig. 1. Proposed hybrid localization approach

We now discuss the proposed approach, comprising localization using RSSI in general, analysis of RSSI using an ML algorithm (random forest), and the use of multilateration with RSSI for localization, in more detail.

2.1 Localization Using RSSI

Localization through RSSI values comprises sending low power signals from the transmitter at an anchor node (a node whose location is known) and receiving the signal using a receiver at an unknown node. The strength of the signal as received at the unknown node is assessed and analysed and conclusions are drawn on the position of the unknown node relative to the anchor node that sends the signal. Usually signals sent from multiple anchor nodes are received and analysed at the unknown node and more accurate localization is achieved. The intensity of signals received at the unknown node decreases with increasing distance from the transmitting anchor node i.e., an unknown node close to the anchor node receives a strong signal, while a distant unknown node receives a weak signal.

Equation 1 is Frii's Free Space Transmission Equation [4] and shows that the received signal strength decreases quadratically with distance from the transmitter.

$$P_r = \frac{P_t G_t Gr \lambda^2}{4\pi d^2} \tag{1}$$

where

P_r: power of signal as received at unknown node
P_t: power of signal as transmitted at anchor node
G_t: gain of transmitter at anchor node
G_r: gain of receiver at unknown node
d: distance between the anchor and unknown node
λ: wavelength of signal.

The power of the signal received at the unknown node is roughly interpreted as the Received Signal Strength Indicator (RSSI) value after incorporating factors specific to the communication technology in use.

The RSSI values for signals received at unknown nodes from the various anchor nodes are collected and stored in a database. A matrix template for RSSI values obtained at each node from every other node in the region of interest is shown in the matrix in Eq. 2. Most of these RSSI values are assigned values of -200 db indicating that the receiving node is beyond the communication range of the sending node.

$$R = \begin{bmatrix} RSSI_{11} & RSSI_{12} & \ldots & RSSI_{1k} \\ RSSI_{21} & RSSI_{22} & \ldots & RSSI_{2k} \\ \vdots & \vdots & \vdots & \vdots \\ RSSI_{n1} & RSSI_{n2} & \ldots & RSSI_{nk} \end{bmatrix} \tag{2}$$

The RSSI values so collected are subsequently analysed by an ML algorithm (random forest in this case) and a multilateration technique for localization.

2.2 Localization Using Machine Learning

The Machine Learning (ML) approach to localization involves training an algorithm with data on a large number of sensor nodes. The data comprises the RSSI values of signals received at each node and the relative location of the node. The algorithm is trained in such a manner that it is able to accurately localize a node that receives relevant signals from at least three anchor nodes (anchor nodes, as mentioned earlier, are nodes whose locations are known). The larger the number of anchor nodes, better the accuracy of localization. The algorithm is trained in an 'off-line' manner such that it is trained before it is put to use for localizing sensor nodes.

There are a large number of ML algorithms that can be employed for the task of localization. We assessed several algorithms and based on experiments chose to use random forest in our work as it gave the best localization accuracy. A comparison of the localization accuracies of the ML algorithms that we experimented with is shown in Sect. 4 that discusses the experiments conducted.

Random forest [5] is an ensemble technique that can perform both regression and classification tasks [6]. A random forest comprises several decision trees which are tree-like structures that divide a dataset on the basis of decisions taken at each node. The decision point or split value at a node is determined as one that provides the maximum information gain. Intuitively, a large information gain implies splitting the data in a manner that the data subsets formed as a result of splitting are more homogeneous i.e. datapoints in each subset formed are closer to each other in terms of attribute values. The decision tree establishes the best split amongst its variables with the intent of maximising information gain. This process of splitting begins at the root and each node applies its own split function to the new input. This is repeated recursively until a terminal node is reached.

Once trained, a decision tree is able to provide an appropriate value to a new datapoint. The random forest comprises several such decision trees and an average of the value assigned by each decision tree is assigned to the new point.

Data for the Random Forest. The first step in localization using the random forest algorithm is collection of data for training the model. The training entails teaching the model to correctly map RSSI values of signals received at a node with the 2D coordinates expressing the location of the node. The 2D coordinates of the nodes constitute the output of the random forest model. The input data consists of the RSSI values at the unknown nodes from various anchor nodes. At each unknown node N_i, we represent the RSSI value of the signal received from anchor node A_j as $RSSI_{ij}$. The input data and output of the model are in the formats shown in matrices 2 and 3 respectively for k unknown sensor nodes and n anchor nodes.

$$O = \begin{bmatrix} x_1 \ x_2 \ \dots \ x_n \\ y_1 \ y_2 \ \dots \ y_n \end{bmatrix} \tag{3}$$

In the matrix 2, the input data $RSSI_{nk}$ corresponds to the RSSI value of the signal received at the nth sensor node from the kth anchor node; whereas in the matrix 3, (x_n, y_n) represent the coordinates of the nth sensor node.

Data Preprocessing. Prior to creation of the random forest, the data collected goes through a quick step of preprocessing. Here a new parameter called γ is considered for each unknown node. The γ parameter indicates the number of anchor nodes for which the RSSI value at the node is not -200 db. In other words, the γ parameter provides information on the number of anchor nodes whose signals reach the particular sensor node. For example, $\gamma = 4$ indicates that the sensor node is within the communication range of 4 anchor nodes.

Only datapoints whose $\gamma \geq 3$ are considered for creation of the random forest. Those with smaller values are removed from consideration. This is because, at least 3 legitimate RSSI values are required for accurate localization with random forest.

Creation of the Random Forest. To create a random forest, small bootstrap samples from the input data with $\gamma \geq 3$ are taken and a decision tree is developed with each sample. A small subset of the RSSI values at a node is considered for each tree. From this small subset of RSSI values, one RSSI value is randomly selected for the root node of the decision tree. A split point of this RSSI value is so selected that it gives the best improvement in terms of variance. For brevity, we do not dwell into the procedure for variance calculation.

Based on the 'best' split point of the feature, the data is divided into two or more parts and these form the child nodes of the root. At each child node again a feature value (in this case RSSI value) is randomly chosen from the small sample and the best split point for this feature value further divides the data. This is continued until a certain number of iterations or until the data is exhausted, whichever comes first. The decision tree so created is combined with a larger random forest that comprises all such decision trees created.

The number of decision trees created in the random forest, called n-estimator is an important parameter and impacts the performance of the model. We experimented with using n-estimators values of 1000, 2000, and 3000. We got the best results with 2000 decision trees and used this value for further computations.

Testing Phase. Of the legitimate RSSI data with values of $\gamma \geq 3$, 90% was allocated for training the model whereas 10% was kept aside for testing the efficacy.

To test the model as well as use it with our real world implementation, the test point is made to go through each of the 2000 decision trees in the random forest. As the test data point moves through each tree and converges at a node in the tree, the x–y coordinates of the datapoint at the node are allocated as the coordinates of the test point.

This is repeated for all 2000 decision trees and finally an average of all the 2000 x and y coordinates is computed and is allocated to the test point.

2.3 Localization Through Multilateration

Multilateration is a localization technique popularly used to localize vehicles in a GPS system. Multilateration depends on the relation between the distance of nodes and their relative location coordinates. To localize one node using multilateration, at least three nodes with known locations (anchor nodes in our case) within the communication range of the unknown node are required. The distance between an anchor node and the unknown is calculated using Friis's Free Space Transmission Equation [4] shown in Eq. 1 that relates the received signal strength value at the unknown node with the distance from the anchor node from which the signal was sent. This distance (which is not the exact distance but a computed approximate distance) is calculated between all the anchor nodes within the communication range of the unknown node and the unknown node. The calculated distance along with the 2D coordinates of the anchor nodes are together employed in the Least Squares Method [7].

Equation 4 shows the expression that needs to be minimised to compute the location of the unknown node. $\tilde{d}_i$ is the distance between the unknown node and the ith anchor node as computed. The bar above d indicates that the value of the distance is not necessarily exact and is diluted by channel noise, obstacles, and other shadowing effects.

$$\text{Minimize } \varepsilon = | \sum_{i=1}^{M} \sqrt{(x_i - x)^2 + (y_i - y)^2} - \tilde{d}_i^2 \qquad (4)$$

M denotes the number of anchor nodes within the communication range of the unknown node. M needs to be at least 3 for proper localization. The square of the computed distance between the unknown node and the anchor node is computed as follow:

$$(x_i - x)^2 + (y_i - y)^2 = \tilde{d}_i^2$$
$$\forall i = 1, \ldots, M$$
$$(x_i - x)^2 - (x_j - x)^2 + (y_i - y)^2 - (y_j - y)^2$$
$$= \tilde{d}_i^2 - \tilde{d}_j^2$$
$$\forall i = 1, \ldots, M; i \neq j$$
$$2x(x_j - x_i) + 2y(y_j - y_i)$$
$$= \left(\tilde{d}_j^2 - \tilde{d}_i^2 \right) - (x_j^2 - x_i^2) - (y_j^2 - y_i^2)$$
$$\forall i = 1, \ldots, M; i \neq j$$

Expressing the equation in the form of a matrix:

$$\begin{bmatrix} 2(x_j - x_1) & 2(y_j - y_1) \\ \vdots & \vdots \\ 2(x_j - x_M) & 2(y_j - y_M) \end{bmatrix} \begin{bmatrix} x \\ y \end{bmatrix} = \begin{bmatrix} \tilde{b}_j \\ \vdots \\ \tilde{b}_M \end{bmatrix}$$

where

$$\begin{bmatrix} \tilde{b}_j \\ \vdots \\ \tilde{b}_M \end{bmatrix} = \begin{bmatrix} \left(\tilde{d}_j^2 - \tilde{d}_i^2 \right) - (x_j^2 - x_i^2) - (y_j^2 - y_i^2) \\ \vdots \\ \left(\tilde{d}_j^2 - d_M^2 \right) - (x_j^2 - x_M^2) - (y_j^2 - y_M^2) \end{bmatrix}$$

The form of the above equation is $A.\bar{x} = \bar{b}$. Using this, the location of the unknown node can be computed by minimising $\|A.\bar{x} - \bar{b}\|^2$. Using the Least Squares equation, the solution to the equation becomes $\hat{x} = \left(A^T A \right)^{-1} A^T \tilde{b}$.

2.4   The Hybrid Approach to Localization

We take a hybrid approach to localization owing to limitations in the ML approach as well as the multilateration approach. The ML approach is effective in accurately localizing a large number of sensor nodes harnessing the locations of just a few anchor nodes. The limitation of the ML approach, however, is that it needs to be trained in advance and can only be employed for one iteration. It cannot be easily trained with the locations of the newly localized nodes and thus cannot be used for further iterations. The ML approach, therefore, is useful when all the unknown nodes are within the communication range of at least 3 anchor nodes. This is usually possible in an indoor setting and is seldom the case with large outdoor locations.

The multilateration approach to localization on the other hand can be readily employed for multiple iterations. Multiple iterations imply that the unknown nodes localized in an iteration become the new anchor nodes for subsequent iterations. The iterations continue until the entire area is covered. This is useful but has the drawback that localizations through multilateration are not very precise and this imprecision increases at every iteration. A very large number of iterations of multilateration localization is therefore not advised.

The hybrid approach proposed in this paper takes the best of both approaches. One iteration of ML localization is first conducted. This results in significant number of unknown nodes getting accurately localized. These newly localized nodes become the new anchor nodes for subsequent localizations using multilateration. A combination of the two approaches enables the coverage of most of the outdoor region of interest.

3   Evaluation

In this section we experimentally assess the working of the random forest algorithm, the multilateration approach to localization separately first, and subsequently as a hybrid combination. We first create a simulated environment to comprehensively validate the approach; and subsequently demonstrate its efficacy on a real-world set-up.

3.1   Dataset and Simulated Environment

To demonstrate the effectiveness of the proposed localization approach, we create a simulated environment and a synthetic dataset. We need to synthesize the data as standard datasets for localization over large areas do not exist. Also, we do not have access to real world deployments of this scale.

We consider a 130×130 m^2 region. A dataset comprising anchor nodes (nodes whose locations are known in advance) and sensor nodes (unknown nodes that need to be localized) deployed within this region was synthesized. A total of $12,321$ sensor nodes were created whose positions are along a 1×1 m^2 grid starting from a position of 10 m from the periphery of the region of interest and extending to a distance of 110 m. This is done along both the horizontal and vertical axes. 8 anchor nodes, whose locations are known, are placed at the periphery of the region of interest. This is a realistic scenario as nodes along the peripheries of real world regions of interest are accessible and their locations can be determined. The locations of the anchor nodes are as follows: $(0, 0)$, $(60, 0)$, $(130, 0)$, $(0, 60)$, $(0, 130)$, $(60, 130)$, $(130, 60)$, and $(130, 130)$. Each anchor node has a defined range over which it can communicate with other sensor nodes.

Table 1. Sensor nodes within communication range of anchor nodes

Number of sensor nodes	Neighbouring anchor nodes
4666	2
3914	3
3622	1
119	0

Table 1 shows the number of sensor nodes that are within the range of communication of different number of anchor nodes.

3.2   Machine Learning (Random Forest) Localization

We choose random forest as the ML algorithm for the first iteration of localization. Of the total of 3914 sensor nodes that are within the communication range of 3 anchor nodes (you may recall that for localization, a node needs to be receiving signals from at least 3 anchor nodes), 90% of the nodes or 3523 nodes are set aside for training of the random forest and 10% or 391 is used for testing.

Localization Accuracy. Table 2 shows the localization results of the random forest algorithm for 10 randomly selected datapoints. In this table (Xactual, Yactual) are the actual coordinates of the datapoints; (Xpred, Ypred) are the predicted coordinates using random forest localization; and Deviation indicates the distance between the actual and predicted locations.

3.3   Multilateration Localization

The other major localization approach employed in this paper is multilateration, as discussed earlier. Multilateration utilises the Least Squares Error technique to accurately localize nodes with distances computed from RSSI values. The advantage of the multilateration approach, in contrast to the ML localization, is that it can be used for multiple iterations.

The downside of localization with multilateration, however, is the inferior localization accuracy as the iterations progress. The first iteration usually returns acceptable accuracy results. This deteriorates because the error in localization at earlier iteration propagates through subsequent iterations.

Table 2. X-Y coordinates, actual vs predicted by random forest

Xpred	Ypred	Xactual	Yactual	Deviation (m)
22.97	16.13	23.0	16.0	0.13
108.99	19.93	109.0	20.0	0.07
13.85	34.11	14.0	34.0	0.18
86.88	23.99	87.0	24.0	0.17
34.15	93.00	34.0	93.0	0.15
102.75	97.84	103.0	98.0	0.29
109.76	98.82	110.0	99.0	0.30
15.79	35.01	16.0	35.0	0.21
16.02	31.90	16.0	32.0	0.10
28.73	85.33	29.0	85.0	0.42

Localization over Iterations. We conducted experiments to understand the extent of deterioration in localization accuracy as the iterations of localization with multilateration progress. To conduct this experiment, we use a 50×50 m^2 sized simulation environment with 8 anchor nodes positioned respectively at $(0,0), (25,0), (50,0), (25,50), (50,50), (0,25), (0,50)$, and $(50,25)$. The sensor nodes localized in the first iteration become the new anchor nodes for the next iteration and localise more sensor nodes. In this way, the nodes over the entire region of interest are localized in three iterations. Tables 3, and 4 respectively show the localization of sensor nodes after the first and second iterations of multilateration. (Xactual, Yactual) are the actual coordinates of the nodes localized and (Xpred, Ypred) are the coordinate values computed using multilateration. Deviation indicates the distance between the actual locations of the sensor nodes and the locations predicted by multilaterion. The values of deviation in the three tables indicate a trend towards deteriorating localization accuracy as the iterations progress.

3.4   The Hybrid Localization Approach

In this paper, we combine the localization potential of random forest localization and multilateration localization seeking to harness the strengths of both. Random forest is utilised in the first iteration and it localizes a large number of sensor nodes with a high degree of accuracy. These newly localized sensor nodes serve as the anchor nodes for the subsequent iterations of localization which is done using multilateration.

Table 5 shows the localization results for 10 random sensor nodes in terms of the predicted coordinates (Xpred, Ypred) and actual coordinates (Xactual, Yactual). The Deviation column shows the distance between the actual locations of the nodes and the locations predicted by the hybrid approach. The results indicate acceptable localization with small deviations from actual locations owing to

Table 3. X–Y coordinates, actual vs predicted by first iteration of multilateration

Xpred	Ypred	Xactual	Yactual	Deviation (m)
10.36	13.36	11	14	0.90
14.24	11.30	15	12	1.03
35.76	12.21	35	13	1.09
37.61	12.30	37	13	0.92
9.60	9.60	10	10	0.56
11.25	35.75	12	35	1.06
13.36	39.63	14	39	0.89
38.94	10.06	39	10	0.08
9.27	39.49	10	39	0.87
36.78	36.78	36	36	1.10

Table 4. X–Y coordinates, actual vs predicted by second iteration of multilateration

Xpred	Ypred	Xactual	Yactual	Deviation (m)
26.72	12.44	27	15	2.57
24.67	12.12	25	11	1.16
16.21	29.60	18	30	1.83
10.06	27.98	10	29	1.02
14.62	26.97	14	28	1.20
17.18	14.31	17	16	1.69
21.00	35.20	22	35	1.01
23.09	34.31	24	34	0.93
31.06	12.01	31	10	2.01
25.29	11.77	25	11	0.82

the initial boost provided to multilateration in terms of a large number of anchor nodes provided by random forest. The hybrid approach, therefore, is seen to be quite useful for localization of nodes in large outdoor spaces.

Table 5. X–Y coordinates, actual vs predicted by hybrid approach

Xpred	Ypred	Xactual	Yactual	Deviation (m)
86.01	47.70	86	48	0.30
68.02	31.26	68	32	0.74
75.06	98.07	75	98	0.09
95.40	73.73	95	74	0.48
77.80	69.20	78	70	0.82
39.90	71.40	39	72	1.08
49.00	75.26	48	76	1.24
56.94	78.91	57	79	0.10
63.81	19.54	64	20	0.49
109.80	47.60	110	48	0.44

4   Conclusion

In this paper, we proposed a hybrid technique for localization of nodes in a Wireless Sensor Network (WSN) without the use of GPS. The major contribution of our approach is that it overcomes the simplifying assumption that every node in the WSN deployment is within the communication range of every other node. Our hybrid approach combines the capability of random forest, a Machine

Learning (ML) algorithm, with a more conventional multilateration algorithm. The random forest algorithm is trained in advance and is able to accurately localize a large number of unknown nodes using just a small number of anchor nodes (nodes whose locations are known in advance). It is difficult to train random forest 'on the go' and hence it cannot be used for subsequent iterations. The nodes localized by random forest, however, are utilised as new anchor nodes and employed for localization of the remaining nodes by the multilateration approach. Multilateration is not as accurate as ML algorithms but can be repeated several time and hence is effective in covering a large deployments. In spite of being a little compromised in terms of accuracy of localization, multilateration does a fairly decent job within the hybrid set-up owing to the initial boost provided by random forest wherein a large number of anchor nodes are created.

We validated the efficacy of the proposed technique using a simulated set-up and with synthetic data. This is because standard data sets for WSN deployments are not available and we were unable to get access to a WSN deployment large enough to validate the idea proposed. The results of localization on the simulated set-up clearly demonstrate the efficacy of the proposed idea.

References

1. Stoleru, R., He, T., Stankovic, J.A.: Range-free localization. In: Poovendran, R., Roy, S., Wang, C. (eds.) Secure Localization and Time Synchronization for Wireless Sensor and Ad Hoc Networks. Advances in Information Security, vol. 30, pp. 3–21. Springer, Boston (2007). https://doi.org/10.1007/978-0-387-46276-9_1
2. Dil, B., Dulman, S., Havinga, P.: Range-based localization in mobile sensor networks. In: Römer, K., Karl, H., Mattern, F. (eds.) EWSN 2006. LNCS, vol. 3868, pp. 164–179. Springer, Heidelberg (2006). https://doi.org/10.1007/11669463_14
3. Zhou, Y., Li, J., Lamont, L.: Multilateration localization in the presence of anchor location uncertainties. In: 2012 IEEE Global Communications Conference (GLOBECOM), pp. 309–314 (2012)
4. Rappaport, T.S: Wireless Communications: Principles and Practice. Prentice Hall PTR, New Jersey (1996)
5. Breiman, Leo: Random forests. Mach. Learn. **45**, 5–32 (2001)
6. Liaw, A., Wiener, M.: Classification and regression by Random Forest. R News **2**, 18–22 (2002)
7. Jo, C., Lee, C.: Multilateration method based on the variance of estimated distance in range-free localisation. Electron. Lett. **52**, 1078–1080 (2016)

An Empirical Analysis on Just-In-Time Defect Prediction Models for Self-driving Software Systems

Jiwon Choi[1] ⓘ, Saranya Manikandan[1], Duksan Ryu[1(✉)] ⓘ, and Jongmoon Baik[2] ⓘ

[1] Department of Software Engineering, Jeonbuk National University, Jeonju, Korea
{jiwon.choi,saranyamanikandan76,duksan.ryu}@jbnu.ac.kr
[2] School of Computing, Korea Advanced Institute of Science and Technology, Daejeon, Korea
jbaik@kaist.ac.kr

Abstract. Just-in-time (JIT) defect prediction has been used to predict whether a code change is defective or not. Existing JIT prediction has been applied to different kind of open-source software platform for cloud computing, but JIT defect prediction has never been applied in self-driving software. Unlike other software systems, self-driving system is an AI-enabled system and is a representative system to which edge cloud service is applied. Therefore, we aim to identify whether the existing JIT defect prediction models for traditional software systems also work well for self-driving software. To this end, we collect and label the dataset of open-source self-driving software project using SZZ (Śliwerski, Zimmermann and Zeller) algorithm. And we select four traditional machine learning methods and state-of-the-art research (i.e., JIT-Line) as our baselines and compare their prediction performance. Our experimental results show that JITLine and logistic regression produce superior performance, however, there exists a room to be improved. Through XAI (Explainable AI) analysis it turned out that the prediction performance is mainly affected by experience and history-related features among change-level metrics. Our study is expected to provide important insight for practitioners and subsequent researchers performing defect prediction in AI-enabled system.

Keywords: Just-in-time defect prediction · Change-metric · Machine learning · Explainable AI

1 Introduction

With the increase in the size and complexity of software systems, it is very important to detect software defects before a software product is released. Defective software can cause serious problems, such as economic problems, or even endangering human life [1]. Software defect prediction (SDP) has been proposed to detect defects and is regraded as one of representative quality assurance techniques. SDP predicts whether new instances of code regions (e.g., files, changes, and methods) have defect(s) using a model built on software historical data [2]. The primary goal of SDP is to effectively allocate limited and valuable software testing resources on fault-prone code regions.

Change-level defect prediction, a.k.a. Just-in-time (JIT)defect prediction, has been used to predict whether a code change (i.e., commits) at the time is a defect or not [2]. Since the identified defect-inducing changes are linked with specific changes, JIT defect prediction can predict defects at a finer granularity than the file-level [4]. Also, changes can be classified as defective or clean as soon as they are committed to the repository. Thus, developers can reduce resources of time and effort to examine code by focusing on defect-prone code changes.

Many approaches have been proposed for predicting change-level defects, mainly performed in open-source projects [6–8]. Hoang et al. [6] proposed a prediction method using cloud infrastructure service and cross-platform application domain data. Zeng et al. [21] used Eclipse JDT and Gerrit project data. However, the JIT defect prediction has never been used in the self-driving software domain. A major bug in self-driving software systems is caused due to incorrect implementation of an algorithm [5]. Since self-driving software defects can endanger people's-lives unlike other non-safety related software domains, it is essential to apply much stronger software quality assurance activities. However, it is unknown whether the existing JIT defect prediction approach is effectively performed well for self-driving software systems. Also, among the 14 change-level features widely used in existing JIT research, features that affect defect-inducing change are still unknown.

We collect open-source self-driving software projects and explore whether the existing JIT defect prediction approach works well in the self-driving software domain. Unlike other software, self-driving software is an AI-enabled system and one of representative systems to which edge cloud service is applied. Edge computing is comprised of computer storage, data management, data analysis and networking technologies. Self-driving vehicles can connect to the edge to improve safety, enhance efficiency, reduce accidents and decrease traffic congestion. The edge-cloud computing model for autonomous vehicles deploys edge devices in the vehicle to reduce latency and power consumption and cloud servers to provide a large amount of computation resources. [22] In addition, we identify the features that affected defect prediction among 14 change-level features using explainable AI.

This paper makes the following contributions:

(1) We collect and label the dataset of the most popular self-driving projects using the MA-SZZ algorithm [12] since there is no autonomous dataset available for predicting JIT defects prediction.
(2) We investigate whether traditional machine learning and state-of-the-art model perform well in predicting defects in self-driving software projects.
(3) We identify important change-level features using explainable AI analysis in self-driving projects.

The rest of this paper is summarized as follows. Section 2 briefly reviews the related work on JIT defect prediction. Section 3 describes the research question, dataset, evaluation metrics, and baseline methods. Section 4 compares the results obtained in this paper. Section 5 presents the threats to validity of our study. Finally, Sect. 6 describes the conclusion and future work.

2 Related Work

Most recent research of JIT defect prediction has been using machine learning algorithms or deep learning methods. Research using machine learning used code change metrics (e.g., number of files modified and number of lines of code added) which are manually designed. Code change metrics are used as an input for a conventional classifier (e.g., Random Forest, Logistic Regression). JIT defect prediction research using deep learning automatically creates features that can represent semantic information of code change and syntactic structure of code.

Hoang et al. [6] automatically extracted meaningful features from commit messages and associated code change (in programming languages) using a convolutional neural network. They reported that the performance of the proposed method can be improved when code change metrics (e.g., the number of added lines) are used together. They first proposed an end-to-end trainable model for JIT defect prediction, but its performance has not been verified in various software projects. Hoang et al. [7] built a hierarchical attention network to embed added and deleted code of each changed file associated with one given commit respectively. However, the model proposed in [7] requires an unlabeled testing dataset for training. Pornprasit et al. [8] used both the code change metrics and the code token frequency of each commit as input data for the Random Forest (RF). The proposed method showed better performance than deep learning approaches [6, 7] for predicting JIT defects. However, their method still needs to improve the recall performance.

Previous studies have used industrial automotive data to predict defects. Altinger et al. [10] presented automotive data based on Matlab/Simulink model, which is an extensive modeling tool for embedded automotive functions. Altinger et al. [11] analyzed the effect of sampling according to the machine learning classifier using the data proposed in [10]. They proposed a defect prediction technique at a file-level. But we focus on defect prediction methods at a change-level defect since changes are usually smaller than files and developers have much less code to inspect to uncover defects [2]. The changes can be timely classified as defective or clean when they are committed to the repository unlike file-level defect prediction.

Self-driving software is one of the AI-enabled systems, and various machine learning models or deep learning frameworks are included [13]. In terms of testing for software quality assurance, traditional software (including automotive software) testing focuses on functional testing, and self-driving software focuses on functional testing of machine learning/deep learning models [14]. However, no study on the defect prediction for self-driving software has conducted yet. Therefore, it is necessary to investigate whether the JIT defect prediction methods used for traditional software are also effective for self-driving software systems.

3   Experimental Setup

3.1   Research Question

RQ1. How Well Do JIT Defect Prediction Approaches Perform on Self-driving Projects?
In this research question, we compare the performance among machine learning algorithms and a state-of-the-art method. To answer this research question, we use Random Forest (RF), Gradient Boosting Decision Tree (GBDT), Logistic regression (LR), and XGBoost. These algorithms have been widely used in defect prediction research [8, 15] and we also check the performance of the state-of-the-art JITLine [8] approach. The detailed information on each algorithm is described in Sect. 3.4.

RQ2. What Factors Affect Performance of Model that Performed Well in RQ1?
In this research question, we identify factors that affected the performance of the model based on the experimental results of RQ1. To answer this question, we perform a sensitivity analysis in terms of (1) input data, (2) preprocessing.

RQ3. What Are the Important Features for JIT Defect Prediction on Self-driving Projects?
We use 14 change-level features that are widely used in JIT defect prediction studies. However, among the 14 change-level features, the features that significantly affect the defect prediction performance were not identified. Therefore, we aim to identify which features affect defect prediction performance in this research question. To answer this research question, we use Shapley Additive explanation (SHAP) [3], an explainable AI technique, to identify important features.

3.2   Dataset

Project Selection. The keywords, '*self-driving*' and '*autonomous driving*', were used to collect data from GitHub repositories. Then, we sort them in descending order by stars. To select the most appropriate project, we establish the following criteria: (1) projects should not be one of these types: tutorials, educational projects, non-language repositories; (2) A repository with no more than 10,000 commits. After filtering with these criteria, we selected the projects with the most top-2 stars. We clone the repository of the selected project for the period from the creation date to January 26, 2022. A summary of these projects can be seen in Table 1.

Data Labeling. Software projects contain many historical changes, so it requires a significant amount of effort to manually find bug-inducing changes [4]. Therefore, the researchers proposed the SZZ(Sliwerski-Zimmermann-Zeller) algorithm to automatically identify bug-inducing changes [17].

Among the various SZZ algorithms, we use the meta-change aware SZZ (MA-SZZ) [12] algorithm. The MA-SZZ algorithm handles meta changes on top of the existing SZZ algorithm (AG-SZZ [19]). The meta changes include branch changes and file properties

Table 1. Summary of self-driving projects.

Project	#Stars	# Changes	# Defective	Def ratio	Short introduction
Carla	7.2k	6,477	2,933	45.28%	Open-source simulator for self-driving
Donkeycar	2.2k	2,359	865	36.67%	Self-driving library

changes [17]. In particular, the data labeled by MA-SZZ have a low false-positive rate and false-negative rate [17], and both Recall and Precision performance are superior to other algorithms [16].

Change-level features 14 change-level features as shown in Table 2 have been used in previous studies [4, 6]. These features proposed by Kamei et al. [18] are divided into five dimensions: diffusion, size, purpose, history, and experience. The diffusion dimension quantifies the distribution within the change, and the size dimension measures the size of the change. The purpose dimension characterizes whether to fix bugs, and the history dimension indicates how developers modify the files within the change. The experience dimension quantifies the change experience of developers who perform change based on the number of changes previously submitted by the developer.

Table 2. Summary of change-level features.

Dimension	Feature	Description
Diffusion	NS	The number of modified subsystems
	ND	The number of modified directories
	NF	The number of modified files
	Entropy	Distribution of modified code across each file
Size	LA	Lines of code added
	LD	Lines of code deleted
	LT	Lines of code in a file before the change
Purpose	FIX	Whether or not the change is a defect fix
History	NDEV	The number of developers that changed the modified files
	AGE	The average time interval between the last and current change
	NUC	The number of unique changes to the modified files
Experience	EXP	Developer experience
	REXP	Recent developer experience
	SEXP	Developer experience on a subsystem

3.3 Evaluation Metrics

Recall is defined as the ratio of instances correctly predicted as defective out of actual defective instances. It is calculated as (1).

$$Recall = TP/(FN + TP) \tag{1}$$

where TP represents true positive, and FN denotes false negative. TP is the number of predicted defective instances whose true label is defective. FN is the number of predicted clean examples whose true label is defective.

Probability of false alarm rate (PF) is referred to as false positive rate (FPR) which is calculated as the ratio of actual non-defective instances predicted incorrectly as defective instances to the all-non-defective instances. FPR can be measured as,

$$PF = FP/(TN + FP) \tag{2}$$

where FP denotes false positive, and TN represents true negative. FP denotes the number of predicted defective instances whose true label is clean. TN is the number of clean instances which are predicted as clean.

Area Under the ROC Curve (AUC). The ROC curve is plotted in a 2-D space with FPR as the x-axis and true positive rate as the y-axis. AUC belongs to a range between 0 and 1, and higher value represents the better performance.

P_{opt} defines the relation between Recall and inspection cost for prediction model. Two further prediction models such as optimal and worst model are required to find this measure. In accordance with actual defects, the changes of optimal and worst models are sorted in descending and ascending order respectively. *Popt* for given prediction model *m*, can be calculated as,

$$P_{opt}(m) = 1 - \frac{Area(optimal) - Area(m)}{Area(optimal) - Area(worst)} \tag{3}$$

where *Area(m)* represents area under the curve corresponding to the model *m*.

Statistical Analysis. We use Cohen's d [20] to statistically determine whether the performances of the two-methods are different. This method is an effect size measure that quantifies the performance difference between the two techniques. Depending on the values of Cohen's d, it can be categorized into four levels as shown in Table 3.

$$Cohen's\, d = \frac{M_1 - M_2}{\sqrt{\frac{\delta_1{}^2 + \delta_2{}^2}{2}}} \tag{4}$$

3.4 Baseline Methods

We build the traditional machine learning models after preprocessing (i.e., min-max normalization and SMOTE oversampling). To reduce experimental bias, baselines are performed via 10-fold cross-validation.

Table 3. Effectiveness levels based on Cohen's d.

Cohen's d	Level
$0 \leq |d| < 0.2$	Negligible (N)
$0.2 \leq |d| < 0.5$	Small (S)
$0.5 \leq |d| < 0.8$	Medium (M)
$|d| \geq 0.8$	Large (L)

Random Forest (RF). RF is a classifier that generates the forest with the multiple numbers of decision trees on several subsets and returns the final prediction by taking the average to improve the accuracy.

Gradient Boosting Decision Tree (GBDT). Gradient Boosting in the ensemble learning method is a machine learning algorithm in which the bunch of models work sequentially. It works on the principle of combining several weak (base) learners to turn up one strong learner. Each base learner is individual decision tree. All the decision trees are connected sequentially to learn the mistakes from previous decision tree models. As a result of this sequential connection, the final model aggregates the outcome of each model, and thus becomes the strong learner reducing the error.

Logistic Regression (LR). Logistic Regression finds the relationship between the variable response and the predictor variables. When used for prediction, Logistic Regression fits data to the logistic curve, and the parameters of logistic regression are estimated based on the maximum likelihood.

XGBoost. The influence of the XGBoost algorithm relies on its scalability, which gives parallel fast learning with high accuracy. The concept behind the XGBoost algorithm is to choose some samples and features to build a weak model (simple model as a decision tree) as the basic classifier. It constructs a new model by learning the residuals from the previous models. The final model is generated by a combination of all previous models into comprehensive models with high accuracy.

JITLine. A JITLine approach [8] is one of the state-of-the-art change-level JIT defect prediction approaches based on machine learning techniques (RF). It predicts the commits which introduce defects and determines the corresponding defective lines with that commit. The key principle behind the JIT-Line approach is building commit-level JIT defect prediction model using Bag-of-Tokens (i.e., extracting source code tokens of code changes as token features) and change-level metrics.

4   Experimental Result

4.1   RQ1: How Well Do JIT Defect Prediction Approaches Perform on Self-driving Projects?

To answer this question, we selected five baselines, for each method we describe in Sect. 3.4. Table 4 presents the experimental results, with the best results among methods highlighted in bold face. From this table, we observe that JITLine and LR outperform other traditional machine learning models. In the Donkeycar project, JITLine shows excellent performance in four evaluation indicators, and LR has the best performance of PF. In the Carla project, JITLine presents superior performance in Recall and P_{opt}, and LR performs well in terms of PF and AUC evaluation indicators. However, there also exists a room to improve performance in all evaluation indicators.

Table 4. Experimental results of RQ1.

Project	Evaluation	RF	GBDT	XGBoost	LR	JITLine
Donkeycar	Recall	0.5575	0.5295	0.5084	0.3194	**0.568**
	PF	0.3622	0.3337	0.3368	**0.2069**	0.2809
	AUC	0.5976	0.5978	0.5857	0.5562	**0.6324**
	P_{opt}	0.6246	0.6293	0.6267	0.6315	**0.6375**
Carla	Recall	0.5068	0.4729	0.38	0.5109	**0.6352**
	PF	0.5336	0.4976	0.4366	**0.3373**	0.475
	AUC	0.4865	0.4876	0.4717	**0.5868**	0.5625
	P_{opt}	0.4665	0.4736	0.4603	0.6322	**0.6375**

We conduct the effect size test of JITLine and other traditional machine learning performances in that JITLine showed superior performance in the effort aware evaluation indicator (P_{opt}) than LR. From Table 5, we observe that there is a large-level performance difference in terms of AUC and P_{opt}. This means that JITLine shows a statistically significant performance difference from other machine learning algorithms.

Table 5. The statistical analysis results of RQ1.

	JITLine vs.			
	RF	GBDT	XGBoost	LR
Recall	2.3334(L)	3.2311(L)	3.0719(L)	2.5984(L)
PF	−0.7640(M)	−0.4197(S)	−0.1133(N)	1.2803(L)
AUC	1.1937(L)	1.1866(L)	1.4541(L)	0.9619(L)
P_{opt}	1.6449(L)	1.5631(L)	1.5977(L)	22.8298(L)

4.2 RQ2: What Factors Affect Performance of Model that Performed Well in RQ1?

To answer this question, we perform a sensitivity analysis of the JITLine approach, which is the best performing method in RQ1. JITLine uses code change features and code token frequency of each commit as input data. We compare the performance when using only code change features and only code token frequencies. In addition, the JITLine method uses SMOTE, an oversampling technique, to solve the class imbalance problem. Therefore, we analyze whether SMOTE affects the performance of self-driving projects.

First, we check the performance difference according to the input data used in the JITLine approach. In Table 6, 'Only metric' means that only the change-level metric is used as input data, 'Only code' means that only the frequency of code tokens of each commit is used, and 'w/o SMOTE' indicates that without SMOTE. The results of performance measures are shown in Table 6. It shows the best performance in Donkeycar project when change-level metrics and code data are used together as suggested by the [8], but in Carla project it shows superior performance when only metric is used. Through this experimental result, we can confirm that the change-level metric rather than the code token frequency affects the performance. The results of the effect size test using Cohen's d (Table 7) show that JITLine significantly improved performance compared to when only code was used and SMOTE was not applied.

Table 6. Experimental results of RQ2.

Project	Evaluation	JITLine	Only code	Only metric	w/o SMOTE
Donkeycar	Recall	0.568	0.4836	0.5967	**0.6831**
	PF	**0.2809**	0.4967	0.4698	0.5164
	AUC	**0.6324**	0.4913	0.5421	0.5585
	P_{opt}	**0.6375**	0.4786	0.6043	0.6327
Carla	Recall	0.6352	0.5475	0.6391	**0.7345**
	PF	0.475	0.5703	**0.3918**	0.5203
	AUC	0.5625	0.4831	**0.6096**	0.5824
	P_{opt}	0.6375	0.4844	**0.6661**	0.6606

Table 7. The statistical analysis results of RQ2.

	JITLine vs.		
	Only code	Only metric	w/o SMOTE
Recall	2.6246(L)	−0.5802(M)	−3.5828(L)
PF	−2.1194(L)	−0.7145(M)	−2.0454(L)
AUC	4.4307(L)	0.6287(M)	1.0337(L)
P_{opt}	76.0749(L)	0.1052(N)	−0.9276(L)

4.3 RQ3: What Are the Important Features for JIT Defect Prediction on Self-driving Projects?

To answer this question, we use SHAP, an explainable AI technique, to identify the features that most influenced LR model. LR is the model that showed the best performance among traditional machine learning models in our RQ1, so we choose LR. We classify the features in Table 8 that had the greatest impact on performance as top-1, top-3, and top-5. In the Donkeycar project and the Carla project, the 'Experience' dimension affects the performance the most, and the developer's recent experience (REPX) is identified as the most important feature. Prior work shows that developers with more experience are less likely to introduce bugs in their changes [22]. The second important dimension is 'Size', and a larger change is more defect-prone since such a change introduces [15]. The third important dimension is 'History', prior studies noted that files previously modified by many developers contain more bugs [9].

Table 8. Experimental results of RQ3.

Dimension	Feature	Top-1		Top-3		Top-5	
		#Projects	#Sum	#Projects	#Sum	#Projects	#Sum
Diffusion	NS	0	0	0	0	0	0
	ND	0		0		0	
	NF	0		0		0	
	Entropy	0		0		0	
Size	LA	0	0	0	1	0	3
	LD	0		1		1	
	LT	0		0		2	
Purpose	FIX	0	0	0	0	0	0
History	NDEV	0	0	0	0	1	1
	AGE	0		0		0	
	NUC	0		0		0	
Experience	EXP	0	2	2	5	2	6
	REXP	2		2		2	
	SEXP	0		1		2	

5 Threats to Validity

We have three internal validities. First, we have chosen a traditional machine learning classifier as our baseline. We use RF, GBDT, LR, and XGBoost, which are widely used in SDP. We plan to add various deep learning models as future work. Second, while we implement the latest research on JIT defect prediction, potential errors may be included in the implementation process. We conducted a peer review of the code to mitigate these threats. Third, we only used SHAP, an explainable AI technique, to identify features that have a significant impact on performance. A library of tree-based models provides algorithms for extracting important features. However, this method has the disadvantage that the feature importance indicator is inconsistent. To improve this problem, the proposed Shapley value maintains consistency, and SHAP uses the Shapley value. We plan to apply other explainable AI techniques to identify important features.

6 Conclusion

Nowadays, the increasing use of software systems is essential to detect defects and ensure the quality assurance technique. The traditional SDP models identify the fault-prone software module at the design level or later. Therefore, many researchers proposed change-level defect prediction for identifying the changes inducing faults at an earlier stage. The JIT defect prediction identifies defects at a satisfactory granularity level than a file-level. However, the existing JIT defect prediction that is effective for safety systems like self-driving software is still unknown. Therefore, the state-of-art JITLine [8] approach, a machine learning-based JIT defect approach applied to 2 different open-source projects in the self-driving domain. The experimental results show that among the five baseline methods conducted, the JITLine defect prediction model and LR perform better than other traditional machine learning models. In addition, the JIT defect prediction model is mainly affected by experience and history-related features.

In future work to improve the quality assurance of safety systems, we will plan to verify the performance of JIT defect prediction based on deep learning models and investigate the comparative analysis of the JIT defect prediction approach.

Acknowledgement. This research was supported by Basic Science Research Program through the National Research Foundation of Korea (NRF) funded by the Ministry of Education (NRF-2022R1I1A3069233) and the Nuclear Safety Research Program through the Korea Foundation Of Nuclear Safety (KoFONS) using the financial resource granted by the Nuclear Safety and Security Commission(NSSC) of the Republic of Korea (No. 2105030) and the MSIT (Ministry of Science and ICT), Korea, under the ITRC (Information Technology Research Center) support program (IITP-2022-2020-0-01795) supervised by the IITP (Institute of Information & Communications Technology Planning & Evaluation) and NRF grant funded by the Korea government (MSIT) (No. NRF-2020R1F1A1071888).

References

1. Jiang, L., Jiang, S., Gong, L., Dong, Y., Yu, Q.: Which process metrics are significantly important to change of defects in evolving projects: an empirical study. IEEE Access **8**, 93705–93722 (2020)
2. Wang, S., Liu, T., Nam, J., Tan, L.: Deep semantic feature learning for software defect prediction. IEEE Trans. Softw. Eng. **46**(12), 1267–1293 (2018)
3. Lundberg, S.M., Lee, S.I.: A unified approach to interpreting model predictions. Adv. Neural Inf. Process. Syst. **30**, 4765–4774 (2017)

4. Ni, C., Xia, X., Lo, D., Yang, X., Hassan, A.E.: just-in-time defect prediction on JavaScript projects: a replication study (2020)
5. Garcia, J., Feng, Y., Shen, J., Almanee, S., Xia, Y., Chen, A.Q.A.: A comprehensive study of autonomous vehicle bugs. In: Proceedings of the ACM/IEEE 42nd International Conference on Software Engineering, pp. 385–396 (2020)
6. Hoang, T., Dam, H.K., Kamei, Y., Lo, D., Ubayashi, N.: DeepJIT: an end-to-end deep learning framework for just-in-time defect prediction. In 2019 IEEE/ACM 16th International Conference on Mining Software Repositories (MSR) (pp. 34–45). IEEE (2019)
7. Hoang, T., Kang, H.J., Lo, D., Lawall, J.: CC2vec: distributed representations of code changes. In: Proceedings of the ACM/IEEE 42nd International Conference on Software Engineering, pp. 518–529 (2020)
8. Pornprasit, C., Tantithamthavorn, C.K.: JITLine: a simpler, better, faster, finer-grained just-in-time defect prediction. In: 2021 IEEE/ACM 18th International Conference on Mining Software Repositories (MSR), pp. 369–379. IEEE (2021)
9. Matsumoto, S., Kamei, Y., Monden, A., Matsumoto, K.I., Nakamura, M.: An analysis of developer metrics for fault prediction. In: Proceedings of the 6th International Conference on Predictive Models in Software Engineering, pp. 1–9 (2010)
10. Altinger, H., Siegl, S., Dajsuren, Y., Wotawa, F.: A novel industry grade dataset for fault prediction based on model-driven developed automotive embedded software. In: 2015 IEEE/ACM 12th Working Conference on Mining Software Repositories, pp. 494–497. IEEE (2015)
11. Altinger, H., Herbold, S., Schneemann, F., Grabowski, J., Wotawa, F.: Performance tuning for automotive software fault prediction. In: 2017 IEEE 24th International Conference on Software Analysis, Evolution and Reengineering (SANER), pp. 526–530. IEEE (2017)
12. Da Costa, D.A., McIntosh, S., Shang, W., Kulesza, U., Coelho, R., Hassan, A.E.: A framework for evaluating the results of the SZZ approach for identifying bug-introducing changes. IEEE Trans. Softw. Eng. 43(7), 641–657 (2016)
13. Peng, Z., Yang, J., Chen, T.H., Ma, L.: A first look at the integration of machine learning models in complex autonomous driving systems: a case study on apollo. In: Proceedings of the 28th ACM Joint Meeting on European Software Engineering Conference and Symposium on the Foundations of Software Engineering, pp. 1240–1250 (2020)
14. Lou, G.: Testing of autonomous driving systems: where are we and where should we go? (2021)
15. Moser, R., Pedrycz, W., & Succi, G.: A comparative analysis of the efficiency of change metrics and static code attributes for defect prediction. In Proceedings of the 30th International Conference on Software Engineering, pp. 181–190 (2008)
16. Rosa, G., et al.: Evaluating SZZ implementations through a developer-informed oracle. In: 2021 IEEE/ACM 43rd International Conference on Software Engineering (ICSE), pp. 436–447. IEEE (2021)
17. Fan, Y., Xia, X., da Costa, D.A., Lo, D., Hassan, A.E., Li, S.: The impact of mislabeled changes by SZZ on just-in-time defect prediction. IEEE Trans. Softw. Eng. 47(8), 1559–1586 (2019)
18. Kamei, Y., et al.: A large-scale empirical study of just-in-time quality assurance. IEEE Trans. Softw. Eng. 39(6), 757–773 (2012)
19. Kim, S., Zimmermann, T., Pan, K., James Jr., E.: Automatic identification of bug-introducing changes. In: 21st IEEE/ACM international conference on automated software engineering (ASE 2006), pp. 81–90. IEEE (2006)
20. Sawilowsky, S.S.: New effect size rules of thumb. J. Mod. Appl. Stat. Methods 8(2), 26 (2009)
21. Zeng, Z., Zhang, Y., Zhang, H., Zhang, L.: Deep just-in-time defect prediction: how far are we? In: Proceedings of the 30th ACM SIGSOFT International Symposium on Software Testing and Analysis, pp. 427–438 (2021)
22. Sasaki, Y., et al.: An edge-cloud computing model for autonomous vehicles. In: 11th IROS Workshop on Planning, Perception, Navigation for Intelligent Vehicle (2019)

Knowledge Sharing in Proactive WoT Multi-environment Models

Rubén Rentero-Trejo⑩, Jaime Galán-Jiménez⑩, José García-Alonso⑩,
Javier Berrocal(✉)⑩, and Juan Manuel Murillo⑩

University of Extremadura, Cáceres, Spain
{rrenterot,jaime,jgaralo,jberolm,juanmamu}@unex.es

Abstract. The main goal of Web of Things (WoT) is to improve people's quality of life by automating tasks and simplifying human-device interactions with ubiquitous systems. However, the management of devices still has to be carried out manually, making it very time-consuming as their number increases. Thus, not reaching the expected benefits. This management overload is higher when users change their environment or encounter new ones in their daily lives as new settings and interactions are required. To reduce the required effort, different learning systems assist in the management of automation tasks. However, they require extensive learning times to achieve personalization and cannot manage multiple environments. New approaches are required to manage multiple environments on the fly. Specifically, this paper focuses on knowledge distillation and teacher-student relationships to transfer knowledge between IoT environments in a model agnostic fashion, allowing users to share their knowledge whenever a new environment is encountered. This approach allowed us to eliminate training times and reach an average accuracy of 94.70%, making models automation effective from their acquisition in proactive Internet of Things (IoT) multi-environments.

Keywords: Knowledge distillation · Mobile devices · Context-aware

1 Introduction

According to the State of IoT 2021 report [21], there are more than 12 billion connected IoT devices nowadays. Equipped with sensors, computing and communication capabilities, these devices can be found everywhere working together to make our daily lives easier. Currently, controlling IoT devices is a simple task, as they are designed to execute simple and specific commands. However, in the near future and due to the growth of this field, these devices will be found in homes, workplaces, vehicles and so on, until everything becomes an IoT environment. People will move through these environments, interacting with their devices while changing their context, requirements and behaviour. This scenario demands IoT environments to proactively react to users' needs anytime, anywhere. Managing so many devices to make them personalized to users will become more complicated and time-consuming than ever, especially if the user needs to manually interact with every device whenever the context or their needs change, or whenever they arrive in an environment [24]. The situation worsens in new environments where users have no previous experiences and personalization does not exist yet. These extra efforts will cause users to perceive the IoT benefits as insufficient since it would not reduce the workload as much as expected.

There is a need for approaches that learn from users' behaviour and the contextual information around them, automating routines and thus avoiding time wasted on trivial manual actions which follow predictable patterns. Systems that provide greater control over other devices already exist on the market, such as the Amazon Echo, Google Nest or Apple Homepod voice assistants. However, these assistants do not support automated learning and serve as yet another programmable actuator [3] (e.g. voice assistants can be configured to automate a task, but cannot learn and assimilate changes by themselves). Some learning systems take advantage of the large amounts of data generated by IoT devices to learn behaviours and provide the desired automation. However, they often require long training times or periods of adaptation and are focused on a single environment [9,17]. For example, learning systems designed for a particular smart-home or room which are not usable 'as is', in any other scenario. Given this downside, out-of-the-box automation and personalization approaches are needed, allowing devices to be used efficiently from the early stages, avoiding manual actions or configurations. At the same time, the learnt knowledge must be reusable, providing the flexibility to face new situations and to experience personalization at all times, even if the environment, conditions or preferences change.

This paper presents an approach to sharing knowledge among the participants of a federation and establishes as the main requirement that knowledge acquired by learning models can be reused by other users. Knowledge sharing focuses on enabling participants to leverage the knowledge acquired by other participants (i.e. past experiences from similar users in similar environments) and use them in their particular environment, therefore avoiding the need to learn everything from scratch. Knowledge distillation [7] techniques are used to extract specific portions of knowledge from complex models and transfer it to new, simpler models. This proposal allows models to effectively share their knowledge, achieving an overall accuracy of 94.70% with brief distillation while often improving the source model performance. To this extent, users can refine their knowledge and share it with others in the context of proactive IoT multi-environments. Thus, reducing the need for interaction with IoT devices.

The paper is structured as follows. Section 2 presents the background and motivations of this work. Section 3 presents our proposal to improve knowledge exchanges between IoT multi-environment models and Sect. 4 presents a common scenario in IoT, the set-up and results. Section 5 presents related works on the field. Finally, discussion and concluding remarks are given in Sect. 6.

2   Motivation

Users demand automation and proactivity from IoT environments to fulfil their needs and preferences while models try to avoid most trivial manual actions by knowing their usual behavioural patterns. However, users do not stay in one single place but move through different environments. The visited environments must be able to react to users, based on their preferences and actions performed in the past. Static nodes are not suitable for this task due to their lack of mobility. Therefore, mobile edge nodes are proposed as learning nodes. They serve as companion devices since they know their users better than anyone, can orchestrate the behaviour of different environments as the main points of interaction, and their computing capabilities fit the automated learning necessities, reducing the dependency on the cloud. Related to this issue, different authors have proposed approaches like mobile-centric models to provide users greater control over their data [5], or an architecture to improve the integration of people within the IoT ecosystem [13]. To this end, mobile devices are proposed as mobile edge nodes to rule over the generated data. Their main role is to act as users' representatives and to be the main learning and decision-making nodes, interacting with IoT devices on their behalf. Since the main goal is personalization, dealing with multiple IoT devices, the way users operate them and the conditions around them give shape to an IoT environment. Learning models need to learn from the user's previous actions in other environments. The use of a common point, such as a mobile device, simplifies this task. However, the first problem to overcome is the lack of data. New users and new environments (i.e. mostly those consisting of devices the user has not previously used) experience a lack of previous data and models can not be trained. As a consequence, users need to generate data based on devices' usage, causing models to be inactive in their early stages and penalizing users' experience due to these adaptation periods [28].

To overcome this limitation, the knowledge of existing users needs to be transferred to other users and leveraged to avoid the initial training phases. Existing models can be exploited in situations where users do not have previous data, or when facing an environment that is different from their usual experience. However, the second problem arises when trying to select specific portions of knowledge. Performing an effective knowledge transfer in situations with ever-changing conditions like IoT environments and ever-evolving models is a challenging task due to the models' heterogeneity. For example, suppose a model which manages 4 different environments with many devices each. Now, if a user wants the functionality of only one environment, relationships between the subset of input features and the subset of output labels of interest cannot be decoupled from the rest of the network. Due to the nature of neural networks (NNs), layers can be deleted or added [8] and their neuron weights can be modified or transferred [12,19], but extracting specific end-to-end relationships is still a challenge (i.e. it cannot be known which specific set of neurons among the whole network produces a specific output).

To solve both issues, the concept of knowledge reusability needs to be extended to every mobile device. By reusing the knowledge assimilated by existent models, users will take advantage of the actions performed by previous users in situations where data is non-existent or insufficient. If the behaviours of **similar users** who have previously visited a **similar environment** are selected, a model capable of managing new environments can be generated. Knowledge Distillation [4] is the main driver of this approach. It allows distillation, extraction and sharing of knowledge (i.e. specific fragments). In exchange for a small training phase, a teacher model trains a student model. This process allows to extract end-to-end relationships by looking at models' outcomes from a model-agnostic perspective while maintaining the original performance. Finally, the student model acquires the processed knowledge and will mimic its teacher. Although this technique has a promising potential, it is usually used for model reduction, which converts a complex model into a simpler, faster and cheaper one, that does the same tasks. However, this process can be modified to make students mimic only specific tasks (i.e. each specific user needs).

Recovering the previous example, this approach allows newcomers to ask for a specific part of knowledge from a similar user. In this way, users acquire a trained and ready-to-use model. Even if some further refinement is needed to reach full personalization, the model will be ready from the early stages without heavy training phases while providing acceptable performance. This perspective avoids traditional learning necessities where time was needed to generate data to train on later, especially for models that need to achieve personalization.

This paper place Knowledge Distillation in the IoT context and extend its traditional use to allow the selection of knowledge fragments from complex models and create new, smaller and task-specific models. First, knowledge distillation techniques are applied to reduce the complexity of a larger and intensively trained model and distil it into a simpler one. Second, available data and the training algorithm are modified, so input features and output labels are reduced to fit the new model and user needs. This avoids providing an overly complex model to a user who is only interested in some specific functionalities, such as the behaviour of a single environment or a subset of devices, and avoids long waits for users when there is a deficit of data.

3   Knowledge Distillation in WoT Environments

This paper applies Knowledge Distillation (KD) to complex and heavily trained models to extract specific fragments of knowledge and transfer them to new and simpler models which fit other users' needs. The goal is to provide users with a personalised and ready-to-use model whenever they discover a new environment. The main components are as follows. 1) A complex, trained model that takes the role of the teacher. 2) A reduced, simpler model that takes the role of the student. 3) A distiller that implements the training algorithm and manages the distillation from teacher to student. Finally, by *complexity* we mean both the configuration and structure of the internal layers of a NN, as well as the number of input features and output labels.

Although distillation involves much less training compared to training a model from scratch, a small amount of data is still required. However, this data can be provided by both the teacher (e.g. a small history of recently performed actions) or the student (e.g. generated data from known preferences or usage data from the actual environment). They are needed to identify the internal relationships from the teacher inputs to the outputs. For privacy reasons, the distiller process takes place in the student mobile device using its data, avoiding the risk of data exposure. As the distiller needs both models, the teacher model is sent to the student (either compiled or as a list of neuron weights) to complete the process. Once the creation of the student model is done, the teacher model is discarded from the student's device. This also implies the student carries the distiller computation, as it will be the main beneficiary at the end of the process.

The process starts with a dataset of information (i.e. tuples of devices usage). After the pre-processing steps, two different datasets are obtained as input data (Fig. 1). Although representing the same information, they are processed differently to feed the two models since the feature space and the label space from both models are different (e.g. if a teacher manages 3 environments but the student is interested in one as Fig. 2 shows, the student dataset will not have any data related other environments or devices, modifying the feature space and the target output labels). More details about inputs are given in Sect. 4.2.

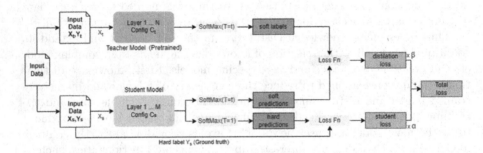

Fig. 1. Distiller workflow. Input data is processed into two datasets to fit networks input and output. Note that Y_t is never used. Configurations C_t and C_s can be different to make the distiller model agnostic and allow model heterogeneity.

The distiller coordinates the training. It performs the operations with the different functions and optimizers to update the weights of the neurons appropriately. The following process is carried out in each training step. First, the input data X_t is used to perform a forward pass on the trained teacher to get the soft labels from a *SoftMax* function and temperature (T). The purpose of the temperature parameter is to soften the logits and smooth the probability distribution to reveal the internal relationships learned from the teacher. The same process is performed with the input data X_s on the student to get soft predictions. To get the *distillation loss* (DL), Kullback-Leibler divergence has been applied to minimize both teacher and student probabilistic outputs (1).

A parallel process takes place to calculate the student loss (SL), being the difference between student predictions and ground-truth using the *softmax* function where $T = 1$ to get the original output, and the *Categorical CrossEntropy* (CCE) loss function (2) as it is a classification problem. Finally, the total loss (3) is obtained by weighting the two different losses (SL, DL) with an α value that ranges between 0 and 1. This total loss is the one used to get the gradients and update the trainable weights of the student NN with the optimizer.

$$DL = KLDivergence(Softmax(pred_t/T), Softmax(pred_s/T)) \qquad (1)$$

$$SL = CCE(Y_s, pred_s) \qquad (2)$$

$$TotalLoss = \alpha * SL + (1 - \alpha) * DL \qquad (3)$$

In our study, the most common situation involves models with different feature spaces and label spaces. Thus, some modifications need to be made to be able to operate with the different probabilistic outputs. The main restriction are operations that involve logits from different models, like DL (1). To make these operations viable, logits that are of no interest to the student need to be discarded to fit teacher and student shapes (e.g. if a student is interested in a specific device like smart tv, data from other devices is meaningless). This way, specific labels can be selected and transferred from one model to another.

In short, this process allows cumbersome and heavily trained models to share a specific part of their knowledge with third parties. It allows knowledge reusability and avoids intense training periods for newcomers and users when visiting new IoT environments since they acquire an immediate and adequate device personalization from the early stages of the model.

4   Validation

The validation of this work is structured as follows. Section 4.1 introduces the studied scenario and the source of our data. Section 4.2 deals with the algorithm technical details and model configurations. Finally, Sect. 4.3 present our results and analyze the proposal performance.

4.1   Scenario

A case study has been proposed with situations similar to the one illustrated in Fig. 2: Suppose a user (U1) that has many IoT devices (e.g. light bulbs, air conditioner, speakers, smart TV) in different IoT environments (e.g. home, office, car). This user can automate them with a learning model installed on his mobile device. Somewhere, another user (U2) enters an environment with the same settings that one specific environment from U1 while having similar preferences. Instead of training from scratch, U2 asks for U1's model, as it is already trained. As U2 is interested in just one environment, the mobile device extracts the knowledge of interest to then automate the newly discovered environment.

To measure the performance of our approach, a large number of datasets are needed. To do so, semi-synthetic data has been prepared following a specific process. First, real data was obtained from a set of real users who regularly interact with IoT devices. Notable differences between them were work and leisure schedules (hours and weekdays), device type preferences, usage, environment changes and occasional patterns. For 3 weeks, they have been provided with an Android app to specify the device, performed action, and environment. This first phase with real data gave us an accurate overview of how users interact with IoT devices and how their daily circumstances affects their behaviour in environments. However, the obtained data were not large enough to train a sufficient amount of learning models. Therefore, this real data was extended to get substantial data for training and testing purposes. TheONE Simulator [10] have been used to simulate human movement patterns. The relevant patterns for this work are those simulating the movements of a person in his day-to-day life through different places. Some examples are daily home-to-work trips and vice versa and occasional trips for leisure, visits or shopping purposes. By modifying its core, this tool allowed us to simulate interactions with IoT devices in different environments. For example, human-device interactions like turning on lights in the morning or at night, setting up alarms, setting up the desired temperature and choosing specific channels and radio stations on TV and speakers. For the sake of completion, 165 user datasets have been generated, being No-IID and unbalanced data, up to a maximum of 1.500 tuples each.

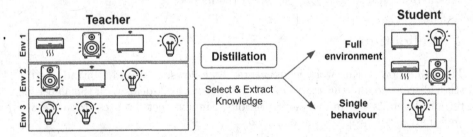

Fig. 2. Situation example where a teacher manages multiple environments (monolithic model) and student, who decides to learn a full environment or just the behaviour of a single device.

4.2   Set-Up

After an exhaustive data processing, each dataset has a maximum of 64 columns, generated from the source data by *One-Hot Encoding*, 54 of them will be taken as input features for NNs. Since we are dealing with a classification problem, the output data are 10 at the most. To set up students datasets (X_s, Y_s), the unused columns and tuples are removed and only the environment of interest for the student remains in the dataset. Teachers configurations vary from just a couple of layers to cumbersome models according to the user needs and their development over time.

For starters (i.e. students), in a previous work [18] we identified that the best performance relies on simple models with 2 hidden layers with 54 nodes each and an ADAM optimizer, which are capable of managing single environments of any kind. As summary, to find the best configuration for our models, different tests were performed on a high heterogeneity federation. The tests consisted of an exhaustive comparison of different NN definitions, changing the depth, complexity, number of layers, nodes, and use of techniques like Batch Normalization or Dropout. The four most relevant configurations were selected and studied in detail before choosing the best one. Additionally, to improve the models quality, a custom filter was designed for teachers, limiting their ability to teach on low-performance stages. Finally, after the distillation is complete, the students have been tested with new data unrelated to teachers and generated in the users' particular environment to check the performance of the reused knowledge under the conditions of new users. For completeness, 50 teachers were selected, which taught one of their environments to 50 students in a 1:1 ratio.

4.3   Results

The teacher models have been evaluated for their ability to transfer knowledge to other models. First, models that were still in the early stages of their development (i.e. less than 85% accuracy on their environments) have been discarded by the quality filter and are therefore not eligible for teaching. Second, the models selected as teachers achieved an average accuracy of 94.04%, and therefore well placed to share their knowledge effectively. Figure 3 shows the fast progress of models when teaching. Also, it is important to note that brief training is needed to achieve good learning. Although it is represented in steps, these data have been obtained in roughly 5 epochs.

New students, taught from the scratch by their respective teachers, obtained an average accuracy of 94.70%. This demonstrates that, overall, all of the resulting models were able not only to maintain the accuracy of their teachers, but also to improve it, as seen in Fig. 4. However, since both environments and users are heterogeneous, there are models that improve the accuracy of their teachers by more than 6%, while some cannot keep up with the teacher and their accuracy worsens by a similar amount in the worst case. Although this last case has rarely occurred in the study, the worst student had a performance of 88%, always comfortably meeting the minimum requirements of the established quality filter. It is an expected outcome, as not every user will ever perfectly match the needs and preferences of another user. At that point, the brief personalization period to fine-tune the model in its entirety would start from this solid base.

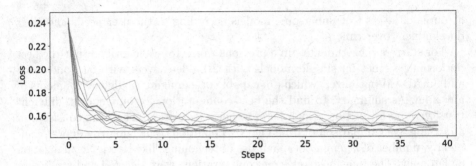

Fig. 3. Example of total loss obtained from a random subset of students. The average loss of all models is shown by the bold red line. For readability, each step represents 5 actual train steps in the algorithm (i.e. 200 steps in total). (Color figure online)

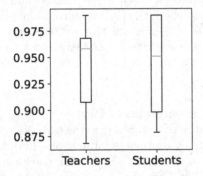

Fig. 4. Teachers and Students final accuracy (%) comparison. White boxes represent 50% of the models. The inner line is the central value (median).

5   Related Works

Although not focused on the IoT field, there are many works dealing with the concept of knowledge reusability, focusing their efforts on making cheaper and faster models capable of maintaining the performance of the original models. For example, in the Natural Language Processing field, Sanh et al. [20] applied distillation to the large-scale model BERT and improved the overall performance in a lighter model called DistilBERT. Aguinaldo et al. [1] studied model compression and its possibilities on Generative Adversarial Networks through KD. Proposed two novel methods and validated them on popular datasets as MNIST, CIFAR-10 and Celeb-A. In the image processing field, works like Yu et al. [27] studied how to efficiently compute image embeddings with small networks. Xiang [26] revisited the KD fundamentals and also proposed a new framework called Evolutionary Embedding Learning for open-set problems, which deepens on the model acceleration problem avoiding the trade-off in model accuracy. In Tang et al. [23] work, KD is first introduced into the recommender systems. Their proposal focuses on learning compact ranking models and is called Ranking Distillation, because the recommendation is expressed as a ranking problem. Polino et al. [15] studied the impact of combining distillation and quantization when compressing Deep NNs and demonstrates how students can reach similar accuracy levels to state-of-the-art full-precision teacher models. Finally, Guo et al. [6] focused their study on collaborative learning, dropping the traditional teacher-student scheme and treating all models as students. It enables parallel computation, fast models and an interesting generalization ability.

For the specific field of IoT environments there are very different approaches. In previous works [18], the authors of this paper focused on federations, leveraging individually generated knowledge to generate a collective benefit. However, as it relies on federated learning (FL), federation models' structures and internal details are limited to the one imposed by the server and do not allow the extraction of fragments of knowledge. Incurring situations where a user ends up with an unnecessary complex model to solve simple situations and vice versa. For example, Savazzi et al. [22] uses FL [12] to collaboratively train a global model that generalizes a federation behaviour, and applies it to massive IoT networks to leverage the mutual cooperation of devices. *Transfer Learning* can also be used to learn some or all parameters in the global model and re-learn them in local models [25], but those models cannot be re-trained for too long to avoid knowledge forgetting. Nascimiento et al. [14] also proposed an architecture that uses a ML model to analyze a dataset or interact with an environment, and also monitors changes in the context. Sangsu et al. [11] propose an approach where mobile devices are also the main learning nodes. It extends FL as an egocentric collaboration in opportunistic networks where devices learn new information from encounters with other devices. Nevertheless, this approach is tied to opportunistic encounters that may or may not occur. Kabir et al. [9] propose an architecture which provides services according to users' choices using machine learning. However, there is no discussion about detecting other environments automatically and the multi-environment concept is kept inside the same home. Bahirat et al. [2] present a data-driven approach to improve privacy. By applying machine learning techniques, default smart profiles are generated and then recommended to other users. Zipperle et al. [29] propose a framework to describe task-based IoT services and their settings in a semantical manner and decouple them from their physical environments. However, still has limitations like the increasing complexity and deteriorating accuracy over time. Finally, recommender systems are a widely used option. Although presenting limitations of mobility between environments and usually focused on a single environment, they take the concept of IoT and Smart-home to a higher level as Smart-cities [16].

6 Conclusions

During the development of this work, the following limitations have been identified: 1) As seen, smart environments can be very different and heterogeneous, same as the needs of the users who frequent them. This fact makes the teacher-student matching a challenging task in some cases. 2) Although KD is a popular technique, it is necessary to control that teachers do not train students for too long. Otherwise, students' performance will be negatively affected. 3) The distillation process can be also carried out teachers. However, this would have disastrous scalability within a federation, since many students can request knowledge from the same teacher, saturating it. In addition, teachers are not rewarded for training students, so it is more fair for the student to make the effort.

Currently, we are improving the association and clustering of similar users and similar environments to ensure that students can take full advantage of the knowledge gained from teachers. In future works, we plan to apply the proposed approach in social environments, where many users need to be taken into account in the same environment and conflicts of interests need to be addressed.

Acknowledgement. This work was funded by the project RTI2018-094591-B-I00 (MCI/AEI/FEDER, UE), the 4IE+ Project (0499-4IE-PLUS-4-E) funded by the Interreg V-A España-Portugal (POCTEP) 2014–2020 program, by the Department of Economy, Science and Digital Agenda of the Government of Extremadura (GR21133, IB18030), and by the European Regional Development Fund.

References

1. Aguinaldo, A., Chiang, P.Y., Gain, A., Patil, A.D., Pearson, K., Feizi, S.: Compressing GANs using knowledge distillation. arXiv abs/1902.00159 (2019)
2. Bahirat, P., He, Y., Menon, A., Knijnenburg, B.: A data-driven approach to developing IoT privacy-setting interfaces. In: IUI 2018, pp. 165–176. Association for Computing Machinery (2018). https://doi.org/10.1145/3172944.3172982
3. Becca, C., Hick, P., Henry, S.L.: The best smart speakers 2021 (2021). https://www.techradar.com/news/best-smart-speakers
4. Gou, J., Yu, B., Maybank, S.J., Tao, D.: Knowledge distillation: a survey. Int. J. Comput. Vis. **129**(6), 1789–1819 (2021). https://doi.org/10.1007/S11263-021-01453-Z/TABLES/6
5. Guillén, J., Miranda, J., Berrocal, J., García-Alonso, J., Murillo, J.M., Canal, C.: People as a service: a mobile-centric model for providing collective sociological profiles. IEEE Softw. **31**(2), 48–53 (2014). https://doi.org/10.1109/MS.2013.140
6. Guo, Q., et al.: Online knowledge distillation via collaborative learning. In: Proceedings of the IEEE/CVF Conference on Computer Vision and Pattern Recognition (CVPR) (2020)
7. Hinton, G.E., Vinyals, O., Dean, J.: Distilling the knowledge in a neural network. arXiv abs/1503.02531 (2015)
8. Hu, H., Peng, R., Tai, Y., Tang, C.: Network trimming: a data-driven neuron pruning approach towards efficient deep architectures. CoRR abs/1607.03250 (2016). http://arxiv.org/abs/1607.03250
9. Kabir, M., Hoque, M.R., Yang, S.H.: Development of a smart home context-aware application: a machine learning based approach. IJSH **9**, 217–226 (2015)
10. Keränen, A., Kärkkäinen, T., Pitkänen, M., Ekman, F., Karvo, J., Ott, J.: Information - The ONE. https://akeranen.github.io/the-one/
11. Lee, S., Zheng, X., Hua, J., Vikalo, H., Julien, C.: Opportunistic federated learning: an exploration of egocentric collaboration for pervasive computing applications. In: PerCom 2021, pp. 1–8 (2021). https://doi.org/10.1109/PERCOM50583.2021.9439130

12. McMahan, H., Moore, E., Ramage, D., Arcas, B.A.: Federated learning of deep networks using model averaging. arXiv abs/1602.05629 (2016)
13. Miranda, J., et al.: From the internet of things to the internet of people. IEEE Internet Comput. **19**(2), 40–47 (2015). https://doi.org/10.1109/MIC.2015.24
14. Nascimento, N., Alencar, P., Lucena, C., Cowan, D.: A context-aware machine learning-based approach. In: CASCON (2018)
15. Polino, A., Pascanu, R., Alistarh, D.: Model compression via distillation and quantization. In: International Conference on Learning Representations (2018)
16. Quijano-Sánchez, L., Cantador, I., Cortés-Cediel, M.E., Gil, O.: Recommender systems for smart cities. Inf. Syst. **92**, 101545 (2020). https://doi.org/10.1016/j.is.2020.101545
17. Reinisch, C., Kofler, M.J., Kastner, W.: Thinkhome: a smart home as digital ecosystem. In: IEEE-DEST 2010, pp. 256–261 (2010)
18. Rentero-Trejo, R., Flores-Martín, D., Galán-Jiménez, J., García-Alonso, J., Murillo, J.M., Berrocal, J.: Using federated learning to achieve proactive context-aware IoT environments. J. Web Eng. (2021). https://doi.org/10.13052/jwe1540-9589.2113
19. Saha, S., Ahmad, T.: Federated transfer learning: concept and applications. Intelligenza Artificiale **15**, 35–44 (2021)
20. Sanh, V., Debut, L., Chaumond, J., Wolf, T.: DistilBERT, a distilled version of BERT: smaller, faster, cheaper and lighter. arXiv abs/1910.01108 (2019)
21. Satyajit Sinha: State of IoT 2021 (2021). https://iot-analytics.com/number-connected-iot-devices/
22. Savazzi, S., Nicoli, M., Rampa, V.: Federated learning with cooperating devices: a consensus approach for massive IoT networks. IEEE Internet Things J. **7**(5), 4641–4654 (2020). https://doi.org/10.1109/JIOT.2020.2964162
23. Tang, J., Wang, K.: Ranking distillation: learning compact ranking models with high performance for recommender system. In: KDD 2018, pp. 2289–2298. Association for Computing Machinery (2018). https://doi.org/10.1145/3219819.3220021
24. Thieme, W.: Why It Is Time to Prioritize IoT Network and Device Management (2020). https://www.iotevolutionworld.com/iot/articles/445675-why-it-time-prioritize-iot-network-device-management.htm
25. Wang, K., Mathews, R., Kiddon, C., Eichner, H., Beaufays, F., Ramage, D.: Federated evaluation of on-device personalization. arXiv abs/1910.10252 (2019)
26. Wu, X., He, R., Hu, Y., Sun, Z.: Learning an evolutionary embedding via massive knowledge distillation. Int. J. Comput. Vis. **128**(8), 2089–2106 (2020). https://doi.org/10.1007/s11263-019-01286-x
27. Yu, L., Yazici, V.O., Liu, X., van de Weijer, J., Cheng, Y., Ramisa, A.: Learning metrics from teachers: compact networks for image embedding. In: CVPR 2019, pp. 2902–2911 (2019). https://doi.org/10.1109/CVPR.2019.00302
28. Zhuang, F., et al.: A comprehensive survey on transfer learning. Proc. IEEE **109**(1), 43–76 (2021). https://doi.org/10.1109/JPROC.2020.3004555
29. Zipperle, M., Karduck, A., Ko, I.-Y.: Context-aware transfer of task-based IoT service settings. In: Arai, K., Kapoor, S., Bhatia, R. (eds.) IntelliSys 2020. AISC, vol. 1252, pp. 96–114. Springer, Cham (2021). https://doi.org/10.1007/978-3-030-55190-2_8

Multivariate Time Series Anomaly Detection Based on Reconstructed Differences Using Graph Attention Networks

Jung Mo Kang and Myoung Ho Kim[✉]

Korea Advanced Institute of Science and Technology, Daejeon, Republic of Korea
{qazec19,mhkim}@kaist.ac.kr

Abstract. Today, many real-world applications generate the amount of multivariate time series data. Monitoring those data and detecting some meaningful events early is important. As one of those tasks, interest in anomaly detection has grown. In recent research, some authors conducted anomaly detection in multivariate time series data by using graph attention networks to capture relationships among series and timestamps respectively. And another author suggested some connections between timestamps called Spatio-temporal connections. In this paper, we combine two ideas jointly and propose another multivariate time series anomaly detection method using series differences between adjacent timestamps. By using the proposed method, we conduct anomaly detection on two public datasets and compare the performance with other models. Also, to check for the possibility of operation on the edge environment, we measure the throughput of our proposed method in the IoT edge gateway that has restricted resources.

Keywords: Multivariate time series data · Anomaly detection · Graph attention networks · IoT edge gateway

1 Introduction

Today, several real-world applications or systems, e.g., sensors installed in the smart factory, generate the amount of data. As the size of generated data has grown more and more, it is one of the important interests how we utilize and analyze this huge data. Although there are several ways to utilize collected data, one of the important tasks is event detection. Event detection is a process of finding the particular event or pattern of event that we have been interested in among the numerous flow of the data. Meanwhile, the type of generated data usually becomes time series data, i.e., multivariate time series data, because the data is generated, collected, or observed periodically. Consequently, event detection is essentially relevant to the time series data domain. Although there exist many types of valuable events in the time series data domain, one of the important events is an anomaly. An anomaly is an event shown differently from the

G. Agapito et al. (Eds.): ICWE 2022 Workshops, CCIS 1668, pp. 58–69, 2023.
https://doi.org/10.1007/978-3-031-25380-5_5

general or expected event pattern. If we can detect anomalies early, we prevent some disasters that will occur in the future and get some benefits. For example, in terms of industrial, detecting anomalies in systems early can save money and time. Moreover, these monitoring and detection can have more benefits in the edge environment because of lower latency. On the other hand, apart from the edge environment, research about anomaly detection in multivariate time series data has been conducted because of the importance of anomaly detection tasks. Especially, after the graph attention mechanism [10] was proposed, some researchers used the graph attention mechanism to detect anomalies in the multivariate time series data. As one of those research, the authors of MTAD-GAT [13] generated graph structure data in terms of series and timestamps respectively, adapted the graph attention mechanism to each graph structure data, and utilized the reconstruction-based method and forecasting-based method together. Consequently, MTAD-GAT showed good performance on two public datasets. In the forecasting field, the author of [14] suggested the Spatio-temporal connection between adjacent timestamps. The author showed the connection can improve the forecasting performance. So, in this paper, we combine these two ideas jointly and suggest another multivariate time series anomaly detection method using series differences between adjacent timestamps. Also, as we mentioned, because monitoring anomaly is one of the valuable tasks in the edge environment, we measured the possibility of the proposed method being executed in restricted hardware resources of the edge environment.

2   Related Works

In this section, we describe some related works about anomaly detection in the multivariate time series domain. At first, the outlier detection algorithm like [1] had been used because the anomaly detection was started from the outlier detection problem. But those outlier detection algorithms couldn't consider both the temporal character of the time series and the complex inner relationship between series. As the result, the forecasting-based method had been used based on the statistical model such as ARIMA to consider the temporal dependency. In recent, however, the deep learning-based method has been widely proposed because of the good computation and inference performance as the universal function approximator. One of the first deep learning-based methods was [5]. This method suggested the LSTM autoencoder architecture and compared the forecasting-based method and reconstruction-based method for the multivariate time series anomaly detection. Next, LSTM-NDT [3] used the forecasting-based method with the LSTM autoencoder and suggested a non-parametric dynamic threshold technique. OmniAnomaly [9] used the GRU autoencoder and variational inference and exploited a planar normalization flow to build a more complex latent distribution from the simple normal distribution. Also, the author adapted the extreme value theory introduced in [8] to set the threshold automatically as possible. MSCRED [12] used the correlation to capture the relationship between series. The author also used the convolution LSTM to reflect temporal property. However, the relationship between series couldn't be perfectly

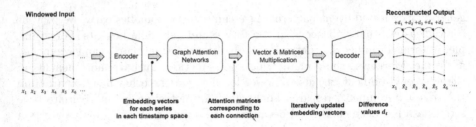

Fig. 1. An overview of the detection process conducted in our neural net model

represented by the linear correlation. So, to represent the relationship between series more correctly, the graph structure data has been used. GDN [2] and MTAD-GAT [13] used the graph attention network (GAT) [10] to consider the relationship between series. Moreover, [13] showed good performance by using the reconstruction-based method and the forecasting-based method together. Inspired by [2,13], our proposed method also uses graph attention networks. But differing from them, we combine the Spatio-temporal connection concept introduced in STJGCN [14] as the temporal connection for improved performance. We propose another reconstruction-based anomaly detection method using series differences between adjacent timestamps. We also measure the execution possibility in the restricted hardware resource assuming the edge environment, unlike previous studies (Fig. 1).

3   Methods

3.1   Problem Definition

In this paper, we address the anomaly detection problem in multivariate time series data. We assume the overlapping sliding windowed input $X_{t+1:t+w} = \{x_{t+1}, \dots, x_{t+w}\}$ with a fixed length of w. Each $x_{t+n,n=1,\dots,w}$ is a k dimension vector and we denote the i-th scalar element of the vector x_{t+n} as x_{t+n}^i. Our purpose is to determine whether the given input $X_{t+1:t+w}$ contains some anomalous parts or not based on the anomaly score $S(X_{t+1:t+w})$. We will describe how we compute the anomaly score in Sect. 3.6.

3.2   Encoder Architecture

Some research [6,13] used the entire series to generate graph structure data, but we build the series relationship graph from the bottom, i.e., timestamp unit. To generate i-th series' embedding vector f_{t+n}^i from x_{t+n}^i scalar value, we use the transpose convolution 1D 4 layers with a kernel size of 7 as an encoder. Also, to capture the diverse range of series information, we use three additional sub-encoders. Specifically, these three sub-encoders consist of convolution 1D [6, 3, 2] layers with the same kernel size of 7, and dilation size of [2, 2, 1] respectively. The first sub-encoder can capture the long-range of series information because 6 layers have large reception fields. The second and third sub-encoders capture the

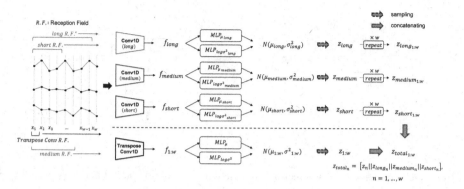

Fig. 2. The process of encoding embedding vectors (The case of $t = 0$)

medium and short range of series information respectively in proportion to the number of layers and dilation sizes. After being generated, embedding vectors are given to MLP layers to compute mean and log variance because we adapt the VAE [4] architecture (Fig. 2).

$$\text{TransConv1D}(x_{t+n}) = f_{t+n}, \ \text{Conv1D}_{type}(X_{t+1:t+w}) = f_{type} \qquad (1)$$

$$\mu_{t+n} = \text{MLP}_\mu(f_{t+n}), \ \log \sigma^2_{t+n} = \text{MLP}_{\log \sigma^2}(f_{t+n}) \qquad (2)$$

$$\mu_{type} = \text{MLP}_{\mu_{type}}(f_{type}), \ \log \sigma^2_{type} = \text{MLP}_{\log \sigma^2_{type}}(f_{type}) \qquad (3)$$

$$z_{t+n} = sample(N(\mu_{t+n}, \sigma^2_{t+n})), \ z_{type} = sample(N(\mu_{type}, \sigma^2_{type})) \qquad (4)$$

$$z_{type_{1:w}} = repeat(z_{type}, w) \qquad (5)$$

$$z_{total_{t+n}} = [z_{t+n} \ || \ z_{long_n} \ || \ z_{medium_n} \ || \ z_{short_n}], \ n = 1, ..., w \qquad (6)$$

In (1), the $f_{t+n} \in \mathbb{R}^{k \times d_f}$ and the $f_{type} \in \mathbb{R}^{k \times d_{type}}$ are embedding vectors. The *type* means each element of {*long, medium, short*}. The d_f and d_{type} mean each series' embedding vector dimensions respectively. The *sample* means sampling and the *repeat* replicates z_{type} latent vector w times. The reason why we need *repeat* is to match the number of z_{type} to the number of z_{t+n}. Because Conv1D$_{type}$ sub-encoders use the windowed input $X_{t+1:t+w}$, f_{type} and z_{type} vectors are generated only once for each *type*. In contrast, the TransConv1D uses each timestamp input and z_{t+n} feature vectors are generated as the number of timestamps, w. Consequently, we use *repeat* to resolve the inconsistency of the length. Next, we use a concatenate operate [...||...] to combine z_{t+n} and z_{type_n} along the series dimension axis. The $z_{total_{t+1:t+w}} \in \mathbb{R}^{w \times k \times d_{total}}$ is a concatenated feature and the value of $d_{total} = d_f + d_{long} + d_{medium} + d_{short}$.

3.3 Graph Attention Mechanism Between Timestamps

As the previous research [2,13] showed, the graph attention network (GAT) can capture the relation between time series. MTAD-GAT [13] generated two graph

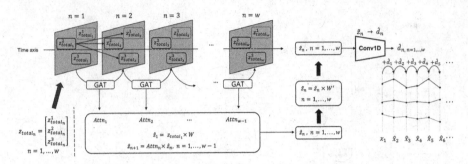

Fig. 3. The process of GATs, vector & matrices multiplication, and differences decoding

structures to capture the series and timestamps relationship, but we combine them as a single graph attention mechanism by using the concept of Spatio-temporal connection [14]. If you see Fig. 3, you can see connections between $z_{total_1}^2$, i.e., the $2nd$ series' embedding vector of $n = 1$ timestamp space, and the entire embedding vectors of $n = 2$ timestamp space. They were introduced as Spatio-temporal connections in [14], but in our proposed method, we use those connections as temporal connections between adjacent timestamps. After assuming the temporal connection exists in every pair of vectors between adjacent timestamp space, we compute attention scores by (7) and (8).

$$e_{p,q,t+n} = \text{LeakyReLU}([z_{total_{t+n}}^p W \| z_{total_{t+n+1}}^q W]a) \tag{7}$$

$$\alpha_{p,q,t+n} = \frac{exp(e_{p,q,t+n})}{\sum_{r=1}^k (exp(e_{p,r,t+n}))} \tag{8}$$

In (7), $W \in \mathbb{R}^{d_{total} \times l}$ is a weight matrix for the linear transform and $a \in \mathbb{R}^{2l \times 1}$ is a shared attention mechanism. l is a linear transform dimension and exp means a natural exponential function. $\alpha_{p,q,t+n}$ is an attention coefficient corresponding to the edge from the latent vector $z_{total_{t+n}}^p$ to the latent vector $z_{total_{t+n+1}}^q$. Also, the $z_{total_{t+n}}^p \in \mathbb{R}^{1 \times d_{total}}$ means a p-th series' latent vector at $(t+n)$-th timestamp space and $z_{total_{t+n+1}}^q \in \mathbb{R}^{1 \times d_{total}}$ indicates a q-th series' latent vector at $(t+n+1)$-th timestamp space. In this process, the graph attention layer may learn the temporal property and series relationship simultaneously.

3.4   Vector and Matrices Multiplication

After getting attention score matrices for all connections between adjacent timestamps, we compute the linear transformed latent feature $\hat{z}_{t+1:t+w}$ by multiplying with attention matrices $Attn_{t+1:t+w-1}$ iteratively. This process can be understood as the consecutive implicit forecasting process because we start from the first latent vector and compute the remaining vectors by considering the relationship between each series, i.e., multiplication with attention matrices. Also, if anomalous data exist in some timestamps, the relationship between normal preceding timestamps and trailing abnormal timestamps may cause incorrect graph attention scores in the previous step. As proceeding with this step, the wrong attention scores may gradually amplify errors and the amplified error can make the model detect an anomaly easier.

$$\hat{z}_{t+n+1} = Attn_{t+n} \times \hat{z}_{t+n}, \ \hat{z}_{t+1} = z_{total_{t+1}} \times W, \ n = 1, ..., w-1$$
$$Attn_{t+n} = \{\alpha_{p,q,t+n} \mid p = 1, ..., k, q = 1, ..., k\}, \ Attn_{t+n} \in \mathbb{R}^{k \times k} \tag{9}$$

3.5 Decoder Architecture

Before we pass the computed latent features to the decoder layer, we first change the dimension of each latent feature $\hat{z}_{t+n}$ from $\mathbb{R}^{k \times l}$ to $\mathbb{R}^{k \times d_{total}}$. To do this, we use a weight matrix $W' \in \mathbb{R}^{l \times d_{total}}$. After each latent feature's dimension comes back, we pass the latent feature to the convolution decoder. Because this process is a reverse version of Sect. 3.2, the convolution 1D 4 layers with kernel size 7 are used instead of transpose convolution. As one important thing in this phase, we don't reconstruct the original input time series data directly. Otherwise, the model may memorize the data rather than learn it. To avoid that, we make the model decode series differences between adjacent timestamps. After finishing the reconstruction of differences, the model finally reconstructs input time series values by adding differences to the first timestamp input value iteratively. And then, we compute the loss function value following (12) and train our model to reduce the loss value. The first term of (12) is a mean squared error between input data and reconstructed data. The second and third terms reduce a gap between the encoder's recognition latent distribution and normal distribution.

$$\tilde{z}_{t+n} = \hat{z}_{t+n} \times W', \ \hat{d}_{t+n} = \text{Conv1D}_{dec}(\tilde{z}_{t+n}) \tag{10}$$

$$\hat{x}_{t+n+1} = \hat{x}_{t+n} + \hat{d}_{t+n}, \ \hat{x}_{t+1} = x_{t+1}, \ n = 1, ..., w-1 \tag{11}$$

$$
\begin{aligned}
Loss = \ & MSE(X_{t+1:t+w}, \hat{X}_{t+1:t+w}) \\
& - \tfrac{1}{2} \sum_{types}(1 + \log \sigma_{type}^2 - \mu_{type}^2 - \sigma_{type}^2) \\
& - \tfrac{1}{2} \sum_{n=1}^{w}(1 + \log \sigma_{t+n}^2 - \mu_{t+n}^2 - \sigma_{t+n}^2)
\end{aligned}
\tag{12}
$$

3.6 Criterion for Detection

We check whether the given windowed input $X_{t+1:t+w}$ contains an anomaly or not based on the last time series value x_{t+w} because we reconstruct the input data by adding reconstructed differences consecutively to the first input value x_{t+1}. If only normal time series data exist in the given windowed input, our neural net model may reconstruct differences between adjacent timestamps with a small error. In contrast, if some anomalous data exist in the given window, our model cannot reconstruct differences well. So, the error will be accumulated and the last time series value may show a huge error compared with the ground truth value. To quantify how the windowed data $X_{t+1:t+w}$ is anomalous, we compute the anomaly score $S(X_{t+1:t+w})$ based on the reconstruction error of the last time series value x_{t+w} by using (13). If the computed anomaly score exceeds the fixed threshold value τ, we regard the windowed data $X_{t+1:t+w}$ to have some anomalies. Otherwise, the windowed data $X_{t+1:t+w}$ is regarded as the normal data.

$$S(X_{t+1:t+w}) = \sqrt{\frac{1}{k}\sum_{i=1}^{k}(x_{t+w}^i - \hat{x}_{t+w}^i)^2} \qquad (13)$$

3.7   Strategy for Setting Threshold Automatically

In this section, we describe how to select the threshold automatically. In the time series domain, the threshold is a key criterion to decide the model's performance. However, the model can't know future inputs. To address this issue, [8] proposed a method to select threshold values automatically based on the Extreme Value Theory (EVT). A summary of the EVT is that the probability distribution of extreme values is similar to each other regardless of the original probability distribution where extreme values are extracted. It means the probability distribution of the extreme score value corresponding anomaly is similar to each other in the training dataset and testing dataset. Consequently, we can adapt the extreme score distribution computed by the training dataset to the test dataset. To use this method, we first set the criterion for peak values among known data, i.e., training data. The author suggested τ_{init} in (14) as a value of 0.98 quantiles [8]. Based on this initial threshold τ_{init}, we can get peak values from the known dataset. Next, we conduct the maximum likelihood estimation over the Generalized Pareto Distribution (GPD) by using observed peak values. The GPD is a generalized probability distribution of tail distributions and we can get a real threshold value z_q by setting the $risk$ value q as desired value, e.g., 10^{-4}. The Eq. (14) is a result of maximum likelihood estimation. $\hat{\sigma}$ and $\hat{\gamma}$ are results from maximum likelihood estimation and N_t means the number of observed peak values. n is the number of total observed values, and q is a $risk$ value. z_q means the quantile value satisfying $P(X > z_q) < q$. This z_q will be used as a fixed threshold τ in the test phase.

$$z_q \simeq \tau_{init} + \frac{\hat{\sigma}}{\hat{\gamma}}\left(\left(\frac{qn}{N_t}\right)^{-\hat{\gamma}} - 1\right) \qquad (14)$$

4   Experiments

4.1   Datasets

In experiments, we used two public datasets in the multivariate time series anomaly detection domain. One is the MSL (Mars Science Laboratory) dataset and the other is the SMAP (Soil Moisture Active Passive) dataset. Both datasets were used in [3] and collected by NASA. Please refer to Table 1 if you want to know the details of these two datasets. Because original datasets don't have validation datasets, we used 30% of training datasets as validation datasets for

Table 1. The details of datasets.

Name	# of items	Dimensions	# of train timestamps	# of valid timestamps	# of test timestamps	Ratio of anomalies
MSL	27	55	40,822	17,495	73,728	10.72%
SMAP	55	25	94,629	40,554	427,617	13.13%

early stopping. We also used both training and validation datasets to select the threshold τ automatically based on the EVT [8].

4.2 Experiment Settings

We implemented the proposed model by using PyTorch and used Adam optimizer with a learning rate of 0.0003 for training. We trained our model during 20 epochs and adopted early stopping when the validation loss exceeds the average of the previous 5 validation losses. We also set the window size $w = 100$ following previous research [9,13] and batch size as 1 following [4]. All training processes were conducted under the Ubuntu 20.04 LTS OS with Intel(R) Core(TM) i7-10700 CPU 2.90 GHz and NVIDIA RTX 3090 with 24 GB VRAM. We also measured the possibility of whether our model can be executed on some devices having restricted hardware resources. We tested our model in the IoT gateway device based on the Odroid N2 model. The IoT gateway has the ARM Cortex-A73 1.8 GHz and Dual-core Cortex-A53 1.9 GHz with 4 GB RAM. Lastly, We empirically used the risk $q = 0.005$ and $\tau_{init} = 0.95$ quantiles for the SMAP dataset and the risk $q = 0.025$ and $\tau_{init} = 0.95$ quantiles for the MSL dataset.

5 Results

5.1 The Performance Comparison

In this section, we compare the proposed method's performance with other multivariate time series anomaly detection models. The metric is an f1-score used widely in the anomaly detection domain. We also quote the [13]'s model performance table because we used the same threshold selection method based on the EVT [8]. The performance comparison result is like Table 2. As you can see, our proposed method shows the best precision and the f1-score performance on the SMAP dataset. However, the proposed method shows the third performance on the MSL dataset. So, we should find the reason why the performance is lower in the MSL dataset in future work. Although we're not sure, we may infer two reasons. According to [14], the author said the Spatio-temporal connection grows up the forecasting performance. And [13] said the forecasting-based anomaly detection methods such as LSTM-NDT and DAGMM show better performance on the SMAP dataset than the MSL dataset. In Sect. 3.4, we may understand that the model implicitly forecasts differences between adjacent timestamps. Consequently, our model may show a better performance on the SMAP data compared

Table 2. The performance comparison for each dataset.

Model	SMAP			MSL		
	Precision	Recall	F1-score	Precision	Recall	F1-score
OmniAnomaly	0.7416	**0.9776**	0.8434	**0.8867**	0.9117	0.8989
KitNet	0.7725	0.8327	0.8014	0.6312	0.7936	0.7031
GAN-Li	0.6710	0.8706	0.7579	0.7102	0.8706	0.7823
MAD-GAN	0.8049	0.8214	0.8131	0.8517	0.8991	0.8747
LSTM-VAE	0.8551	0.6366	0.7298	0.5257	0.9546	0.6780
LSTM-NDT	0.8965	0.8846	0.8905	0.5934	0.5374	0.5640
DAGMM	0.5845	0.9058	0.7105	0.5412	**0.9934**	0.7007
MTAD-GAT	0.8906	0.9123	0.9013	0.8754	0.9440	**0.9084**
Proposed	**0.9379**	0.9257	**0.9318**	0.8316	0.9225	0.8747

with the MSL data because of the Spatio-temporal connection and the property of the SMAP dataset. The other reason may be a property of differences. In the time series data analysis, getting the difference between adjacent timestamps is one way of transforming non-stationary time series into stationary time series. In the stationary time series case, statistical indices such as mean and variance don't change over time. That makes sometimes the stationary time series be looked like a random signal such as white noise. It makes also the stationary time series hard to be forecasted in long term. So, we have a plan to conduct a test such as KPSS to check for the stationary property of reconstructed differences. Additionally, there may exist some other reasons that lower the model performance in the MSL data set, e.g., incorrect graph structure generation method, or absence of the neural net model to capture the temporal property.

5.2   The Throughput Measurement of the Proposed Model

As we mentioned in the introduction and abstract, in the monitoring system, utilizing the edge environment may be useful. However, one of some problems in the edge environment is the restricted device performance. So we measured the throughput to check for the execution possibility of the proposed method in the restricted hardware resources. Specifically, we checked the throughput of our proposed model by using the tqdm library displaying batch iterations per second or seconds per batch iteration. We used a single batch in both training and testing and the single batch corresponds to a single-window data. Therefore the iterations per second can be understood as the throughput of our proposed method. As a result, in the IoT edge gateway described in Sect. 4.2, our proposed method shows 2.24 iterations per second on the SMAP dataset. It means our proposed method can conduct detection for 2.24 windows with a window length $w=100$ per second. In the MSL dataset case, the tqdm library shows 1.07 iterations per second. Because the MSL dataset consists of 55 series compared with

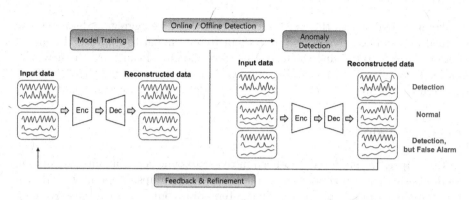

Fig. 4. The entire process of training, detection, feedback, and refinements.

25 series of the SMAP data, the MSL data requires more computation and this causes the lower throughput performance. So, if we deploy our anomaly detection model in the small IoT edge gateway, the proposed model can be operated normally when the gap of taking raw data input is larger than 1 s without considering other overhead. That condition seems hard to be satisfied, but one solution is to use a non-overlapping sliding window mechanism. When we suppose the gap between every new raw input data is 1 s, the overlapping sliding window mechanism has to process windowed input within every 1 s. However, in the non-overlapping sliding window mechanism, the proposed model doesn't need to produce the detection output within every 1 s because the model can have spare time about 100 s before getting the next windowed input. Fortunately, because some recent research [7, 11] also shows good performance in the non-overlapping sliding window mechanism, we will consider the non-overlapping sliding window mechanism in future work.

5.3 Feedback and Refinement Process

Although we used the reconstruction-based method to detect anomalies in this paper, in fact, it is a drawback of the reconstruction-based method that the model cannot correctly distinguish the input data not seen in the training phase. In other words, in the test or detection phase, if the model encounters the data that doesn't appear during the training, the model may regard the data as an anomaly. But the data also can be normal. To avoid this situation, we should periodically collect those false alarm cases and retrain the model. This feedback and refinement process can be represented in Fig. 4. First, the model is trained on the collected multivariate time series data regarding as normal. Second, the model conducts detection in the online or offline environment. The online environment means real-time, and the offline means not real-time but collected data during some periods. Third, whenever the model detects anomaly candidates, the human expert may confirm whether candidates are real anomalies or not. In Fig. 4, the model correctly detects the anomaly in the first input data but makes a false alarm on the third input data. Lastly, we aggregate data that are turned out as false alarms and give them to the model to improve the model performance by retraining them. In this step, the model can learn the new normal data patterns and recognize them as normal. By repeating these feedback and refinement steps, we can improve the model's performance gradually.

6   Conclusion

In this paper, we proposed another multivariate time series anomaly detection method using the difference between adjacent timestamps. We jointly combined the graph attention concept and Spatio-temporal connection concept. We conducted experiments on the two public datasets in the multivariate time series anomaly detection domain and the proposed method showed better performance than the baseline model [13] in one dataset. We also measured the proposed method's possibility that can be executed in the small restricted hardware resources device such as the edge environment. And we suggested another direction to improve the throughput of the proposed method. Lastly, we suggested the feedback and refinement process to improve and maintain the model's performance. However, as you have seen, there are some remaining issues in this research. We will find the specific reason why the model's performance is lower in the MSL dataset, and we will measure the throughput of the proposed method in the restricted hardware environment again after retraining the model in a non-overlapping sliding window mechanism.

Acknowledgements. This research was supported by the MSIT (Ministry of Science and ICT), Korea, under the ITRC (Information Technology Research Center) support program (IITP-2020-0-01795) supervised by the IITP (Institute of Information & Communications Technology Planning & Evaluation). This work was supported by the Bio-Synergy Research Project (2013M3A9C4078137) of the MSIT (Ministry of Science and ICT), Korea through the NRF. This work was supported by the National Research Foundation of Korea (NRF) grant funded by the Korea government (MSIT) (No. 2020R1A2C1004032).

References

1. Breunig, M.M., Kriegel, H.P., Ng, R.T., Sander, J.: LOF: identifying density-based local outliers. SIGMOD Rec. **29**(2), 93–104 (2000). https://doi.org/10.1145/335191.335388
2. Deng, A., Hooi, B.: Graph neural network-based anomaly detection in multivariate time series. In: Proceedings of the AAAI Conference on Artificial Intelligence, vol. 35, no. 5, pp. 4027–4035 (2021). https://ojs.aaai.org/index.php/AAAI/article/view/16523
3. Hundman, K., Constantinou, V., Laporte, C., Colwell, I., Soderstrom, T.: Detecting spacecraft anomalies using LSTMs and nonparametric dynamic thresholding. In: Proceedings of the 24th ACM SIGKDD International Conference on Knowledge Discovery Data Mining. ACM (2018). https://doi.org/10.1145/3219819.3219845

4. Kingma, D.P., Welling, M.: Auto-encoding variational bayes (2013). https://doi.org/10.48550/ARXIV.1312.6114

5. Malhotra, P., Ramakrishnan, A., Anand, G., Vig, L., Agarwal, P., Shroff, G.: LSTM-based encoder-decoder for multi-sensor anomaly detection (2016). https://doi.org/10.48550/ARXIV.1607.00148

6. Shang, C., Chen, J., Bi, J.: Discrete graph structure learning for forecasting multiple time series (2021). https://doi.org/10.48550/ARXIV.2101.06861

7. Shen, L., Li, Z., Kwok, J.: Timeseries anomaly detection using temporal hierarchical one-class network. In: Larochelle, H., Ranzato, M., Hadsell, R., Balcan, M., Lin, H. (eds.) Advances in Neural Information Processing Systems, vol. 33, pp. 13016–13026. Curran Associates, Inc. (2020). https://proceedings.neurips.cc/paper/2020/file/97e401a02082021fd24957f852e0e475-Paper.pdf

8. Siffer, A., Fouque, P.A., Termier, A., Largouet, C.: Anomaly detection in streams with extreme value theory. In: Proceedings of the 23rd ACM SIGKDD International Conference on Knowledge Discovery and Data Mining, KDD 2017, pp. 1067–1075. Association for Computing Machinery, New York (2017). https://doi.org/10.1145/3097983.3098144

9. Su, Y., Zhao, Y., Niu, C., Liu, R., Sun, W., Pei, D.: Robust anomaly detection for multivariate time series through stochastic recurrent neural network. In: Proceedings of the 25th ACM SIGKDD International Conference on Knowledge Discovery Data Mining, KDD 2019, p. 2828–2837. Association for Computing Machinery, New York (2019). https://doi.org/10.1145/3292500.3330672

10. Veličković, P., Cucurull, G., Casanova, A., Romero, A., Liò, P., Bengio, Y.: Graph attention networks (2017). https://doi.org/10.48550/ARXIV.1710.10903

11. Xu, J., Wu, H., Wang, J., Long, M.: Anomaly transformer: time series anomaly detection with association discrepancy (2021). https://doi.org/10.48550/ARXIV.2110.02642

12. Zhang, C., et al.: A deep neural network for unsupervised anomaly detection and diagnosis in multivariate time series data. In: Proceedings of the AAAI Conference on Artificial Intelligence, vol. 33, no. 01, pp. 1409–1416 (2019). https://doi.org/10.1609/aaai.v33i01.33011409. https://ojs.aaai.org/index.php/AAAI/article/view/3942

13. Zhao, H., et al.: Multivariate time-series anomaly detection via graph attention network (2020). https://doi.org/10.48550/ARXIV.2009.02040

14. Zheng, C., Fan, X., Pan, S., Wu, Z., Wang, C., Yu, P.S.: Spatio-temporal joint graph convolutional networks for traffic forecasting (2021). https://doi.org/10.48550/ARXIV.2111.13684

First International Workshop on the Semantic WEb of Everything (SWEET 2022)

Preface

The First International Workshop on the Semantic WEb of EveryThing (SWEET 2022) was held in Bari (Italy) on July 8th, 2022, in conjunction with the 22nd International Conference on Web Engineering (ICWE 2022).

SWEET was organized to give researchers and practitioners an opportunity to discuss and interact about realistic penetration of Artificial Intelligence techniques and technologies in the Web of Things, with particular attention to pervasive contexts.

Seven presentations were given in the two technical sessions of the workshop. A total of 23 authors from 7 institutions in 3 different continents participated in the event. All presentations were given in person, but SWEET 2022 adopted a hybrid model so as to allow people to listen and intervene remotely as well.

A wide span of innovative models, architectures, algorithms and applications was presented, as well as strategies for optimizing performance and scalability. The discussions following each presentation was very fruitful, allowing the participants to explore current and future perspectives with respect to the following problems:

- How can we integrate the Web of Things with Semantic Web technologies and tools?
- How can we use ontologies and semantic annotations to enhance real world pervasive devices, applications and services?
- How can we exploit reasoning and planning in Web of Things scenarios?
- How can we integrate machine learning efficiently in pervasive large-scale scenarios with high volumes of data?
- What IoT technologies are able to support the Semantic Web of Everything evolution?

Semantic Web technologies for mobile, embedded and ubiquitous computing were the focus of several talks. Further contributions concerned other Artificial Intelligence (AI) areas, including machine learning, natural language processing, argumentation and artificial vision. The proposed approaches often integrated AI with other research fields, such as ambient intelligence, robotics and blockchain. Discussed application areas included Industry 4.0, healthcare, smart mobility, sustainability, and infrastructures management.

We were pleased with the quality of the submitted papers, the oral presentations and the discussions emerged during the workshop. We also received a good feedback from the attendees about their satisfaction with the experience. We are sincerely grateful to all contributors for their participation. Special thanks go to ICWE 2022 organizers, and particularly to the Workshop Chairs Cinzia Cappiello and Azzurra Ragone, for their constant support before, during and after the event.

We hope to continue and improve on every aspect of the workshop in future SWEET editions, in order to promote the mutual exchange of ideas and possibly even new research collaborations to bring Semantic Web and AI technologies everywhere and to everything.

September 2022

Giuseppe Loseto
Hasan Ali Khattak
Michele Ruta
Floriano Scioscia

A Decentralized Environment for Biomedical Semantic Content Authoring and Publishing

Asim Abbas[1] , Steve Fonin Mbouadeu[1] , Fazel Keshtkar[1] ,
Hasan Ali Khattak[2], Tahir Hameed[3] , and Syed Ahmad Chan Bukhari[1]([✉])

[1] Collins College of Professional Studies, Department of Computer Science,
St. John's University, New York City, NY, USA
{abbasa,steve.mbouadeu19,keshtkaf,bukharis}@stjohns.edu
[2] SEECS, National University of Sciences and Technology (NUST),
Islamabad, Pakistan
hasan.alikhattak@seecs.edu.pk
[3] Management Department, Girard School of Business, Merrimack College,
North Andover, MA, USA
hameedt@merrimack.edu

Abstract. The portable document format (PDF) is currently one of the most popular formats for *offline* sharing biomedical information. Recently, HTML-based formats for *web-first* biomedical information sharing have gained popularity. However, machine-interpretable information is required by literature search engines, such as Google Scholar, to index articles in a context-aware manner for accurate biomedical literature searches. The lack of technological infrastructure to add machine-interpretable metadata to expanding biomedical information, on the other hand, renders them unreachable to search engines. Therefore, we developed a portable technical infrastructure (goSemantically) and packaged it as a Google Docs add-ons. The "goSemantically" assists authors in adding machine-interpretable metadata at the terminology and document structural levels While authoring biomedical content. The "goSemantically" leverages the NCBO Bioportal resources and introduces a mechanism to annotate biomedical information with relevant machine-interpretable metadata (semantic vocabularies). The "goSemantically" also acquires schema.org meta tags designed for search engine optimization and tailored to accommodate biomedical information. Thus, individual authors can conveniently author and publish biomedical content in a truly decentralized fashion. Users can also export and host content with relevant machine-interpretable metadata (semantic vocabularies) in interoperable formats such as HTML and JSON-LD. To experience the described features, run this code with Google Doc URL: github.com/ahmadchan/gosemantically.git.

Keywords: Structured data · Biomedical semantics · Structured data publishing · FAIR biomedical data · Biomedical content authoring

G. Agapito et al. (Eds.): ICWE 2022 Workshops, CCIS 1668, pp. 75–86, 2023.
https://doi.org/10.1007/978-3-031-25380-5_6

1   Introduction and Background Work

Recently, due to the unprecedented growth in biomedical research and clinical practices, a vast amount of biomedical content has been produced in research articles, clinical notes, and biomedical reports. According to the 2018 online molecular biology database collection, PubMed now has 1737 large-scale biological databases and over 30 million citations for biomedical literature, with a tenfold rise every year [1]. Efficient practices for accessing biomedical publications are essential to timely disseminating knowledge from the scientific research community to peer investigators and other healthcare practitioners. One of the most popular formats for disseminating scientific information (offline) is the portable document format (PDF) [2,3]. For online scientific literature, a few HTML-based formats have lately been proposed [4].

The following sections detail the recently proposed tools to promote scientific article authoring and publishing through semantic technology in a decentralized environment. The dokieli tool [5] is a client-side, browser-based publishing and annotating decentralized tool. It was created to generate HTML+RDF annotation notices in scientific texts. The generated "live" articles are interoperable and independent of dokieli since it adheres to W3C open web platform standards and best practices. A dokieli article is an HTML page that allows the user to insert raw data in the Turtle, JSON-LD, or TriG nano-publication formats (see Table 1). Additionally, users can apply the dokieli-specific CSS and JavaScript packages to any HTML page, triggering a user annotation creation environment. Research Publications in Simplified HTML (RASH) [6], a framework similar to dokieli, was designed to accommodate the Web-first style for publishing HTML-based academic articles. The RASH team set out to establish an easy-to-use web-based tool for sharing academic publications with embedded semantic annotations while remaining compatible with traditional publishing workflows [6]. The assessment research revealed various challenges with RASH adoption and HTML adoption in general for non-technical users. Other features, such as the ability to convert from/to current formats like OpenXML, are also required for it to be widely adopted (see Table 1). Authorea[1] is a collaborative writing platform that enables scholars to write, collaborate, host data, and publish their work online. Authorea produces output in four different formats: PDF, LaTeX, DOCX, and a zipped bundle containing a large number of HTML pages (see Table 1). ScholarMarkdown is a framework for creating academic publications in a lightweight HTML syntax that is immediately converted to HTML+RDFa and printed to PDF into a conventional scientific template through browser (see Table 1). It provides syntactic sugar for citing articles, writing arithmetic calculations, and other purposes [7]. FidusWriter[2] is another Web-based application that creates HTML academic articles using a wordprocessor-like interface. While the particular format is not specified, it does allow users to convert the HTML

---

[1] https://www.authorea.com/.
[2] https://www.fiduswriter.org/.

text written in the program to EPUB and LaTeX (In addition to HTML) (see Table 1).

The non-existence of the technological infrastructure required to add machine-interpretable information into growing publications makes them unable to access literary search engines like Google Scholar. As a result, researchers and practitioners are confronted with various information accessibility issues. Search engines require meta-data to accurately index contents in a context-aware fashion for accurate biomedical literature searches and to facilitate secondary meta-analysis. Incorporating machine-interpretable semantic annotations at the pre-publication stage (during authoring) of biomedical content and retaining them throughout online publication is always desired and contribute to the broader semantic web vision [8, 9]. On the other hand, these complicated procedures need a high level of technical and/or domain understanding. The primary source of the semantic content enrichment process is biomedical annotators. These biomedical annotators employ biomedical ontologies from public libraries like BioPortal [10] and UMLS [11] to convert unstructured material into a structured format by associating content with the proper ontology concept. We propose "goSemantically," a lightweight Google Docs add-on that allow researchers to add semantic metadata at the terminology and document structural levels without any prior technological expertise. For that, we designed a comprehensive strategy to semantically enrich biomedical textual content by annotating it with semantic metadata from appropriate ontologies at the word/token level. Users are given an interface to link schema.org metadata tags with document constructions like introduction and body sections to improve the document structure semantically. Furthermore, the proposed infrastructure allows users to download semantically enhanced content in various compatible formats for hosting and sharing on a decentralized basis. Finally, the incorporated semantic metadata makes it easier for search engines to index the elevated biomedical material for intelligent semantic search.

The rest of the paper is organized as a proposed methodology. Following that, we discuss the design application demonstration scenario and outcomes. Finally, a conclusion is discussed.

Table 1. A comparison of goSemantically with existing HTML-oriented formats for scholarly papers according to five distinct features.

Format	Syntax (HTML)	Semantic annotation (RDF, RDFa, JSON-LD XML, Turtle)	WYSIWYG editor	Conversion from (DOCX, PDF, ODT, LaTeX)	Conversion to (DOCX, PDF, EPUB, ODT, LaTeX, HTML)
dokieli	✓	✓	✓	x	✓
RASH)	✓	✓	✓	✓	✓
Authorea	✓	x	✓	✓	✓
ScholarMarkdown	✓	x	✓	x	✓
Fiduswriter	✓	x	✓	x	✓
goSemantically	✓	✓	✓	✓	✓

2   Proposed Methodology

Recent advances in web technology can be utilized to enhance the semantic quality of scientific journal articles by improving links to other resources, adding descriptive metadata to aid article discovery, and defining the meaning of concepts and terms in the article [12]. In addition, it allows users access to "lively" content in the form of interactive figures, re-orderable reference lists, document summaries, and downloadable numerical datasets. The proposed "goSemantically" is a lightweight Google Docs add-on to assist biomedical practitioners and researchers uplift unstructured biomedical content by automatically suggesting the appropriate ontology vocabularies for semantic annotation at content and structural levels. Subsequently, an array of Schema.org compliant web publishing options are provided to the users to export their semantically enhanced content in various interoperable formats for hosting and sharing in a decentralized fashion. The following section explains the content-level semantic enrichment and structural-level semantic enrichment process as shown in Fig. 1.

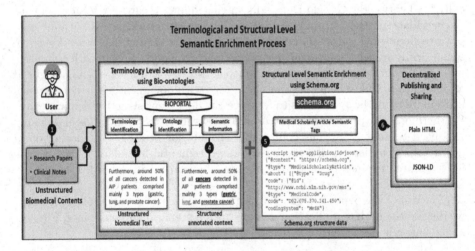

Fig. 1. Proposed architecture and workflow of goSemantically

2.1   Terminology-Level Semantic Enrichment Process

The practice of adding semantic metadata to content is called semantic tagging. Various technologies, methods, and techniques are used to enrich content with semantic metadata at the content or terminology level [13]. In the biomedical domain, biomedical annotators are widely utilized for content-level semantic annotations [14]. These annotators often adopt biomedical ontologies repositories available publicly, such as Bioportal [10] and UMLS [11]. However, challenges and issues exist in automating the semantic annotation and enhancement process, primarily accuracy and speed. Furthermore, a lack of a user-friendly framework makes the semantic enrichment process harder. As a result, in the proposed application, we used an NCBO Bioportal resources [15] web service that analyzes raw textual metadata, tags them with appropriate biomedical ontology concepts, and delivers an initial set of semantic annotations. Adding a layer of secondary semantic metadata to the biomedical scholarly article content makes the machine search engines more intelligent. Further semantic enrichment processes include (1) the Google Doc editor interface, (2) biomedical terminology identification, and (3) ontological semantic information extraction. We believe that this level of information is critical in the semantic enrichment of biomedical content to improve search engine indexing of biomedical scholarly articles.

- **Google Doc Editor Interface:** The "goSemantically" Google add-ons provide user-friendly authoring environments for users and authors of various backgrounds and expertise through the Google Docs editor, a web-based interface. Authors can import existing biomedical text or start typing directly in Google Doc editor.
- **Biomedical Terminology Identification:** Terminology identification and extraction from unstructured biomedical content are fundamental steps toward biomedical content semantic annotation in the biomedical domain. We utilize the BioPortal's Open Biomedical Annotator (OBA) [16] API to identify biomedical terms. The OBA accepts the user's free text and feeds it forward as input to a concept recognition tool. The concept recognition tool utilizes Mgrep services developed by NCBI [16] and ontology-based dictionary constructed from UMLS [11] and NCBO [15] ontologies. The tool identifies the biomedical terms by following the string matching approach. The output is a set of biomedical terminologies and ontologies to which the terms belong. To study further the OBA concept recognition tool, we recommend studying the following article [17].
- **Ontological Semantic Information Extraction:** Semantic information extraction is the process of extracting insight and detailed information about biomedical terminology utilizing biomedical ontology repositories such as UMLS [11] and Bioportal [10]. An ontology is a collection of concepts and the semantic relationships among them. In the proposed work, we leverage the Bioportal Ontology web service [15], a repository containing over 729 ontologies in the biomedical domain. The biomedical text provided to "goSemantically" is mapped to Bioportal [15] to identify the relevant ontologies, acronyms, definitions, and ontology links for individual terminologies that are best matched based on the context. This semantic information is displayed in the "goSemantically" annotation panel for human interpretation and understanding. The "goSemantically" allows users to author this semantic information based on their knowledge and experience, such as choosing appropriate ontology from the list, suitable acronym, removing semantic information or annotation for explicit terminology, etc. Finally, this metadata information is embedded into the document. Such a level of semantic information improves connectivity consistency and provides a formal, structural, relational, and conceptual representation of the biomedical contents or terminologies [18].

The embed and export feature takes the newly generated semantic information and adds that to the HTML document heading for search engine understanding and interpretation.

2.2 Structural-Level Semantic Enrichment Process

Structured data is a standardized format for providing information about a page and classifying the page's content. Various technologies are used to prepare structured data, such as schema.org [19]. We utilized Schema.org, a collaborative community-defined set of vocabularies designed to create structured web content from many domains. These community-agreed sets of vocabulary are endorsed by Google, Yahoo, Yandex, and Bing to improve the indexing of web pages [20, 21]. Schema.org vocabulary provides explicit clues or definite identifiers about the meaning of the page to search engines by including structured information on the page. For example, what is the title of the article, who are the authors of the article, affiliation, section, and related content of each section, and other details? There are hundreds of different markup types contained by schema.org because there are so many additional questions people turn to search engines to answer. These markup types are arranged in a hierarchy, where the most commonly used types of schema.org are Creative Works, Event, Health and MedicalTypes, Organization and Person, etc. We utilized Health and Medicaltypes tags in the proposed application, which is useful for publishers wishing to mark up health and medical content on the web. The Health and Medicaltypes further expand into MedicalCondition, Drug, MedicalGuideline, MedicalWebPage, and MedicalScholarlyArticle (See Fig. 2). As we aim to contribute to the semantic uplifting of the medical scholarly article at the structural level to enhance its discoverability, interactivity, openness, and (re) usability for humans and machines, we choose the MedicalScholarlyArticle schema type further see Fig. 2. The MedicalScholarlyArticle schema type has various properties that provide a brief description to the biomedical content, such as publicationType, abstract, keywords, publisher, etc. see Fig. 2.

In "goSemantically", on the right side of the sidebar, is a structural level button to initiate the structural level semantic enrichment process, see Fig. 4. A dropdown list of checkboxes with the MedicalScholarlyArticle properties label will appear see Fig. 4(3). The user is free to select any MedicalScholarlyArticle properties suitable to the article contents, user knowledge, and observations. Later these properties with semantic content are embedded into the article heading to assist for quick search and indexing, such as what the article is about, abstract, authors, institution affiliation, sponsor or funding agencies, etc. see Fig. 2. Subsequently, the MedicalScholarlyArticle properties checkbox was checked, and a list of text fields appears containing a MedicalScholarlyArticle type property placeholder that indicates the user to input relevant semantic content as presented in Fig. 4(4). A user is not allowed to leave any text fields empty, or a user can go back and unchecked the property checkbox unwanted. Successively filling in the chosen properties text field, the user is free to generate structural level content by clicking on "Generate Structural Content" see

Fig. 4(4). Finally, the structural level contents are generated in JSON-LD format, the language code for HTML pages or search engines. This JSON-LD format structural level content is embedded directly in the HTML file's <head> tag. The notation used for "@context" and "@type" attributes is to specify the vocabulary in schema.org.

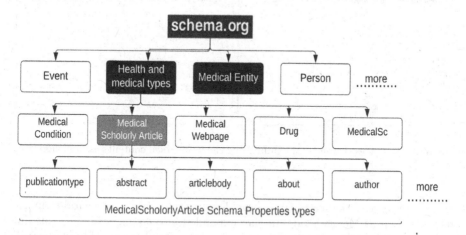

Fig. 2. Schema.org schema hierarchical structure for MedicalScholarlyArticle property types

3 A Decentralized Authoring and Publishing

In a decentralized environment, applications run independently of a centralized interconnected system. Additionally, decentralization enables authors to create and select their own semantics, for example, by annotating RDF with their own vocabulary. Following this, documents or contents can be linked to one another as well as their schemas in a decentralized way [5]. We demonstrated the "goSemantically", a browser-based application which provides a decentralized environment for users to author and publish semantically enhanced data in plain HTML and JSON-LD formats see Fig. 3. The schema.org website provides the semantic markup tag. Extending the schema.org MedicalEntity and MedicalScholarlyArticle tags "goSemantically" allows users to download and publish the content. In addition, the MedicalScholarlyArticle provides a document-level structural-semantic markup such as publicationType, abstract, articlebody, etc. (See Fig. 2 and Fig. 3).

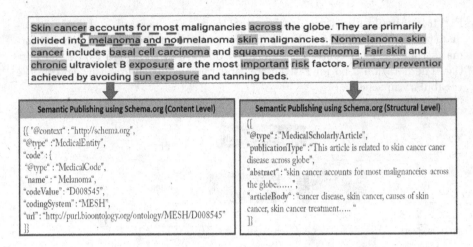

Fig. 3. Proposed Modeling for the publishing the biomedical contents using Schema.org

In contrast, MedicalEntity provides content-level structural-semantic markups such as MedicalCode, further expanded into coding system, name and link see Fig. 3. Finally, we merged terminology level and structural level semantic markup by extending Schema.org to publish the biomedical contents online. The "goSemantically" enables users to publish biomedical content automatically by using proposed semantic markups in plain HTML, and JSON-LD format. As a result, the published web pages will preserve both the structural and content-level semantics of the biomedical data see in Fig. 3.

4   Results and Example Case Study

To assess the efficacy of the "goSemantically", we experience three unstructured clinical datasets supplied by the i2b2 National Center, Partners Healthcare, and Beth Israel Deaconess Medical Center. According to the i2b2/VA challenge organizers' guidelines, the dataset comprised discharge summaries that were manually annotated for three categories of clinical concepts (problem, treatment, and test). There are 97 clinical notes in Partners Healthcare, 73 clinical notes in Beth Israel Deaconess Medical Center, and 256 notes in the i2b2 National Center's test dataset [22]. The unstructured notes were used for experimentation, and the gold dataset was used for analysis.

A sensitivity index is used to measure the performance of "goSemantically" for biomedical content recognition and identification; see Eq. 1. For experimentation purposes, we randomly choose twenty documents from each dataset. We constructed results for individual datasets and then averaged all results to measure the system-level performance. At the individual dataset level, the Beth dataset obtained a high sensitivity score of 93.81% compared to the Partners and i2b2 Test data and an accepted level sensitivity score of 92.06% obtained by the "goSemantically" at the system level. We noticed some points during experimentation where the "goSemantically" should improve. First, we noticed that the "goSemantically" does not recognize biomedical content having stop word compositions such as "her disease," "his cancer," etc. The other point we noticed is that the application is not generalized towards biomedical abbreviations such as "heart rate (HR)", "cerebral palsy (CP)" etc. and content having numbers such as "RBC-21-50" that deliver information about red blood cells in a body or blood, and "atenolol 50 mg" that delivers information about tablet dosage used for high blood pressure treatment. Overall, the "goSemantically" performs well and identifies the biomedical content in unstructured clinical documents with high and acceptable accuracy, as shown in Table 2.

$$Sensitivity = \frac{Number\ of\ true\ positive}{(Number\ of\ true\ positive\ +\ Number\ of\ true\ Negative)} \quad (1)$$

Table 2. goSemantically Annotation performance on the i2b2 dataset for Biomedical content recognition.

Data source	True positive	False negative	Sensitvity
Beth Medical Center	197	13	93.81%
Partners Healthcare	193	17	91.90%
i2b2 Test Dataset	190	20	90.48%
Overall Result	580	50	92.06%

We illustrated the "goSemantically" user interface and functionalities in Sect. 4.1 and 4.2, while processing a biomedical research article as example case study. As shown in Fig. 4(2,3) the "goSemantically" interface comprises of two main buttons: (a) Content Level and (b) Structural Level to enhance biomedical content borrow from Pubmed.org. Each button functionalities is explained below:

4.1   Terminology Level

1. Any biomedical text from Pubmed.org may be copied and pasted into the Google Doc editor. A cancer disease article [23] is used to demonstrate the application see Fig. 4(1).
2. Subsequently, click on Annotate button on the "goSemantically" sidebar.
3. Upon retrieving the annotations, users may amend them in the Google Doc editor by clicking on each context. For example, the user can pick an appropriate ontology from a list by selecting the "Not satisfied with this annotation" button. The "Removing annotation" button deletes the proposed annotation for the context see Fig. 4 (2).

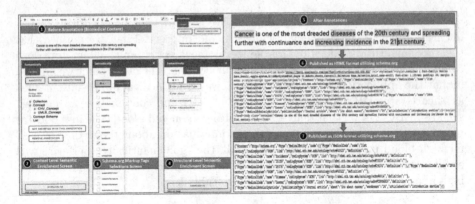

Fig. 4. Demonstration Scenario and User Interface of the goSemantically Google add-ons

4. When a user clicks on an annotated concept, its pref-label, recommended ontology, concept definition, and a tree browser of ontology vocabularies emerge see Fig. 4(2). From the tree browser, the user chooses the appropriate ontology vocabulary.
5. The loading symbol disappears, and the highlights appear on the text, indicating that annotation retrieval is complete see Fig. 4(5).

4.2　Document Structural Level

1. Subsequently, terminology level annotation users are enabled to initiate structural level annotation.
2. In Fig. 4(3), click the Structural Level button.
3. A list of MedicalScholarlyArticle schema types emerged in a drop-down menu see Fig. 4(3).
4. The user is enable to select the appropriate MedicalScholarlyArticle properties from the drop-down list in see Fig. 4(3).
5. A list of text fields appears which contain a MedicalScholarlyArticle schema type properties placeholder that indicates that the user should provide appropriate information see Fig. 4(4).
6. Finally, the user clicks the structure content button, in results MedicalScholarlyArticle and MedicalEntity properties type content is coupled see Fig. 4(4).
7. A download button is enabled for the user to download the content and publish it in plain HTML and JSON-LD format, as shown in the see Fig. 4(6,7). Finally, the content is ready to be hosted and published online.

5　Conclusion

Daily vast amounts of data are produced in the biomedical domain in research papers and clinical notes that contain much helpful information. However, the lack of machine-interpretable metadata remains inaccessible to search engines for information retrieval and knowledge extraction. Therefore, it is unquestionably desirable to incorporate machine-interpretable semantic annotations at the pre-publication stage of biomedical content and maintain them throughout online publishing. As a result, we created "goSemantically," a lightweight Google Docs add-on that allow researchers to add semantic metadata at the content and structure levels with minimal technical experience. The goSemantically holistic method elevates syntactic biomedical content by automatically annotating it with the relevant ontology vocabulary at the sentence level. Furthermore, users may intuitively assign structural-level schema.org metadata. Additionally, the proposed infrastructure lets users download semantically enriched information in various web-first compliant formats for decentralized hosting and sharing. Consequently, the semantic information makes it easier for search engines to index the increased biological material for intelligent semantic search thanks to the included semantic information.

Acknowledgement. This work is supported by the National Science Foundation grant ID: 2101350.

References

1. Rigden, D.J., Fernández, X.M.: The 2018 nucleic acids research database issue and the online molecular biology database collection. Nucleic Acids Res. **46**(Database issue), D1 (2018)
2. Shotton, D., Portwin, K., Klyne, G., Miles, A.: Adventures in semantic publishing: exemplar semantic enhancements of a research article. PLoS Comput. Biol. **5**(4), e1000361 (2009)
3. Brady, E., Zhong, Y., Bigham, J.P.: Creating accessible PDFs for conference proceedings. In: Proceedings of the 12th Web for All Conference (W4A 2015), pp. 34–37. ACM (2015). https://doi.org/10.1145/2745555.2746665
4. Spinaci, G., et al.: The RASH JavaScript editor (RAJE) a wordprocessor for writing web-first scholarly articles. In: Proceedings of the 2017 ACM Symposium on Document Engineering, pp. 85–94 (2017)
5. Capadisli, S., Guy, A., Verborgh, R., Lange, C., Auer, S., Berners-Lee, T.: Decentralised authoring, annotations and notifications for a read-write web with dokieli. In: Cabot, J., De Virgilio, R., Torlone, R. (eds.) ICWE 2017. LNCS, vol. 10360, pp. 469–481. Springer, Cham (2017). https://doi.org/10.1007/978-3-319-60131-1_33
6. Peroni, S., et al.: Research articles in simplified HTML: a web-first format for HTML-based scholarly articles. PeerJ Comput. Sci. **3**, e132 (2017)
7. Lin, T.T.Y., Beales, G.: ScholarlyMarkdown Syntax Guide. Guide (2015). http://scholarlymarkdown.com/
8. Warren, P., Davies, J., Brown, D.: The semantic web-from vision to reality. ICT futures: delivering pervasive, real-time and secure services, , pp. 55–66 (2008)
9. Mbouadeu, S.F., Keshtkar, F., Bukhari, S.A.C.: Semantically: a framework for structured biomedical content authoring and publishing. In: ISWC (Posters/Demos/Industry) (2021)
10. Whetzel, P.L., et al.: BioPortal: enhanced functionality via new web services from the national center for biomedical ontology to access and use ontologies in software applications. Nucleic Acids Res. **39**(Suppl. 2), W541–W545 (2011)

11. Humphreys, B.L., Lindberg, D.: The UMLS project: making the conceptual connection between users and the information they need. Bull. Med. Libr. Assoc. **81**(2), 170 (1993)

12. Abbas, A., et al.: Biomedical scholarly article editing and sharing using holistic semantic uplifting approach. In: The International FLAIRS Conference Proceedings, vol. 35 (2022)

13. Mbouadeu, S.F., et al.: A sociotechnical framework for semantic biomedical content authoring and publishing. In: The International FLAIRS Conference Proceedings, vol. 35 (2022)

14. Abbas, A., et al.: Clinical concept extraction with lexical semantics to support automatic annotation. Int. J. Environ. Res. Public Health **18**(20), 10564 (2021)

15. Jonquet, C., et al.: NCBO annotator: semantic annotation of biomedical data. In: International Semantic Web Conference, Poster and Demo Session, Washington DC, USA, vol. 110 (2009)

16. Jonquet, C., Shah, N.H., Musen, M.A.: The open biomedical annotator. Summit Transl. Bioinform. **2009**, 56 (2009)

17. Dai, M., et al.: An efficient solution for mapping free text to ontology terms. AMIA Summit Transl. Bioinform. **21** (2008)

18. Abbas, A., et al.: Meaningful information extraction from unstructured clinical documents. Proc. Asia-Pac. Adv. Netw. **48**, 42–47 (2019)

19. Guha, R.V., et al.: Schema.org: evolution of structured data on the web. Queue **13**(9), 10–37 (2015). https://doi.org/10.1145/2857274.2857276

20. Michel, F.: "The bioschemas community", Bioschemas & Schema.org: a lightweight semantic layer for life sciences websites. In: Biodiversity Information Science and Standards, vol. 2, p. e25836 (2018). https://doi.org/10.3897/biss.2.25836

21. Mbouadeu, S.F., et al.: Towards structured biomedical content authoring and publishing. In: 2022 IEEE 16th International Conference on Semantic Computing (ICSC). IEEE (2022)

22. Uzuner, Ö., South, B.R., Shen, S., DuVall, S.L.: 2010 i2b2/VA challenge on concepts, assertions, and relations in clinical text. J. Am. Med. Inform. Assoc. **18**, 552–556 (2011)

23. Hausman, D.M.: What is cancer? Perspect. Biol. Med. **62**(4), 778–784 (2019)

AI for Food Waste Reduction in Smart Homes

Giovanni Mezzina[✉], Dionisio Ciccarese, and Daniela De Venuto

Department of Electrical and Information Engineering, Politecnico di Bari, 70124 Bari, Italy
{giovanni.mezzina,dionisio.ciccarese,daniela.venuto}@poliba.it

Abstract. Globally, one of the most economically impacting problems in the modern era concerns food waste on the consumer side. In this framework, the here-proposed work stems from the idea of combining the potential of a modern smart home with the need to reduce domestic food waste. For this purpose, the paper proposes a food waste reduction (FWR) architecture composed of a smart sensing network and an actuation system. The sensing network is realized via intelligent sensor nodes able to real-time assess the monitored food shelf life and the storage condition, as well as localize them in the environment. If bad conditions of storage are recognized, the sensor node is able to call for actuation system intervention. This latter system includes a robot platform that can localize food, manipulate it, and guarantee better storage conditions to preserve its shelf life. Experimental tests on 50 operations show that in more than 60% of cases, the automatic operations have been successfully completed starting from the sensor node call for intervention, up to the object manipulation routine to ensure an adequate storage condition of the food. The promising results achieved by the present pilot study pave the way for investigations on a new main goal in the smart homes' framework, i.e., automatic food waste management.

Keywords: Smart homes · Assistive robotics · Food waste

1 Introduction

The *smart* home concept was born to provide human users with a fully (or semi-) automatic environment able to satisfy four main goals: improved wellness, security, comfort, and reduced energy waste [1]. For decades, these objectives remained unaltered, while the technological advances continuously impacted the functions of the smart home due to the electronic device cost reduction, the increment of computational capabilities, and so on [1, 2]. These technological advances culminate in ecosystems composed of several small computing devices spread in the domestic environment, capable of gathering home and user information and actuating a set of services based on personal needs (e.g., see Google Home or Alexa by Amazon).

In this context, several solutions have been proposed at the state of the art, gathering attention from industry and academia. Most of them focus on algorithms dedicated to the so-called home energy management system (HEMS) [1]. These are algorithms that employ data from sensors distributed in the home environment, to find a procedure able to optimize the energy consumption, e.g., by controlling the kitchen, temperature,

G. Agapito et al. (Eds.): ICWE 2022 Workshops, CCIS 1668, pp. 87–99, 2023.
https://doi.org/10.1007/978-3-031-25380-5_7

air conditioning, and lighting system [3]. In this context, also smart actuators have been introduced and interconnected with the sensing network. Some examples are smart thermostats, plugs, light bulbs, and so on.

Only recently, robots have been included in the smart home framework [4–9]. This is because robots have widely diffused in an assistive context, where their presence became essential for assisting users in rehabilitation [7] or for elderly people care purposes. In this context, robots have been employed as personal assistants of the users, or as a gateway to centralize the interface for smart home devices [4, 8].

Despite the growing number of state-of-the-art solutions concerning wellness, security, comfort, and energy waste, at date, only a few solutions have been proposed for food waste reduction in smart homes [10–12]. However, the totality of the proposed solutions is based on the users' habits analysis, and intelligent management of the refrigerator, limiting the mitigation actions to warnings or advice [10–12].

To bridge this gap, in this paper we propose a robotics-based architecture, to be included in a smart home framework, able to minimize the food waste by carrying out actions to compensate for the bad habits of the human component in terms of food preservation. The proposed architecture exploits data from a wireless network of custom sensor nodes that monitor the local temperature, relative humidity, light, acceleration, and angular velocity. The sensor node, connected to critical foods or beverages, can calculate in real-time their shelf life, monitoring the onset of drastic reductions in the average life of the food. This capability allows the sensor to alert the assistive robot about the estimated food position in the home, and to call for proper actions to stop or slow the shelf-life reduction. In the proposed pilot study, the mitigation action consists of manipulating the good, picking and releasing it in a more adequate place (e.g., a fridge or a dry and cold shelf).

The paper is organized as follows. Section 2 outlines the food waste reduction architecture. Section 3 describes its implementation, while Sect. 4 shows and discusses some relevant experimental results. Section 5 is devoted to concluding remarks.

2   The Food Waste Reduction Architecture

Figure 1 shows an overview of the proposed Food Waste Reduction (FWR) architecture. Specifically, as per Fig. 1, it can be divided into two main parts: the Sensing Network and Actuation System. The Sensing Network consists of a set of sensor nodes designed to monitor local temperature, relative humidity, light, acceleration, and angular velocity. For the proposed use case, the realized sensor node is fixed on the food to be monitored (see Fig. 1). Then, the first three parameters (i.e., temperature, relative humidity, and light) are used to on-board calculate the shelf life (SL) of the monitored food, by exploiting a 1st order kinetic Arrhenius model [13]. It should be specified that the realized sensor nodes have been designed to allow the user to modify the decay model on each node, by *over-the-air* updating them with custom equations for the SL computation.

The nodes enabled for the monitoring return every N seconds (N = 30 s in this application) the SL parameter to the assistive robot, informing it about the dynamic expiration date.

Fig. 1. Food waste reduction architecture overview

Every time, an object equipped with the sensor node is moved from the initial position (i.e., refrigerator), the onboard microcontroller starts estimating the relative displacement by implementing an inertial navigation algorithm employing data from the 3-axis accelerometer and 3-axis gyroscope implemented on the board. When no movements are revealed through the gyroscope data, the sensor node stores the final position and starts monitoring the SL. If during the monitoring, the quality decay model (i.e., SL parameter) experiences a sharp reduction (e.g., red trace in Fig. 1) due to poor food storage procedure (e.g., food outside the fridge for a long time span), the sensor node activates a timer with a preset timeout. If no movements are recorded until the timeout (i.e., 5 min in this application), the food is labeled as not properly stored. This status leads to a call for robot intervention. This is the action field of the Actuation System in Fig. 1. In this application, the Actuation System consists of a personal care robot employed for assistive purposes: Pepper by SoftBank Robotics. Specifically, the native Source Localization And Mapping system of the Pepper robot has been used to navigate in the home environment, while the object manipulation capabilities exploit a framework introduced in our previous work [14].

When the sensor node raises the intervention of the Pepper, the robot queries the node about its estimated relative position. Next, pepper calculates the absolute position of the monitored food in the world frame and moves toward the zone identified by the displacement estimation. The robot stops in a so-called approaching area where it starts scanning the area through the frontal camera. Then, it starts a semantic segmentation of the image from the RGB camera through a pre-trained YOLOv3 object detector algorithm [14]. Once the object is identified in the frontal space, the robot centers on the object and starts the manipulation routine.

It consists of a dedicated algorithm that drives the hand, or the hands, to grab the object. The grabbing operations are based on data from a 3D sensor equipped on the Pepper robot [14]. Finally, the robot must be able to safely navigate towards the adequate place for the food placement, returning it.

3   The FWR Architecture Implementation

3.1   The Sensing Network

3.1.1   The Sensor Node

The sensor node employed for the specific use case is shown in Fig. 2. It consists of a low-cost and currently available components printed circuit board based on an ATMega328PB-AU by Microchip. The microcontroller works at 16 MHz and interfaces a sensor dedicated to temperature (T) and relative humidity (RH) recording, an Ambient Light Sensor (ALS), and an Inertial Measurement Unit (IMU).

All sensors chosen for the design embed (on-chip) both the analog circuitry for the measurement-signal conditioning and a controller for I2C communication [15–17].

Specifically, the employed T/RH sensor is a low power/high accuracy digital sensor of the HDCx family by Texas Instrument. It shows an RH accuracy of ±2% (typical) with very low interchangeability (<0.3%) in the humidity range above 95%. The T sensor accuracy is ±0.2 °C (typical) with peaks of +0.5 °C at the limits of the working region, i.e., −40 °C to 125 °C. The device allows 14-bit measurement resolution, but 12 bits are used for the present application, with a subsequent consumption of 1.3 μA @ 1sps. The chosen light sensor is an ALS from the OPTx family of Texas Instrument. It has been chosen to have a spectral response that tightly matches the photopic response of the human eye, including significant infrared rejection. Measurements are ensured from 0.01 lux up to 83k lux, with a built-in and automatic full-scale setting feature (0.3 lux typical resolution). The device I2C interface provides up to 23-bit measurement resolution, but 12 bits are used for the present application, with consumption of 1.8 μA @ 1sps.

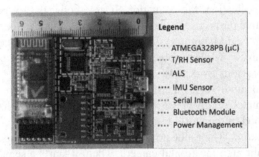

Fig. 2. Sensor node snapshot

The employed IMU sensor is the GY-521 module based on MPU6050 by TDK-Invensense [18]. The MPU6050 is a MEMS-based IMU sensor that includes a 3-axis accelerometer, 3-axis gyroscope, a temperature sensor, and a processor to manage write/read operations on the registers and the I2C interface (with interrupt). The ADCs employed for the 3 accelerometers and 3 gyroscopes have 16 bits of resolution with adjustable full-scale range. The on-board temperature sensor is used to compensate for drifts of the measurement. The device consumption can approach 10 mA (maximum) when all the 6 registers (accelerometers + gyroscopes) are queried in parallel. Finally, the sensor node exploits a Bluetooth Low Energy (BLE) interface to send data to the defined gateway. The board is also set up for Wi-Fi communication via TCP-IP protocol.

Each sensor node uses a 3.7 V LiPo battery for power supply. Let us consider: (i) a LiPO battery capacity of 2000 mAh; (ii) one read every 30 s from all the sensors and their BLE transmission; (iii) a continuous gyroscopes data recording and displacement calculation; (iv) no sleep mode for the serial interface circuitry. Considering the above-mentioned condition, the node can work for a minimum of 50 days (worst case).

The nodes' firmware is design to be updated via a dedicated GUI exploiting an *over-the-air* framework [19].

There are two sensor node versions: the integral one (see Fig. 2) that measures 60 mm × 48 mm and a compact version (without serial interface) that measures 39 mm × 48 mm.

3.1.2 The Shelf-Life Prediction Model

The sensor node acquires temperature, relative humidity, and ambient light intensity every 30 s. These data are processed by the on-board microcontroller to determine the SL of the monitored food. In the current form, each node implements a reprogrammable algorithm for the SL assessment. The basic model used for the proposed use case is the 1st order Arrhenius model, an empirical law that describes the temperature dependence in a simple chemical reaction [13]. The chosen model, inspired by [13], starts with the determination of the decay rate, named k:

$$k(T) = k_{ref} \cdot e^{-\frac{Ea}{R}\left(\frac{1}{T} - \frac{1}{T_{ref}}\right)} \tag{1}$$

where k_{ref} is the decay rate value at a dedicated reference temperature T_{ref}. It depends on a parameter known as pre-exponential factor that varies in function of the food to be monitored. E_a is the activation energy and R is the gas constant. The activation energy is a kinetic parameter strictly related to the specific food [13].

The second step consists of finding a measurement of the food quality, named $c(k)$. It can vary with the application. For example, firmness is considered a good quality metric for the SL assessment of fresh-cut vegetables [13]. A first-order approximation of this quality factor is:

$$c(k) = c_{eq} + c_0 e^{-kt} \tag{2}$$

where c_0 is the initial quality value, c_{eq} is the quality factor at an equilibrium value, and t is the storage time. Once $c(k, t)$ is known, SL can be calculated as per:

$$SL(t) = \frac{1}{k} ln\left(\frac{c(k, t)}{C_{eq}}\right) \cdot \alpha_{RH} \cdot \alpha_{AL} \tag{3}$$

where α_{RH} and α_{AL} are corrective factors (ranging from 0 to 1) related to the impact of humidity and light intensity on the selected quality metric [13].

3.1.3 The Displacement Computation

When the monitored food moves from its initial (and nominal) position, the microcontroller on the activated node starts estimating the displacement along the x and y-axis in real-time. The trigger of the first movement is revealed by a sudden change in a selected gyroscope data (energy-saving operation). Once triggered, the node implements a so-called Inertial Navigation System (INS), a self-contained navigation technique that exploits data from accelerometers and gyroscopes to track the position of the monitored object with respect to the initial coordinates. In this context, raw data from the IMU sensors on the node must undergo two steps: signal filtering and signal processing [20]. The first step is necessary because accelerometer and gyroscope outputs are intrinsically noisy [20].

Noisy signals can have a deleterious effect on the double integration of acceleration that leads to the displacement estimation. For this reason, several algorithmic filters have been introduced in the INS context. The most used are the Kalman filter, the noise filter, and the simple moving average filter [21, 22].

For the specific application, a discrete Kalman filter for accelerometer noise reduction has been selected. The Kalman filter is an algorithm that describes a recursive solution for data filtering problems. Typically, it receives and computes the input measurements and, based on these, it estimates the actual value of the inter-state variables. As a linear-quadratic problem estimator, the resulting estimate is statically optimal with respect to any quadratic error estimation function. Since the Kalman filter is recursive, it is not necessary to store all the past data, because it uses the last value of the previous state, repeating the operations. It allows a useful implementation of this algorithm in real-time systems [21]. The discrete Kalman filter has been implemented according to the procedure proposed in [19]. The filtered data are, thus, subject to the signal processing step. This step realizes a double integration of the acceleration data. For this purpose, several numerical integration algorithms have been tested, with particular focus on close Newton-Cotes formulas. For the proposed case study, the trapezoidal rule has been chosen among the analyzed integration algorithms, due to its suitability in real-time data processing applications. Nevertheless, trapezoidal rule prerequisite is noise-less inputs. This condition is still difficult to be achieved even with filtered data due to DC components that introduce slope on the first integration and exponential behavior on the second one. To avoid this drift, a Finite Impulse Response (FIR) high pass filter with cutoff frequency of 1 Hz has been implemented downward the Kalman filter. If no changes in gyroscope data are recorded in a time span of 5 s, the object is labeled as "still". In this latter case, the microcontroller stops computing the displacement, storing the last calculated one. The stored position is, thus, employed for the potential call for robot intervention.

3.2 The Actuation System

3.2.1 The Robot Platform

The assistive robot platform, employed for the proposed case study, is the Pepper Y20 model by SoftBank Robotics. Pepper Y20 is supplied with an Intel ATOM Z530 1.6 GHz processor. One gigabyte of RAM and 2 GB of Flash memory have been allocated for navigation and object manipulation procedures. The developed routines run on Pepper's native operating system, NAOqi OS [22]. For proper working, the object manipulation routine exploits two RGB cameras and a 3D depth sensor as per Fig. 3. The RGB cameras are two OV5640 by Omnivision. The OV5640 provides a maximum resolution of 5 Mp with 55.2° of the horizontal field of view (FOV), 44.3° of vertical FOV, and a diagonal FOV of 68.2°. The designed routine exploits an output set to kVGA (640*480 px) with 10 fps. The 3D sensor used by the system is an ASUS Xtion with 0.3 Mp of resolution. The Xtion provides 58° of horizontal FOV, 45° of vertical FOV, and a diagonal FOV of 70°. The depth camera output has been set to be kQVGA (320*240 px) with 5 fps. For navigation purposes, Pepper is equipped with 3 sets of 15 pulsed lasers. These sets cover frontal, left, and right directions, ensuring, singularly, a vertical FOV of 40° and a horizontal FOV of 60°.

3.2.2 The Navigation Routine

In the proposed application, the navigation routine has been entrusted to the native AL Navigation API provided by the NAOqi [23]. The AL Navigation API embeds several methods for obstacle avoidance, safe trajectory planning, and unknown environment exploration and localization. At the first use, the robot enables the exploration method. It consists of investigating the surrounding in a circle of programmable radius. In this context, the robot starts moving from its absolute initial position (0, 0) enabling the built-in SLAM algorithm for the 2D position computation. To improve the native SLAM algorithm precision, a novel procedure of body rotation angle correction has been introduced in this application. It consists of evaluating the discrepancy between the target rotation angle and the actual rotation of the robot. It allows compensating for bad rotation management by reducing the odometry error. Once the exploration is completed, Pepper stores a 2D matrix representing the extracted map. The robot is now able to identify the absolute position of the place selected as the target for each kind of monitored food (e.g. refrigerator or cold and dry shelf). Accordingly, when the sensor node records a sharp reduction of the SL parameter, and -jointly- no movements related to the monitored food, it will send the estimated coordinates of the monitored object with the call for intervention. Pepper can, thus, estimate the absolute position of the object, or at least a rough estimate of it. Pepper will move toward the identified area starting the object manipulation routine.

3.2.3 The Object Manipulation Routine

The object manipulation routine is entrusted to a procedure proposed and characterized in our previous work [14]. Briefly, it consists of three main steps: (i) Shelf Scanning (ii) Tag Extraction, and (iii) Object -vs-Hand Coverage Routine.

Shelf Scanning. Once the shelf height is estimated, the RGB camera frames are sent to a real-time object detection routine based on the "You Only Look Once" YOLOv3 method [14, 24]. The object detection model pre-training has been carried out offline and consisted of data collection and preparation, model training, inference testing, and model extraction. YOLOv3 oversees extracting a number of bounding boxes returning,

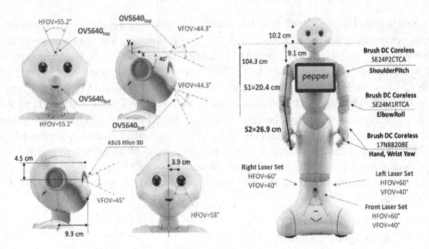

Fig. 3. Assistive robot platform overview

for each of these, the probability that the box contains an object and the probability that the object belongs to a specific class.

Tag Extraction. During this step, the robot moves towards the object, by keeping the selected YOLOv3 tag in the center of the image and progressively adjusting the head frame. The arm selected for the grabbing is led to the position shown in Fig. 4.a. The RGB image from the top camera and the fixed YOLOv3 tag are resized with the 3D image resolution (via bilinear interpolation). Only the area covered by the YOLOv3 tag (Fig. 4.b) is selected for further analysis. The central anchor point of the YOLOv3 Tag is used to extract a reference distance from the depth map of the 3D sensor. This distance fixes a specific color in the colormap (i.e. red in Fig. 4.b), then the depth threshold for the segmentation is set to 5 mm, and the colormap limits are restricted in the close proximity of the reference value. Figure 4.b shows the initial blob vision from the position of Fig. 4.a. The area included in the red blob determines 100% of the uncovered object. The designed routine stores the number of red pixels from depth map.

Object vs-Hand Coverage Routine. Once the number of red pixels is set, the hand moves on the selected object, partially covering it, from the 3D sensor point of view (see Fig. 4.c). Pepper progressively assesses the number of remaining red pixels. If the remaining number is about ~ 40–45% (right hand) of the initial coverage, the hand stops moving, and the grabbing routine starts running. More details about the Object-vs-Hand Coverage Routine and its characterization are available in [14].

4 Experimental Results

The above-presented FWR architecture has been tested in a laboratory environment to assess the effectiveness of the involved operations. For this purpose, two sensors' nodes have been employed for the tests. Both nodes have been programmed to implement an

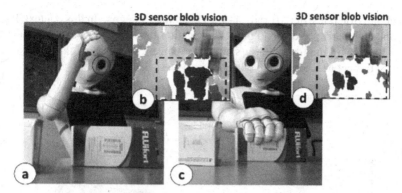

Fig. 4. Object-vs-hand coverage routine for object manipulation

SL model proposed in [13]. One node is moved in places subjected to direct sunlight (to trigger a sudden decay), while the second one is to the target place for storage.

As proof of concept, the nodes have been fixed to easily manageable packages as characterized in our previous works [14, 25, 26]. Overall, 50 operations of displacement have been carried out, followed by a call for intervention toward the robot platform.

4.1 Displacement Estimation and Scanning

As stated in Sect. 3.1.3, each sensor node implements a displacement computation algorithm based on the cascade of a Kalman filter, an approximate FIR filter, and a double integration step based on the trapezoidal rule. During the 50 recovery operations, the exact target coordinates have been derived for the estimate error assessment. On average, an error of $20.81 \pm 10.87\%$ has been recorded between the estimated and the actual coordinate along the x-axis, while an error of $15.25 \pm 8.77\%$ has been extracted along the y-axis. A scatterplot of the errors is reported in Fig. 5.a.

Figure 5.b analyzes the number of successful recovery operations started with a correct automatic scanning of the area via YOLOv3. In 26% of the cases (13/50), the position estimates from the node did not allow a proper scanning operation, preventing the successful completion of operations. In 74% of cases (37/50) the operations proceeded to the second step, i.e., the navigation toward the object and its manipulation.

4.2 Navigation System Characterization

According to Sect. 3.2.2, the navigation routine is based on the AL Navigation API provided by the NAOqi supported by a body rotation angle correction introduced in this application. To characterize the mapping error reduction achieved with the routine, the robot did three calibration tests: (i) three complete turns on itself by exploiting only the built-in functions; (ii) three complete turns on itself by exploiting built-in functions and the correction system with a tolerance of 0.02 rad and (iii) a tolerance of 0.01 rad. Figure 6.a shows the results of the analysis in the three cases. It can be noticed that in the first two cases the three turns (red, blue, and black) present a drift among each other. The third subplot (tolerance of 0.01 rad) shows a good match degree. In this context, Fig. 6.b shows the cumulative error in 30 min of navigation for each laser beam (15 total laser beams) composing the frontal laser set. It is possible to notice how the reconstruction error with respect to x and y, in the latter case, is less than 2 cm.

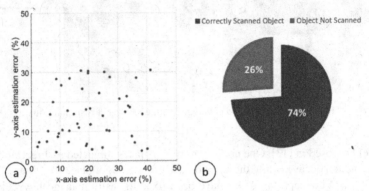

Fig. 5. Displacement Estimation Characterization. (a) scatter plot of estimates errors (x and y axes); (b) successful rate in robot scanning procedure.

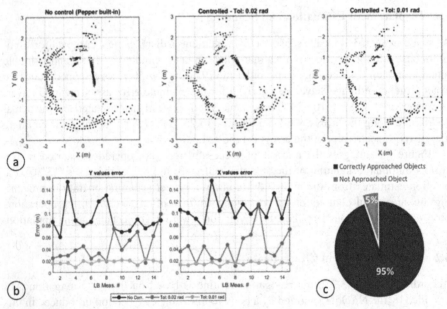

Fig. 6. Navigation Routine Characterization. (a) Rotation Angle Correction System calibration. (b) Cumulative estimation error. (c) Success rate of navigation operations

The object approach operation driven by the navigation routine has been triggered in 37/50 cases as stated in the previous section. In this context, 35/37 (95%) operations concluded this phase with a proper object approach (Fig. 6.c).

4.3 Manipulation Routine Success Rate

The Object vs-Hand coverage routine for the object manipulation optimized for Pepper robot has been widely characterized in our previous work [14]. However, considering the proposed application, the implemented manipulation routine led to 30/35 successfully completed operations (i.e., 86%), concluding the operations to reduce the food waste. Specifically, 24 out of 35 operations have been carried out with the right hand, while 11 out of 35 operations have been realized via the left hand. The five grab-bing errors are distributed as follows: 4 errors are related to left-hand operations, while 1 error concerns right-hand operations. This latter operation (right-hand-based grabbing) was demonstrated to be more reliable than left-hand-based ones.

5 Conclusions

The proposed FWR architecture minimizing the food waste through actions that compensate for the bad habits of the human component in terms of food preservation can drastically reduce the waste, which is nowadays a crucial point. The proposed system exploits data from a wireless network of custom sensor nodes that monitor physical parameters like temperature, humidity, and light, assessing their impact on the expiration date of food. These sensor nodes are fixed on critical foods or beverages packages, to real-time calculate their shelf life. The onset of sharp reductions in the average life of the food triggers a robot intervention that carries out mitigation actions, which consist of manipulating the good, picking, and releasing it in a more adequate place. The FWR architecture has been experimentally tested in a laboratory environment. Fifty operations of food displacement have been carried out, to trigger the shelf-life degradation and lead to a robot intervention. The whole mitigation chain has been successfully completed in 30 out of 50 cases (i.e., 60%). The most relevant source of error (i.e., 26%) lies in a wrong displacement estimation, followed by the 10% that concerns bad grabbing operations. Ultimately, the FWR architecture has shown promising results that can further enhance the capabilities of smart homes, creating a sustainable environment and alleviating the economic impact of consumer-side food waste.

References

1. Badar, A.Q., Anvari-Moghaddam, A.: Smart home energy management system–a review. Adv. Build. Energy Res. **16**(1), 118–143 (2022)
2. Büyük, M., Avşar, E., İnci, M.: Overview of smart home concepts through energy management systems, numerical research, and future perspective. Energ. Sources, Part A: Recovery, Utilization, and Environ. Eff. 1–26 (2022)
3. Dong, B., et al.: Technology evolution from self-powered sensors to AIoT enabled smart homes. Nano Energy **79**, 105414 (2021)
4. Khan, A.T., Li, S., Cao, X.: Human guided cooperative robotic agents in smart home using beetle antennae search. Sci. China Inf. Sci. **65**(2), 1–17 (2022)
5. Khan, A.T., Li, S., Cao, X.: Control framework for cooperative robots in smart home using bio-inspired neural network. Measurement **167**, 108253 (2021)

6. Peng, J., Ye, H., He, Q., Qin, Y., Wan, Z., Lu, J.: Design of smart home service robot based on ROS. Mob. Inf. Syst. 2021 (2021)

7. Annese, V.F., De Venuto, D.: Fall-risk assessment by combined movement related potentials and co-contraction index monitoring. In: 2015 IEEE Biomedical Circuits and Systems Conference (BioCAS), pp. 1-4 (2015). https://doi.org/10.1109/BioCAS.2015.7348366

8. Santhanaraj, K.K., Ramya, M.M., Dinakaran, D.: A survey of assistive robots and systems for elderly care. J. Enabling Technol. (2021)

9. Do, H.M., et al.: RiSH: a robot-integrated smart home for elderly care. Robot. Auton. Syst. 101, 74–92 (2018)

10. Wu, H.H., Chuang, Y.T.: Low-cost smart refrigerator. In: 2017 IEEE International Conference on Edge Computing (EDGE). IEEE (2017)

11. Cappelletti, F., et al.: Smart strategies for household food waste management. Procedia Comput. Sci. 200, 887–895 (2022)

12. Roe, B.E., et al.: A randomized controlled trial to address consumer food waste with a technology-aided tailored sustainability intervention. Resour. Conserv. Recycl. 179, 106121 (2022)

13. De Venuto, D., Mezzina, G.: Spatio-Temporal optimization of perishable goods' shelf life by a pro-active WSN-based architecture. Sensors 18, 2126 (2018). https://doi.org/10.3390/s18 072126

14. Mezzina, G., De Venuto, D.: RGB and 3D-segmentation data combination for the autonomous object manipulation in personal care robotics. In: 2021 16th International Conference on Design & Technology of Integrated Systems in Nanoscale Era (DTIS), pp. 1–6 (2021). https://doi.org/10.1109/DTIS53253.2021.9505128

15. Blagojevic, M., Kayal, M., Gervais, M., De Venuto, D.: SOI hall-sensor front end for energy measurement. IEEE Sens. J. 6(4), 1016–1021 (2006). https://doi.org/10.1109/JSEN.2006.877996

16. De Venuto, D., Castro, D.T., Ponomarev, Y., Stikvoort, E.: Low power 12-bit SAR ADC for autonomous wireless sensors network interface. In: 2009 3rd International Workshop on Advances in Sensors and Interfaces, pp. 115–120 (2009) https://doi.org/10.1109/IWASI.2009.5184780

17. De Venuto, D., Stikvoort, E., Castro, D.T., Ponomarev, Y.: Ultra low-power 12-bit SAR ADC for RFID applications. In: 2010 Design, Automation & Test in Europe Conference & Exhibition (DATE 2010), pp. 1071–1075 (2010). https://doi.org/10.1109/DATE.2010.545 6968

18. Fedorov, D.S., et al.: Using of measuring system MPU6050 for the determination of the angular velocities and linear accelerations. Autom. Softw. Enginery 11(1), 75–80 (2015)

19. Biccario, G. E., Annese, V. F., Cipriani, S., De Venuto, D.: "WSN-based near real-time environmental monitoring for shelf life prediction through data processing to improve food safety and certification. In: 2014 11th International Conference on Informatics in Control, Automation and Robotics (ICINCO), pp. 777–782 (2014). https://doi.org/10.5220/000510 2407770782

20. Treffers, C., van Wietmarschen, L.: Position and orientation determination of a probe with use of the IMU MPU9250 and a ATmega328 microcontroller (2016)

21. Welch, G., Bishop, G.: An introduction to the Kalman filter, pp. 127–132 (1995)

22. De Venuto, D., Annese, V.F., Mezzina, G., Defazio, G.: FPGA-based embedded cyber-physical platform to assess gait and postural stability in parkinson's disease. IEEE Trans. Compon. Packag. Manuf. Technol. 8(7), 1167–1179 (2018). https://doi.org/10.1109/TCPMT.2018.2810103

23. Pandey, A.K., Gelin, R.: A mass-produced sociable humanoid robot: Pepper: the first machine of its kind. IEEE Robot. Autom. Mag. 25(3), 40–48 (2018)

24. Mao, Q.C., et al.: Mini-YOLOv3: real-time object detector for embedded applications. IEEE Access **7**, 133529–133538 (2019)
25. De Venuto, D., Annese, V.F., Mezzina, G., Ruta, M., Di Sciascio, E.: Brain-computer interface using P300: a gaming approach for neurocognitive impairment diagnosis. In: 2016 IEEE International High Level Design Validation and Test Workshop (HLDVT), pp. 93–99 (2016). https://doi.org/10.1109/HLDVT.2016.7748261
26. De Venuto, D., Annese, V.F., Defazio, G., Gallo, V. L., Mezzina, G.: Gait analysis and quantitative drug effect evaluation in Parkinson disease by jointly EEG-EMG monitoring. In: 2017 12th International Conference on Design & Technology of Integrated Systems in Nanoscale Era (DTIS), pp. 1–6 (2017). https://doi.org/10.1109/DTIS.2017.7930171

Cowl: A Lightweight OWL Library
for the Semantic Web of Everything

Ivano Bilenchi[ID], Floriano Scioscia[✉][ID], and Michele Ruta[ID]

Polytechnic University of Bari, Via Edoardo Orabona 4, (I-70125) Bari, Italy
{ivano.bilenchi,floriano.scioscia,michele.ruta}@poliba.it

Abstract. The Semantic Web of Everything, a blend of the emerging Internet of Everything and well-established Semantic Web paradigms, demands efficient cross-platform knowledge management technologies and tools, able to span the wide variety of devices it aims to support. This paper presents *Cowl*, a C library for processing Web Ontology Language (OWL) 2 ontologies, designed for strict portability and efficiency constraints. Its architecture is described and main optimization strategies are outlined. Results of a preliminary experimental campaign validate its effectiveness by comparing it with other state-of-the-art OWL toolkits.

Keywords: Web ontology language · Semantic web · Internet of everything

1 Introduction and Motivation

The Semantic Web of Things (SWoT) [22] integrates Semantic Web technologies in Internet of Things (IoT) contexts, by associating ontology-based annotations to devices, objects, and phenomena, and by supporting automated reasoning procedures to infer implicit knowledge. The ever-increasing pervasiveness and miniaturization of IoT devices is leading to the so-called *Internet of Everything* (IoE) [5], where living beings, objects, places and processes are interconnected and generate data streams. This evolution requires a parallel progress of SWoT methodologies, algorithms and tools toward a *Semantic Web of Everything* (SWoE), which should encompass devices, applications and services from Web scale to micro- and nano-scale.

The extreme volatility of devices, connections and resources in the SWoE calls for Knowledge Representation and Reasoning (KRR) implementations locally available even on severely resource-constrained nano- and micro-devices (classified as Class 0 and Class 1 devices in [3], respectively), without depending on auxiliary systems. Supporting Semantic Web standards like Resource Description Framework (RDF) [20] and Web Ontology Language (OWL) 2 [15] in SWoE contexts, however, is hardly feasible with existing tools, which have been mostly designed for conventional computing architectures (and possibly ported to mobile platforms): the architectural and resource-consumption gaps are too wide. Novel approaches and solutions are therefore needed.

G. Agapito et al. (Eds.): ICWE 2022 Workshops, CCIS 1668, pp. 100–112, 2023.
https://doi.org/10.1007/978-3-031-25380-5_8

This paper presents *Cowl*, a lightweight C library for working with OWL ontologies and Knowledge Bases (KBs). It is distributed under the Eclipse Public License, Version 2.0[1], to promote its adoption both in the research community and in industry. Cowl has been designed for wide portability, including not only workstations and mobile computing devices, but specifically embedded devices with severe processing and memory resource limitations. In order to achieve this goal, it is written in pure standard C11 [10] with no compiler- or platform-specific features. Cowl supports the full OWL 2 specification for KB parsing and arbitrarily complex queries to retrieve KB elements. Core architectural choices and implementation optimizations aim at maximum memory savings, while guaranteeing robustness and ease of use for C developers. An early performance analysis has been carried out by comparing Cowl with three state-of-the-art OWL 2 manipulation tools, in order to provide a preliminary validation of the feasibility of exploiting the proposed library in resource-constrained settings.

The remainder of the paper is as follows: Sect. 2 discusses relevant related work, while Sect. 3 describes Cowl architecture and optimizations; experiments are reported in Sect. 4, before the conclusion.

2 Related Work

The Semantic Web landscape has historically relied on Java runtime environments, as the most popular libraries and tools are written in the Java programming language. The *OWL API* [9] is likely the most widely adopted library for OWL-based *Knowledge Base Management Systems* (KBMS) and applications [2,14]. *Apache Jena*[2] provides ontology manipulation primitives for *Resource Description Framework* (RDF) [20], *RDF Schema* (RDFS) and OWL models, and an inference Application Programming Interface (API) to support reasoning and rule engines; the *Protégé-OWL API* [11] is built on top of Jena and is particularly effective for developing graphical applications. More recently, OWL support has been brought to the Python platform by *OWLready2* [12], an ontology-oriented programming toolkit able to manipulate OWL ontologies and their constructs as Python objects, as well as reasoning over them via modified versions of the *HermiT* [7] and *Pellet* [23] reasoners.

Even though the aforementioned projects are mature and have wide adoption in the Semantic Web community, their use on SWoE devices is unpractical for two key reasons: (i) they are based on the Java Standard Edition (SE) and Python runtimes, which preclude their use on platforms that do not support them; (ii) they were designed for conventional computing contexts, with plenty of processing and memory resources.

The *owlcpp* [13] open-source C++ library supports OWL parsing and querying via a RDF triple store developed on top of the *Redland* [1] application framework, and reasoning through the *Fact++* [25] engine. While the C++ implementation theoretically supports embedded devices, it has two major drawbacks: (i)

---

[1] Eclipse Public License - v2.0: https://www.eclipse.org/legal/epl-2.0/.
[2] Apache Jena project: https://jena.apache.org/.

its core data model is a RDF triple store, which is generally harder to use than OWL abstractions, as queries must be performed over RDF graphs rather than on structured OWL axioms; (ii) it only supports parsing ontologies serialized in RDF/XML, implying the availability of *Extensible Markup Language* (XML) and RDF parsers, further increasing code size and memory demand.

The *OWL API for iOS* [18] is an Objective-C OWL library targeted at Apple devices, providing mobile application developers with familiar interfaces for working with OWL Knowledge Bases (KBs), as it is largely based on the widely adopted Java OWL API. Paired with the *Mini-ME Swift* reasoner [19], it has enabled the development of SWoT applications and services on the iOS operating systems family. Nevertheless, its focus on Apple technologies makes it unsuitable for other target platforms.

As evidenced by this rundown of available OWL manipulation tools, none of the existing frameworks fits the SWoE use case. In this regard, the selection of a suitable programming language and runtime environment proves to be crucial. C is a sensible choice, as it is the most widely used language on IoT devices [8]. This is corroborated by its successful use as the core language of the *Tiny-ME* [17] SWoE-oriented reasoner.

3   Knowledge Representation in the SWoE

Cowl[3] is a lightweight API for working with OWL ontologies. It provides a complete C implementation of the OWL 2 specification [15], and can be compiled both as a static and a dynamic linking library. As previously motivated, one of the most critical prerequisites for a SWoE library is multi-platform support, which Cowl strives to achieve by means of the following architectural and implementation choices:

- it is written in standard C11 with no compiler-specific extensions or platform-specific API calls. It can therefore be deployed to any platform for which a C compiler is available, including microcontrollers and embedded boards;
- it is self-contained, with no external runtime dependencies other than uLib[4], which provides most of its basic data structures;
- it strives to be fast and have a small memory footprint, in order to be suitable to run on resource-constrained devices.

Details about Cowl architecture and optimizations are described in what follows.

3.1   Architecture

The architecture of the Cowl library is illustrated in Fig. 1 and described in the following subsections.

---

[3] Cowl home: http://swot.sisinflab.poliba.it/cowl.

[4] uLib repository: https://github.com/IvanoBilenchi/ulib.

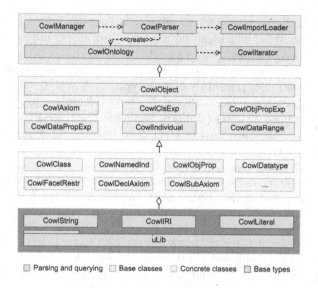

Fig. 1. Cowl architecture

Data Model. Cowl's data model is mostly made of opaque structs, which keeps users from modifying their internal state. This in turn allows for its second fundamental property, which is immutability: as shown in what follows, an immutable data model enables optimizations that would otherwise be more difficult to implement.

The hierarchical nature of the OWL 2 specification is mirrored throughout the API by making extensive use of *pseudo-inheritance* for C structs, a technique that exploits specific features of the C language in order to mimic class inheritance in object-oriented programming and provide a basic form of type safety. As the C specification ([10], Sect. 6.7.2.1-15) guarantees that there is no padding at the beginning of a struct –*i.e.*, its memory address is the same as that of its first member–, if structs are nested so that the struct acting as the base type (the "superstruct") is the first member of the one acting as derived type (the "substruct"), then casts between pointers of the two types are legal. In order to allow for dynamic casts at runtime, pseudo-inheritance can be enhanced by adding a *type enumeration* field to the base struct, as shown in Listing 1, which makes the concrete substruct type explicitly known to the programmer. In the context of the Cowl API, adopting these techniques means it is possible, for example, to cast a `CowlClass` (modelling OWL classes) to `CowlClsExp` (OWL class expressions), and back. If the API returns a base struct type such as `CowlClsExp`, and the programmer is unsure about its concrete subtype, they can check it via the provided `*_get_type` functions, which return the value of the type member, and cast accordingly.

The whole data model is built on top of the `uLib` library, which provides basic types such as strings, vectors, hash maps, and so on. Other than those inherited from `uLib`, Cowl provides a few base types of its own:

- `CowlObject`, the base type for all objects. It contains information about the specific object type, which can be used for type casts, and reference count, both embedded in a single integer field.
- `CowlString`, the string type, is essentially an immutable, reference-counted wrapper around `UString`, uLib's string type.
- `CowlIRI`, representing *International Resource Identifiers* [6]. IRIs basically extend the syntax of URIs (Uniform Resource Identifiers) to a wider set of characters, and they are used in OWL 2 to identify ontologies and many of their elements.
- `CowlLiteral`, modelling OWL literals. They represent data values such as strings or integers, and are analogous to typed RDF literals [20].
- `cowl_ret`, an enumeration acting as the return code type for API functions that can fail.

Although Cowl's architecture is mostly oriented toward the efficient usage of hardware resources, significant effort went into ensuring ease of use by means of a moderate degree of type safety: as reported in the specification [15], OWL constructs can be grouped into families, which the library models as appropriate base pseudo-classes (in parentheses):

- **Axioms** (`CowlAxiom`): statements that specify what is true in the domain the ontology represents;
- **Class expressions** (`CowlClsExp`): the OWL equivalent of complex concepts in Description Logics, they represent sets of individuals by formally specifying conditions on their properties;
- **Individuals** (`CowlIndividual`): instances of the knowledge domain, which can be either *named* or *anonymous*, depending on whether they have an explicit, globally unambiguous name;
- **Object property expressions** (`CowlObjPropExp`): relationships between pairs of individuals. In OWL, they can be either *object properties* or their *inverse* counterpart.
- **Data property expressions** (`CowlDataPropExp`): relationships between individuals and literals.

Each of the previous base classes has multiple subclasses, a subset of which is shown in Fig. 1, labeled as *concrete classes*. In order to keep the library code section small, some of them map multiple OWL constructs, whose specific type can be queried by calling `*_get_type` functions: as an example, `CowlNAryClsAxiom` represents both *equivalent* and *disjoint classes* axioms, and `CowlNAryBool` models both the *intersection* and *union* of class expressions. This part of the data model is extensive but straightforward, as it is essentially a mapping of the OWL data model to C structs[5].

Ontology parsing and querying. KB parsing can be carried out via the `cowl_manager_read_*` functions of `CowlManager`, which is the library entry point for managing ontology documents. Cowl makes use of uLib's input streams,

---

[5] Cowl data model: http://swot.sisinflab.poliba.it/cowl/api/owl.

```
enum MyType {
    MT_A, MT_B
};
struct SuperClass {
    enum MyType type;
};
```

```
struct SubClassA {
    struct SuperClass super;
};
struct SubClassB {
    struct SuperClass super;
};
```

Listing 1: Pseudo-inheritance for C structs.

enabling the deserialization of ontologies from files, memory buffers, or even network streams. Multiple built-in or user-provided parsers are architecturally supported by means of the CowlParser interface, though built-in support is currently limited to the *functional OWL syntax* [15] through a lexer and parser generated using *Flex*[6] and *Bison*[7].

The OWL 2 specification allows for ontologies to import other ontologies, which may involve retrieving them from the network or loading them from mass storage. Cowl delegates imports retrieval to the end user by means of the CowlImportLoader interface: by providing an instance of this struct to the manager or globally, loading of arbitrary ontology imports can be implemented by populating the struct with a pointer to a function, which must return the ontology having the requested IRI.

Parsing a serialized KB produces a CowlOntology object, which can be seen as a set of CowlAxiom instances, and whose member functions allow querying the ontology for knowledge stored therein. Internally, CowlOntology stores axioms in a vector, and populates multiple hash-based collections acting as indices, which are used to optimize queries.

The base mechanism for querying a CowlOntology is to invoke its iterator member functions, each of which accepts a CowlIterator instance. CowlIterator is a wrapper around a function that is called for every element matched by the query. By providing a generic context pointer, one can plug any custom data structure, which allows for arbitrarily complex queries. The iterator function returns a boolean that can be used to control iteration: by returning true iteration goes on to the next element, while returning false causes it to stop. This is useful if, for example, one wants to find the first element matching certain criteria.

3.2   Optimizations

Most of the optimizations implemented in Cowl are aimed at reducing memory usage. Efficient memory management is particularly difficult in the context of OWL data models, as the same construct (*e.g.*, an OWL class) may be referenced by multiple other constructs, making it hard to know when it can be safely

---

[6] Flex home: https://www.gnu.org/software/flex.
[7] Bison home: https://www.gnu.org/software/bison.

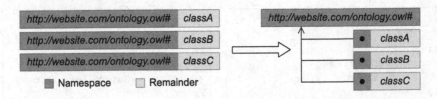

Fig. 2. Efficient IRI storage.

deallocated. A straightforward solution would be avoiding references altogether and ensuring that each super-construct has its own copy of every sub-construct, allowing their lifespans to be tied together, though this has the obvious drawback of requiring additional memory. Given the SWoE-dictated requirement of running on nano-scale devices, sharing instances of equal constructs through references is strongly desirable, hence Cowl adopts the *reference counting* technique for memory management: each construct has a `ref_count` integer member, which is increased (the construct is *retained*) for each new reference to it, and decreased (the construct is *released*) when the construct holding that reference is destroyed. The object can be deallocated safely whenever the reference count reaches zero, as this entails that no other object is referencing it. Control over the reference count of each construct is granted by means of specific implementations of the `retain` and `release` primitives provided for every available type. By virtue of the combination of immutability and reference counting, a construct wanting to safely reference a shared instance of some other construct can simply *retain* it and be sure it will not be mutated or deallocated until it is *released*.

Instance sharing is implemented in Cowl through *interning*, *i.e.*, distinct objects are stored in an *instance pool*, and constructor functions always return shared instances. Other than for entities and IRIs, the library transparently applies conditional interning to strings that are likely to be referenced multiple times, such as common language constructs.

One of the most substantial memory optimizations concerns the storage of IRIs: an IRI can be usually split into a *namespace*, which avoids name conflicts by relating the resource to a certain domain, and a *local name*, which identifies a specific resource within its namespace. Since the namespace part is often shared by multiple IRIs, it is possible to significantly reduce the overall size of their in-memory representations by ensuring that they share a reference to the same namespace instance. In order to allow this, `CowlIRI` is internally composed of two strings, the *namespace* and *remainder* (see Fig. 2). Every time an IRI is created from its string representation, Cowl parses it in order to determine a suitable namespace-remainder split according to the XML namespaces specification [4], and conditional string interning is exploited to allow sharing of the namespace part.

Further optimizations are aimed at reducing the turnaround time of parsing and queries. As an example, since the library makes extensive use of instance pools and entity indices, a significant amount of time is spent in lookups and insertions into hash-based data structures, resulting in a high volume of hash computations and equality checks. The combination of interning and data immutability allows for a significant speed boost for both operations: since interned objects are equal if and only if they are the same instance (*i.e.*, they have the same memory address), the address itself is a perfect hash and equality checks can be implemented as pointer comparisons. Furthermore, hash caching can be exploited to speed up equality checks for strings: since equal strings must have equal hashes, if their hashes differ it can be concluded that they are different. By caching string hashes, expensive equality checks are only necessary if two strings have equal hashes and lengths, while most checks can be skipped.

4 Feasibility and Effectiveness

Performance evaluation is a necessary requisite to validate Cowl's suitability for the heterogeneous contexts and platforms required by the SWoE. A preliminary experimental campaign has involved comparing it to the following state-of-the-art OWL ontology manipulation toolkits: OWL API (version 5.1.20), OWL-ready2 (0.37), and owlcpp (0.3.3). The EVOWLUATOR [21] framework has been leveraged for test automation, exploiting its ability to invoke command line tools over arbitrary OWL datasets and gather performance metrics concerning turnaround time and memory usage. To be integrated into EVOWLUATOR, all libraries have been wrapped in straightforward command line tools that accept the path to the ontology as an argument. The testbed is a 2021 Apple MacBook Pro 16"[8]. All reported performance results are the average of 5 cold runs.

The dataset used for the tests consists of 109 knowledge bases, extracted from the 2014 *OWL Reasoner Evaluation Workshop* (ORE2014) competition corpus[9] as follows: all ontologies in functional-style have been considered and sorted by size, then one sample has been extracted at each MB boundary (if available). Tests concern ontology parsing and querying time, and peak memory usage. The following queries have been selected for benchmarking: (Q1) retrieval of all axioms in the ontology; (Q2) retrieval of all classes in the ontology and, for each class, retrieval of all subclass axioms directly referencing it as the subclass or superclass.

Before presenting the results of the experimental campaign, it is important to point out a few key differences among the evaluated tools:

- They support different OWL serializations: the OWL API features parsers for most syntaxes in literature; OWLready2 only supports RDF/XML, OWL/-XML and Turtle; owlcpp is limited to RDF/XML, while Cowl currently only features a functional syntax parser. The libraries have therefore been configured as follows: OWLready2 and owlcpp have been run on RDF/XML documents, while the OWL API and Cowl have processed their functional syntax variants. This is apparent from data points in the scatterplots, spanning larger ontology sizes for tools using the RDF/XML serialization.

---

[8] Apple M1 Max System-on-Chip with 64 GB RAM, 1 TB SSD, macOS Monterey 12.3.

[9] ORE2014 corpus: http://dl.kr.org/ore2014.

```
SELECT *
WHERE {
    { ?a_class rdfs:subClassOf ?b_class . }
    UNION
    { ?b_class rdfs:subClassOf ?a_class . }
    FILTER (!isBlank(?a_class))
}
```

Listing 2: Retrieval of all subclass axioms for each class from a triple store.

– They adopt different data model architectures: the OWL API and Cowl provide a direct mapping to OWL axioms and constructs, while OWLready2 and owlcpp store ontologies in RDF triple stores. This entails that ontology queries have considerably different implementations, with significant influence on performance.

Figure 3 shows peak memory usage metrics, computed as the *maximum resident set size* (MRSS) of the process, *i.e.*, the value stored in the ru_maxrss field of the structure populated by the getrusage[10] POSIX call. Cowl exhibits a significantly lower memory footprint than all other tools, with the margin being especially wide when compared to the non-native OWL API and OWLready2 libraries. All libraries follow a roughly linear trend for memory occupancy in relation to ontology size, even though absolute values on Class 0 and Class 1 nodes [3] may be different from the adopted testbed with 64-bit architecture.

Figure 4 reports results on turnaround times for ontology parsing. Similar considerations apply here, with Cowl outperforming the other tools, and all libraries behaving linearly in relation to ontology size. The OWL API performs remarkably well with regards to parsing time, even outperforming the native owlcpp library, albeit at the cost of a consistently and significantly higher memory usage than all other tested toolkits.

Figure 5 displays turnaround times for the retrieval of all axioms. Cowl is consistently faster than the other frameworks; interestingly, the OWL API is almost able to match owlcpp. As the query entails iterating over all constructs in the KB, triple store based tools are penalized, as they must process a larger number of constructs, since OWL axioms are generally encoded through multiple RDF statements.

Figure 6 shows turnaround times for the retrieval of all subclass axioms for all classes: owlcpp is the top performer, followed by Cowl, while the OWL API and OWLready2 exhibit very similar, much higher figures. The results were expected, as this query strongly relies on access to constructs that directly reference specific entities, therefore it can be easily answered by triple stores with the simple SPARQL [24] query in Listing 2. Axiom-based tools, on the other hand, must populate auxiliary indices in order to speed up references to specific OWL entities, and may still end up processing unrelated axioms.

---

[10] getrusage man page: https://linux.die.net/man/2/getrusage.

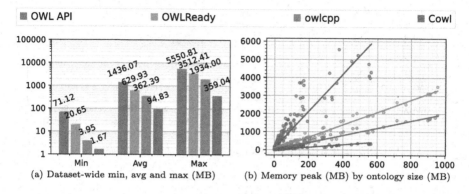

(a) Dataset-wide min, avg and max (MB)   (b) Memory peak (MB) by ontology size (MB)

Fig. 3. Peak memory usage

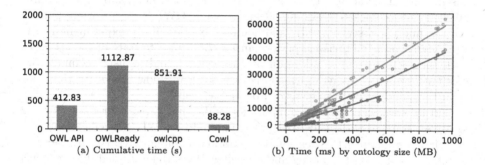

(a) Cumulative time (s)   (b) Time (ms) by ontology size (MB)

Fig. 4. Parsing time

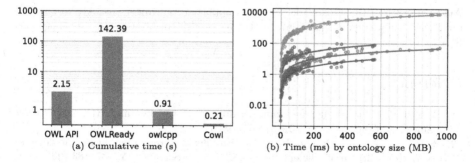

(a) Cumulative time (s)   (b) Time (ms) by ontology size (MB)

Fig. 5. Retrieval of all axioms

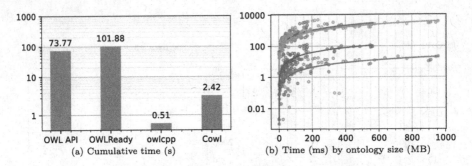

Fig. 6. Retrieval of all subclass axioms for all classes

5   Conclusion and Future Work

The paper has presented Cowl, a lightweight multi-platform OWL manipulation library targeted at the Semantic Web of Everything. Architectural choices and careful optimization aim to achieve both wide portability and high resource efficiency. Nevertheless, Cowl supports the whole OWL 2 specification, parsing KBs in functional-style syntax, and complex queries. Early experimental tests have been conducted to assess performance with respect to state-of-the-art tools, with satisfactory results. Adoption by the research and industry communities –fostered by a permissive open-source license– will allow demonstrating that robustness and ease-of-use goals can be met as well.

Future work concerns the support for additional parsers for more OWL 2 syntaxes, starting with RDF/XML as mandated by OWL 2 specifications [16], as well as a fundamental extension of the library to support KB editing and serialization in addition to parsing and querying. Ports to embedded devices (such as *Arduino*[11] and *Pixhawk*[12] microcontroller families) will be carried out, and their usefulness validated through use cases. Finally, more thorough performance evaluations will be carried out on SWoE target device classes, including energy consumption.

Acknowledgments. This work has been supported by project TEBAKA (TErritorial BAsic Knowledge Acquisition), funded by the Italian Ministry of University and Research.

References

1. Beckett, D.: The design and implementation of the Redland RDF application framework. Comput. Netw. **39**(5), 577–588 (2002)
2. Bobed, C., Yus, R., Bobillo, F., Mena, E.: Semantic reasoning on mobile devices: do Androids dream of efficient reasoners? J. Web Semant. **35**, 167–183 (2015)

---

[11] Arduino home: https://www.arduino.cc.
[12] Pixhawk home: https://pixhawk.org.

3. Bormann, C., Ersue, M., Keranen, A.: Terminology for Constrained-Node Networks. RFC 7228, Internet Engineering Task Force (2014)
4. Bray, T., Hollander, D., Layman, A., Tobin, R., Thompson, H.S.: Namespaces in XML 1.0. Recommendation, W3C (2009). http://www.w3.org/TR/xml-names/
5. Dinc, E., Kuscu, M., Bilgin, B.A., Akan, O.B.: Internet of everything: a unifying framework beyond internet of things. In: Harnessing the Internet of Everything (IoE) for Accelerated Innovation Opportunities, pp. 1–30. IGI Global (2019)
6. Duerst, M., Suignard, M.: Internationalized Resource Identifiers. RFC 7228, Internet Engineering Task Force (2005). https://rfc-editor.org/rfc/rfc3987.txt
7. Glimm, B., Horrocks, I., Motik, B., Stoilos, G., Wang, Z.: HermiT: an OWL 2 reasoner. J. Autom. Reason. **53**(3), 245–269 (2014)
8. Hahm, O., Baccelli, E., Petersen, H., Tsiftes, N.: Operating systems for low-end devices in the internet of things: a survey. IEEE Internet Things J. **3**(5), 720–734 (2015)
9. Horridge, M., Bechhofer, S.: The OWL API: A Java API for OWL ontologies. Semant. Web **2**(1), 11–21 (2011)
10. International Organization for Standardization: C11 Standard, ISO/IEC 9899:2011. Draft, ISO (2011)
11. Knublauch, Holger, Fergerson, Ray W.., Noy, Natalya F.., Musen, Mark A..: The Protégé OWL plugin: an open development environment for semantic web applications. In: McIlraith, Sheila A.., Plexousakis, Dimitris, van Harmelen, Frank (eds.) ISWC 2004. LNCS, vol. 3298, pp. 229–243. Springer, Heidelberg (2004). https://doi.org/10.1007/978-3-540-30475-3_17
12. Lamy, J.B.: Owlready: ontology-oriented programming in python with automatic classification and high level constructs for biomedical ontologies. Artif. Intell. Med. **80**, 11–28 (2017)
13. Levin, M.K., Cowell, L.G.: owlcpp: a C++ library for working with OWL ontologies. J. Biomed. Semant. **6**(1), 35 (2015)
14. Matentzoglu, N., Leo, J., Hudhra, V., Sattler, U., Parsia, B.: A survey of current, stand-alone OWL reasoners. In: 4th OWL Reasoner Evaluation Workshop (ORE). CEUR Workshop Proceedings, vol. 1387, pp. 68–79. CEUR-WS (2015)
15. Parsia, B., Motik, B., Patel-Schneider, P.: OWL 2 Web Ontology Language Structural Specification and Functional-Style Syntax (Second Edition). W3C recommendation, W3C (2012). http://www.w3.org/TR/owl2-syntax/
16. Parsia, B., Rudolph, S., Krötzsch, M., Patel-Schneider, P., Hitzler, P.: OWL 2 Web Ontology Language Primer (Second Edition). W3C Recommendation, W3C (2012). http://www.w3.org/TR/owl2-primer
17. Ruta, M., et al.: A multiplatform reasoning engine for the semantic web of everything. J. Web Semant. **73**, 100709 (2022)
18. Ruta, Michele, Scioscia, Floriano, Di Sciascio, Eugenio, Bilenchi, Ivano: OWL API for iOS: early implementation and results. In: Dragoni, Mauro, Poveda-Villalón, María, Jimenez-Ruiz, Ernesto (eds.) OWLED/ORE -2016. LNCS, vol. 10161, pp. 141–152. Springer, Cham (2017). https://doi.org/10.1007/978-3-319-54627-8_11
19. Ruta, Michele, Scioscia, Floriano, Gramegna, Filippo, Bilenchi, Ivano, Di Sciascio, Eugenio: Mini-ME swift: the first mobile OWL reasoner for iOS. In: Hitzler, P., et al. (eds.) ESWC 2019. LNCS, vol. 11503, pp. 298–313. Springer, Cham (2019). https://doi.org/10.1007/978-3-030-21348-0_20
20. Schreiber, G., Gandon, F.: RDF 1.1 XML syntax. Recommendation, W3C (2014). http://www.w3.org/TR/rdf-syntax-grammar/

21. Scioscia, F., Bilenchi, I., Ruta, M., Gramegna, F., Loconte, D.: A multiplatform energy-aware OWL reasoner benchmarking framework. J. Web Semant. **72**, 100694 (2022)
22. Scioscia, F., Ruta, M.: Building a semantic web of things: issues and perspectives in information compression. In: Proceedings of the 3rd IEEE International Conference on Semantic Computing, pp. 589–594. IEEE Computer Society (2009)
23. Sirin, E., Parsia, B., Grau, B.C., Kalyanpur, A., Katz, Y.: Pellet: a practical OWL-DL reasoner. Web Semant.: Sci. Serv. Agents World Wide Web **5**(2), 51–53 (2007)
24. The W3C SPARQL Working Group: SPARQL 1.1 Overview. Recommendation, W3C (2013). https://www.w3.org/TR/sparql11-overview/
25. Tsarkov, Dmitry, Horrocks, Ian: FaCT++ description logic reasoner: system description. In: Furbach, Ulrich, Shankar, Natarajan (eds.) IJCAR 2006. LNCS (LNAI), vol. 4130, pp. 292–297. Springer, Heidelberg (2006). https://doi.org/10.1007/11814771_26

Features and Capabilities
of a Blockchain-Based Ridesharing
Enhanced with Semantics

Filippo Gramegna[1], Arnaldo Tomasino[1], Giuseppe Loseto[2],
Floriano Scioscia[1](✉), and Michele Ruta[1]

[1] Polytechnic University of Bari, 70125 Bari, Italy
{filippo.gramegna,arnaldo.tomasino,floriano.scioscia,
michele.ruta}@poliba.it
[2] LUM University "Giuseppe Degennaro", 70010 Casamassima, BA, Italy
loseto@lum.it

Abstract. The integration of blockchain platforms with Artificial Intelligence (AI) technologies is increasingly frequent in research and industry. Semantic Web technologies provide peculiar opportunities, since they have been devised for information interoperability at Web scale and enable intelligent software agents for knowledge-driven task automation and decision support. The paper presents a blockchain platform extending Hyperledger Sawtooth with Knowledge Representation and Reasoning features. Semantic Smart Contracts allow annotated resource registration, discovery –leveraging non-standard inference services for semantic matchmaking–, explanation –exploiting logic-based justification provided by the adopted inferences– and selection. A prototypical semantic-enhanced ridesharing service has been built to validate the proposed framework and a time-series data collection infrastructure has been deployed for performance analysis.

Keywords: Semantic matchmaking · Distributed ledger technologies · Time-series data analysis · Intelligent transportation systems

1 Introduction

In conventional distributed databases, a trusted intermediary is needed to ensure transaction integrity. This can be a strong limitation for several classes of applications, including Intelligent Transportation Systems (ITSs) and marketplaces open to the general public. To overcome this issue, *blockchain* has emerged as a family of data structures and protocols for peer-to-peer *trustless* distributed transactional systems. Blockchain platforms approve transactions by means of peer-to-peer *consensus* protocols. Transactions are usually grouped in *blocks*, which are appended sequentially. Alternative emerging proposals are based on Directed Acyclic Graphs (DAGs), and an overall lively landscape of research on *Distributed Ledger Technologies* (DLTs) is envisioning various kinds of architectural and algorithmic variations.

G. Agapito et al. (Eds.): ICWE 2022 Workshops, CCIS 1668, pp. 113–124, 2023.
https://doi.org/10.1007/978-3-031-25380-5_9

Many DLTs can host *Smart Contracts* (SCs), *i.e.*, programs encoding and enforcing terms of an agreement among two or more parties as executable procedures. This fosters the integration of DLTs with Artificial Intelligence (AI) technologies. In particular, Semantic Web technologies –grounded on formal Knowledge Representation and Reasoning– appear as strong candidates for enhancing DLTs, since they have been devised to grant information interoperability at Web scale and to enable intelligent software agents for data-driven task automation or user decision support, a role which can be played by SCs in DLTs.

This paper proposes a semantic-enhanced blockchain platform for Service-Oriented Architectures (SOAs) and resource marketplaces. The proposal extends the *Hyperledger Sawtooth* project[1] [1] with semantic SCs for managing the registration, discovery, explanation and selection steps of service/resource lifecycle. Discovery exploits semantic matchmaking by means of non-standard inference services, capable of ranking a set of available resources by semantic affinity w.r.t. a request, where the request and the resources are annotated referring to a common domain ontology. The adopted inferences also grant logic-based explanation of outcomes, thus having the users trust not only the blockchain platform for transaction security, but also AI facilities by virtue of interpretable results.

In order to validate the correctness and usefulness of the proposal, a prototypical semantic-enhanced *ridesharing* (a.k.a. *carpooling*) service has been built. It allows detailed specification of vehicle and driver characteristics as well as passenger preferences, finding the best matches. For performance analysis of the proposed prototype, a time-series data analysis architecture has been deployed.

The remainder of the paper is as follows. Section 2 recalls the main aspects of Hyperledger Sawtooth. then Section 3 describes in detail the proposed framework. The ridesharing service is presented in Sect. 4, while Sect. 5 outlines the time-series data analysis infrastructure. A discussion of related work is in Sect. 6, before conclusion.

2   Background: Hyperledger Sawtooth

The proposed framework leverages the Hyperledger Sawtooth blockchain, an open source distributed ledger originally aimed for enterprise applications [1]. Sawtooth architecture provides a high decoupling among components, particularly suitable for IoT scenarios to enable transaction processing and data validation on heterogeneous devices. Moreover, the clear separation between application and functional system layers allows developers to write Smart Contracts (SCs) logic in multiple high-level programming languages. In Sawtooth, a client initially signs transactions and groups them into a *batch*, which is the atomic unit of change. If one of the transactions fails, the entire batch is aborted. Signed batches are then sent to a peer node, called *validator*, which is responsible for: (i) processing transactions in parallel in order to improve performance, and (ii) publishing blocks of batches according to a consensus protocol [2]. Available

---

[1] Hyperledger Sawtooth: https://www.hyperledger.org/use/sawtooth.

consensus protocols are the Proof of Elapsed Time (PoET) –an extended version of the Practical Byzantine Fault Tolerance (PBFT) algorithm–, Raft and Devmod, a simplified random-leader algorithm useful only for development and testing purposes [3]. Furthermore, the blockchain global state is stored and synchronized in a single instance of a *Merkle-Radix tree* on each validator, where each leaf address refers to serialized data related to a specific state change in a transaction.

3   Knowledge Representation for Blockchain

This section outlines the proposed DLT architecture and semantic-enhanced Smart Contracts exploiting a Description Logics-based matchmaking framework [10] to implement semantic tasks.

3.1   Knowledge-Based Distributed Ledgers

Figure 1 depicts the functional blocks of the Hyperledger Sawtooth architecture[2] enhanced with semantic capabilities. The main components are:

- a set of **Transaction Processors** (TPs) executing transactions according to the rules associated with a *Transaction Family* (TF). A TF defines a transaction payload format, a model for storing information in the global state and a procedure for validating transactions and updating the state based on the payload;
- **Validator Nodes** which manage the global state and contain other subcomponents to be able to: (i) interact with TPs, (ii) coordinate the communication with their peers to apply the consensus procedure, (iii) verify incoming blocks and create new ones;
- **Clients** which query Validator Nodes to know the state of the blockchain and submit batches. A REST API (REpresentational State Transfer Application Programming Interface) acts as a gateway between Clients and Validator Nodes, communicating through the *ZeroMQ* protocol[3]. Alternatively, Clients can directly talk to a Validator Node exchanging ZeroMQ messages.

The proposed framework extends the functionalities of basic TPs, providing a set of SCs that are able to manage assets annotated w.r.t. a domain ontology and perform semantic tasks. According to the modeled scenario, assets can represent physical or digital resources, as well as service instances. To orchestrate semantically annotated assets, a specific TF has been defined with the implementation of the corresponding Smart Contract Processor. It interfaces with the *Tiny-ME* reasoning engine [10] to carry out the *Registration, Discovery, Explanation* and *Selection* semantic-enabled SCs described below. Using a blockchain substratum guarantees that outcomes are validated by consensus and data is always distributed consistently and synchronized among all participants in the network.

---

[2] Sawtooth documentation: https://sawtooth.hyperledger.org/docs/1.2/.

[3] ZeroMQ: https://zeromq.org/.

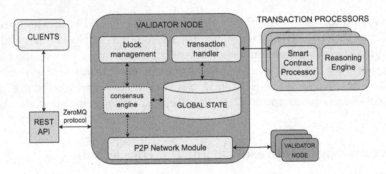

Fig. 1. Semantic-enhanced blockchain architecture

3.2 Semantic-Enabled Smart Contracts

Semantic-enabled SCs are able not only to retrieve a set of resources compliant with a given request, but also to rank them according to a relevance score. In fact, in advanced scenarios full matches are rare and incompatibility often occurs when matching articulate descriptions. In order to achieve a granular ranking of potential and partial matches, non-standard inference services that enhance classic *Satisfiability* and *Subsumption* checks are exploited. Given a request R and a resource S annotated w.r.t. a common ontology $\mathcal{T}$:

- if the *Satisfiability* check concludes R and S are not compatible (*i.e.*, their conjunction is unsatisfiable), **Concept Contraction** returns: (i) what part G (*Give up*) of R clashes with S, (ii) a contracted version K (*Keep*) of the original request such that it is compatible with S;
- if the *Subsumption* check determines that S does not fully satisfy R (*i.e.*, S is not more specific than R), **Concept Abduction** identifies a concept H (*Hypothesis*) representing what is missing in S in order to reach a full match, in the Open World Assumption.

Furthermore, penalty functions based on the Conjunctive Normal Form for DL concept expressions can be associated to both G and H, in order to compute a semantic distance of each available resource w.r.t. a given request. The introduced semantic-enabled SCs are as in what follows:

- **Registration.** As depicted in Fig. 2, to store a specific resource into the blockchain, a Client sends a registration transaction to a Validator Node specifying: (i) the resource Uniform Resource Identifier (URI); (ii) its semantic description as a concept expression w.r.t. a reference ontology; (iii) the ontology URI; (iv) other context-related information (*e.g.*, resource price). The ontology URI is essential to uniquely identify the target resource space, because multiple domains can coexist and associated ontologies can be stored in the same blockchain. Then the Validator invokes the `Registration` SC, which carries out a consistency check to verify the involved resource is satisfiable w.r.t. the referred ontology. If it fails, the transaction is aborted, otherwise a confirmation is sent back to the Client.

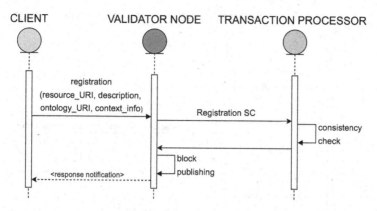

Fig. 2. Registration SC sequence diagram

- **Resource Discovery.** In order to search for (a set of) items, as depicted in Fig. 3, the requester sends a discovery transaction to a Validator, detailing: (i) the URI of the reference ontology; (ii) the semantic description of the request, specifying desired features and constraints; (iii) other contextual information (*e.g.*, minimum semantic relevance threshold, maximum number of results to be returned or the price the requester is willing to pay). The Discovery SC is triggered by the Validator Node and a semantic matchmaking task [10], based on the Concept Abduction and Concept Contraction inference services, is carried out comparing the request annotation with the descriptions of all the available resources. A list of ranked resource URIs is returned to the Client.

- **Explanation.** This optional step allows a requester to get a justification of the discovery outcome and is useful to trigger a request refinement process. Referring to the sequence diagram in Fig. 3, the submitted explanation transaction specifies the semantic description of the request and the URI of the discovered resource. The Explanation SC invoked by the Validator Node replies with the related matchmaking outcome explanation, structured as: (i) semantic affinity score in the [0,1] interval, computed by means of the semantic penalty and other domain-dependent contextual parameters, (*i.e.* physical distance, price); (ii) a description of the related reasoning outcome, in terms of G, K or H concept expressions.

- **Selection.** After receiving a set of results, the requester can choose the desired resource(s). The Client submits a selection transaction specifying the resource URI and optional contextual data. The Selection SC is thus invoked: it is responsible to update the selected resource description with additional compatible features resulting from the request as well as to reply with a properly usable resource representation, *e.g.*, an interface endpoint or a further SC to be invoked.

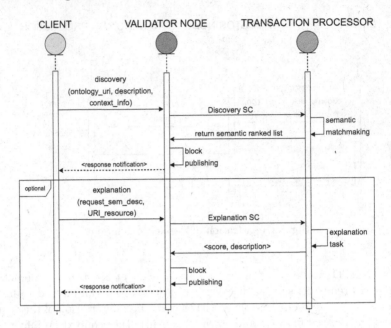

Fig. 3. Resource discovery and explanation SCs sequence diagram

Regardless of the matchmaking result, each completed transaction is published on the blockchain, exploiting the consensus algorithm for robustness, traceability and accountability purposes.

4　RideMATCHain: An Advanced Ridesharing Service

A practical example is described from a prototypical carpooling service named *RideMATCHain*[4], in order to better explain and underline the benefits of the proposed framework. Let us suppose a heterogeneous group of people is sending requests from different places and at various times to a ridesharing service in order to reach their destinations. For example, let us consider two drivers currently available for ridesharing through the service with their cars. The problem consists in matching every passenger with the car better fulfilling their requirements, considering user preferences and compatibility issues. All passengers and vehicles are described according to a prototypical ontology, whose taxonomy of concepts is depicted in Fig. 4. Whenever possible, classes have been reused from *SUMO-OWL* (the OWL translation of the Suggested Upper Merged Ontology) [7], *e.g.*, `Automobile`, `AgeGroup`. Each available ride is a resource, represented as an asset stored into the blockchain with a semantic annotation split into two parts: the first one is constant over time and summarizes the set of vehicle features relevant to the service and the driver's profile; the second part

---

[4] GitHub repository: https://github.com/sisinflab-swot/ridematchain.

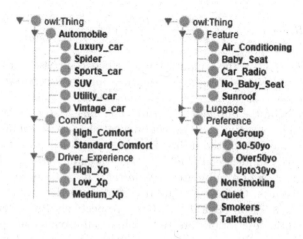

Fig. 4. Reference ontology top-level classes

specifies information about available space for passengers and their luggage. An excerpt of the annotations linked to each car is shown below in Manchester syntax [4]:

SUV1: SUV and (accepts only NonSmoking) and (has_Feature only (Car_Radio and Air_Conditioning and Baby_Seat)) and (comfort_Level only High_Comfort) and (driver_Experience only High_Xp) and (available_Seats exactly 6) and (available_Capacity exactly 650)

Small_CityCar1: Utility_Car and (has_Feature only (Sunroof and No_Baby_Seat)) and (comfort_Level only Standard_Comfort) and (driver_Experience only High_Xp) and (available_Seats exactly 1) and (available_Capacity exactly 200)

Resource descriptions have been registered, distributed and synchronized as assets among all participants in the blockchain, by means of the Registration SC described in Sect. 3.2. For the sake of simplicity, to show how the ridesharing service works, let us consider a single step iteration. *A user, headed downtown with her baby, is looking for a car with two seats, one of which equipped with baby seat. She would like to travel comfortably in an air-conditioned, quiet and non-smoking environment.* In formulas:

R ≡ (accepts only (NonSmoking and Quiet)) and (has_Feature only (Baby_Seat and Air_Conditioning)) and (comfort_Level only High_Comfort) and (driver_Experience only High_Xp) and (available_Seats min 2)

In order to take into account passenger-car and passenger-passenger constraints, the framework invokes the Discovery SC, which in turn triggers the semantic matchmaking task detailed in [10]. After a pre-filtering step, exploited to discard cars with a heading diverging from that of the passenger, the matchmaking finds which vehicles of the fleet best meet the specified requirements. The returned list of resources is ranked according to the following *utility function*:

$$u(R, C) = 100[1 - \frac{s\_penalty(R, C)}{s\_penalty(R, \top)}(1 + \frac{distance(R, C)}{max\_distance})]$$

where $s\_penalty(R, C)$ is the semantic distance between passenger profile R and car annotation C; this value is normalized dividing by $s\_penalty(R, \top)$, which is the distance between R and the *universal concept* $\top$ (a.k.a. *Top* or *Thing*) and depends only on the ontology structure. The *max_distance* contextual data is used to take into account the car geographical distance, combined as weighting factor. The purpose of the utility function is also to convert the semantic distance score to a more user-friendly [0, 100] ascending scale. It is important to notice that in case of a full match $s\_penalty(R, C) = 0$ hence $u(R, C) = 100$ regardless of distance. Outcomes, ranked according to the utility function, are 90.2 and 76.2 for SUV1 and Small_CityCar1, respectively As evident, SUV and passenger semantic descriptions are very similar: all atomic concepts, universal quantifiers and unqualified number restrictions on roles are compatible. Conversely, passenger requirements are not compatible with the small city car: the user can get an explanation for this from the Explanation SC by means of the *Concept Contraction* reasoning task:

G: (has_Feature only (Baby_Seat)) and (available_Seats min 2)

The best match for the passenger is with SUV1, so she is assigned to it. When the passenger/car association is confirmed, the passenger's preferences (modelled in the filler of the accepts object property) are appended in conjunction with the SUV annotation. This task is performed by the Selection SC that enables the interaction with the selected resource and updates its semantic description (modifications are underlined):

SUV1: SUV and (accepts only (NonSmoking and Quiet)) and (has_Feature only (Car_Radio and Air_Conditioning and Baby_Seat)) and (comfort_Level only High_Comfort) and (driver_Experience only High_Xp) and (available_Seats exactly 4) and (available_Capacity exactly 350)

The selection transaction allows renewing the blockchain internal status and repeating the allocation task for the remaining passengers, verifying any incompatibility constraints.

5 Time Series-Based Performance Analysis

Time-series data analysis tools have been integrated in the overall system architecture to measure hardware and operational performances of the implemented framework. This approach is useful to monitor and detect potential faults within a complex distributed system such as a blockchain.

5.1 Components and Deployment

In order to collect time-series metrics, the following new components have been deployed in the architecture described in Sect. 3.1:

- **InfluxDB**[5], an open-source time-series database that acts as a collector for timestamped data. It stores time series data in a set of *measurements*, comparable to tables of a relational database. A measurement's record, a.k.a. *point*, refers to a specific observation and has a timestamp in addition to values organized in columns. InfluxDB has been chosen due to its high compatibility with both the *Telegraf* metrics collection tool and the *Grafana* dashboarding system.
- **Telegraf**[6], a server agent able to collect a set of predefined metrics from different data sources (databases, systems or IoT sensors) and forward them to multiple types of Data Base Management Systems. A configuration file contains details regarding *InfluxDB* connection, database and operations. The main advantage is that it has a small memory footprint and does not affect performances of the system where it is executed.
- **Grafana**[7], a Web-based open-source visualization tool useful to get a comprehensive view of all the collected parameters through a set of charts. Graphs show data according to predefined queries on a specific data source and can be organized in different dashboards.

Figure 5 clarifies the components interconnection: InfluxDB and Grafana are deployed as separate *Docker*[8] containers, while Telegraf runs as a background process within a Validator Node container, which also provides the required configuration file. All application services have been defined and orchestrated through *Docker Compose*[9].

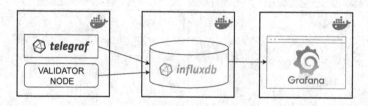

Fig. 5. Deployment of metrics collection components

5.2 Computed Metrics and Data Visualization

The data collection process involves three different groups of parameters:

- measures related to the hardware where the Telegraf process is running. Referring to the diagram depicted in Fig. 5, they include the performance of the container where the Validator Node process runs: CPU load, available memory, hard disk activities (*i.e.*, percentage of waiting time for I/O tasks, disk

---

[5] InfluxDB: https://www.influxdata.com/.

[6] Telegraf: https://www.influxdata.com/time-series-platform/telegraf/.

[7] Grafana: https://grafana.com/.

[8] Docker: https://www.docker.com/.

[9] Docker Compose: https://docs.docker.com/compose/.

read/write speed); operating system information (*i.e.*, the number of context switches that the system underwent);

- metrics directly retrieved by the Validator Node process, such as: number of blocks; pending, committed and published transactions in a time interval; data rates of exchanged messages and response times. While starting a Validator Node process, a set of parameters can be specified in order to collect and send proper data to the InfluxDB instance.
- performance related to the semantic tasks described in Sect. 3.2. They are directly collected by the implemented semantic-enabled SCs and measure the average time taken to complete a single semantic task of registration, discovery, explanation and selection.

As shown in Fig. 6, metrics can be organized in different *Grafana* visualizations dashboards and are useful for trend analysis regarding the operations of the blockchain with respect to the user needs and behaviors.

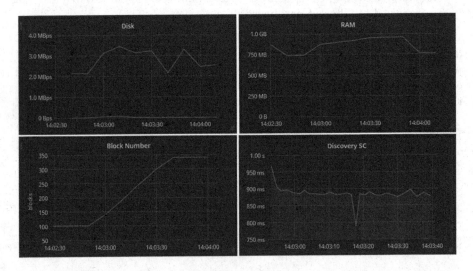

Fig. 6. Visualizations for system and blockchain related metrics

6   Related Work

In order to comply with requirements and needs in ITS, blockchains are leveraged to enable novel transparent and trustless interaction models [9]. Previous modeling approaches have been extended to combine IoT with blockchain technologies for different ITS scenarios [5,14]. The main goal is to explore and improve data exchange, interoperability and cooperation among the various actors. SCs prove particularly useful in this perspective, as they help managing the mapping of new resources and a reliable storage of their (often complex) data [12,13].

The approach in [11] has exploited Semantic Web technologies to provide blockchain assets with a semantic-based structured representation to leverage SCs for improving information interoperability among heterogeneous hosts. The advantages of trustworthiness and traceability offered by a blockchain infrastructure have also been enhanced with semantic-based services to discover and negotiate available resources. In Liu *et al.* [6], decentralized energy and charging service marketplaces for electric vehicles and Smart Grid integration are presented as the most suitable scenarios for such services. Despite the benefits blockchain could offer in the automotive domain, many issues are still open.

Standardization of information models is required for interoperability and data sharing, but it can be hindered by the historically competitive and secretive nature of the automotive sector. Initiatives have been recently launched to take steps ahead against this limitation. A hierarchically organized information model about vehicles data, as well as an architecture for a cloud-based Big Data marketplace, has been proposed in the *AutoMat* [8] Horizon 2020 project, albeit still not relying on a blockchain substratum. Conversely, the BMW Group *VerifyCar* project, based on the *VeChainThor*[10] blockchain, has introduced an experimental platform where up-to-date information about mileage, accident history, inspections, maintenance procedures and other useful information related to the lifecycle of a vehicle are stored and can be properly accessed by authorized parties at any time and cannot be tampered with.

7   Conclusion

The paper has introduced a semantic-enhanced DLT platform, based on the Hyperledger Sawtooth blockchain. Semantic Smart Contracts have been integrated to manage the fundamental steps of the lifecycle of semantically annotated resource descriptions: registration, discovery and selection. The adoption of non-standard inference services for semantic matchmaking non only provides a fine-grained ranking of resources w.r.t. a request, but also enables an explanation SC to make discovery outcomes fully interpretable. A prototypical ridesharing service has been built on top of the proposed platform in order to validate the correctness and usefulness of the proposal, while a performance analysis architecture has been defined and deployed.

Future work includes three main directions: exploit the devised time-series data collection infrastructure to carry out thorough experimental performance analysis, even involving resource-constrained IoT nodes, in order to validate the computational feasibility and scalability of the proposal; extend the blockchain architecture with further semantic SCs to provide more advanced resource management capabilities, including resource composition, substitution, and negotiation; expand the ridesharing prototype toward a viable commercial proposition.

---

[10] VeChain Foundation: VeChain Whitepaper 2.0 - Creating valuable TXs (December 2019) https://www.exodus.com/assets/docs/vechain-whitepaper.pdf.

Acknowledgments. This work has been supported by Italian Ministry of Economic Development R&D project BARIUM5G (Blockchain and ARtificial Intelligence for Ubiquitous coMputing via 5G).

References

1. Aggarwal, S., Kumar, N.: Hyperledger. In: Advances in Computers, vol. 121, pp. 323–343. Elsevier (2021)
2. Ampel, B., Patton, M., Chen, H.: Performance modeling of hyperledger sawtooth blockchain. In: 2019 IEEE International Conference on Intelligence and Security Informatics (ISI), pp. 59–61 (2019)
3. Cachin, C., Vukolić, M.: Blockchain consensus protocols in the wild. In: 31 International Symposium on Distributed Computing, pp. 19–34 (2017)
4. Horridge, M., Patel-Schneider, P.: OWL 2 Web Ontology Language Manchester Syntax (Second Edition). Note, W3C (2012). http://www.w3.org/TR/owl2-manchester-syntax/
5. Humayun, M., Jhanjhi, N., Hamid, B., Ahmed, G.: Emerging smart logistics and transportation using IoT and blockchain. IEEE Internet Things Mag. 3(2), 58–62 (2020)
6. Liu, H., Zhang, Y., Yang, T.: Blockchain-enabled security in electric vehicles cloud and edge computing. IEEE Netw. 32(3), 78–83 (2018)
7. Mascardi, V., Locoro, A., Rosso, P.: Automatic ontology matching via upper ontologies: a systematic evaluation. IEEE Trans. Knowl. Data Eng. 22(5), 609–623 (2009)
8. Pillmann, J., Wietfeld, C., Zarcula, A., Raugust, T., Alonso, D.C.: Novel common vehicle information model (CVIM) for future automotive vehicle big data marketplaces. In: Intelligent Vehicles Symposium (IV), pp. 1910–1915. IEEE (2017)
9. Pureswaran, V., Brody, P.: Device democracy: Saving the future of the Internet of Things. Technical report, IBM Institute for Business Value (2014)
10. Ruta, M., et al.: A multiplatform reasoning engine for the semantic web of everything. J. Web Semant. 73, 100709 (2022)
11. Ruta, M., Scioscia, F., Ieva, S., Capurso, G., Di Sciascio, E.: Semantic blockchain to improve scalability in the Internet of Things. Open J. Internet Things (OJIOT) 3(1), 46–61 (2017)
12. Valtanen, K., Backman, J., Yrjölä, S.: Creating value through blockchain powered resource configurations: analysis of 5G network slice brokering case. In: 2018 IEEE Wireless Communications and Networking Conference Workshops, pp. 185–190. IEEE (2018)
13. Xu, W., et al.: Internet of vehicles in big data era. IEEE/CAA J. Automatica Sinica 5(1), 19–35 (2017)
14. Yuan, Y., Wang, F.Y.: Towards blockchain-based intelligent transportation systems. In: 2016 IEEE 19th International Conference on Intelligent Transportation Systems (ITSC), pp. 2663–2668. IEEE (2016)

Semantic-Based Decision Support for Network Management and Orchestration

Saverio Ieva, Davide Loconte, Agnese Pinto, Floriano Scioscia(✉),
and Michele Ruta

Politecnico di Bari, via Edoardo Orabona 4, (I-70125) Bari, Italy
{saverio.ieva,davide.loconte,agnese.pinto,floriano.scioscia,
michele.ruta}@poliba.it

Abstract. Software-Defined Networking exploits Network Function Virtualization to face the challenges of modern enterprise networks, integrating cloud and Internet of Things deployments. Conventional methodologies are often inadequate, whereas novel approaches based on Artificial Intelligence can achieve the required levels of flexibility and scalability. This paper presents a network orchestration and management framework based on Semantic Web languages and technologies. The proposal adopts a two-level ontology design: (i) a novel translator automatically generates a low-layer ontology from the YANG network information model; (ii) a high-level domain ontology is introduced to model the contextual scenario knowledge. In early tests, a prototypical implementation of the proposed framework has exploited SWRL rules to check network requirements against metrics and constraints, in order to detect violations and provide context-aware suggestions for corrective actions.

Keywords: Semantic web · Automated reasoning · Software-defined networks · YANG data modeling · SWRL

1 Introduction

The fast-paced growth of cloud computing –increasingly in hybrid cloud configurations– and of Internet of Things (IoT) deployments is revolutionizing the traditional management of enterprise networks, with emerging issues of configurability, dynamism and scalability. To overcome these constraints, network topology and communication capabilities have to be controlled in a fine-grained fashion to quickly schedule the allocation of resources needed to provide on-demand services. The Software-Defined Networking (SDN) paradigm, based on Network Function Virtualization (NFV), aims at tackling these challenges: core network components are implemented as software-based services, so they can be virtualized without requiring specialized hardware. In this way, it is possible to precisely control and scale the network components to meet user demands.

On top of low-level standard protocols for network modeling and configuration, Artificial Intelligence (AI) can improve upon conventional capabilities and

G. Agapito et al. (Eds.): ICWE 2022 Workshops, CCIS 1668, pp. 125–136, 2023.
https://doi.org/10.1007/978-3-031-25380-5_10

tools. In such perspective, this paper proposes a Decision Support System (DSS) for network management and orchestration based on a novel approach, integrating Semantic Web technologies and automated reasoning. The framework is based on a two-level ontology, with the generation of a low-level ontology from available network information models expressed in YANG (Yet Another Next Generation) [1] and the subsequent mapping of low-level descriptions –annotated from data collected from network nodes– to high-level entities. The final Knowledge Base (KB) is enriched with Semantic Web Rule Language (SWRL) [5] rules to execute specific actions, such as detecting requirement violations and suggesting corrective actions.

The remainder of the paper is structured as follows: Sect. 2 discusses related work, while Sect. 3 describes how the system builds the KB starting from the low-level information model. In Sect. 4 the overall framework is outlined, and early validation is provided by means of a case study in Sect. 5, before conclusion.

2 Related Work

In latest years, several approaches have been proposed for AI-driven network management and orchestration. Many research works have exploited Machine Learning techniques to address issues in network management [9]. In [17] the traditional Open Shortest Path First (OSPF) routing protocol is extended with Reinforcement Learning techniques for SDN. Analogously, in [19] an energy-efficient routing algorithm based on RL has been introduced to optimize the energy consumption of a Software-Defined Wireless Sensor Network.

A relevant set of works has leveraged automated reasoning for network orchestration. In [3] a semantic-based network policy verification system has been proposed, based on standard inference services and SWRL rules [5]. The domain ontology allows modeling NFV policies as a constraint or a set of constraints. However, only consistency checking has been used to validate network policies. In [12] a framework for semantic-aware SDN orchestration in IoT scenarios has been proposed for optimal allocation w.r.t. security policies. The orchestration engine is able to detect possible network conflicts, by integrating an optimization algorithm, which considers both security aspects and resource usage. A similar framework has been presented in [14] using SWRL to detect structural integrity of deployed Virtual Network Functions (VNFs). However, both systems are tightly coupled to the monitored network, i.e., the overall VNF information model is not completely mapped into the ontology representation, or only aggregated statistical data are considered.

Ontology-based approaches bridge the semantic gap between low-level network information models and high-level network representations, while also allowing knowledge sharing among domain experts. In [6], a NFV ontology has been proposed to model the basic aspects of VNF descriptions, but it has not been used to optimize the network configuration exploiting automated reasoning techniques. Moreover, in the aforementioned works the reference ontology has been usually designed by domain experts, in order to describe the network entities and their relationships in a complex and structured way. The approach proposed here focuses, instead, on the definition of an automated knowledge extraction process, which can be exploited to generate the ontology from a standard network information model.

3   Knowledge Representation for Software Defined Networks

The adopted methodology for automatic translation from network information model to domain ontology is described in what follows.

3.1   The YANG Knowledge Model

The YANG [1] data modelling language has been originally developed to define the configurations and the schema manipulated by the Network Configuration Protocol (NETCONF) [4]. According to the YANG specification, schema definition is composed by *modules* and *submodules*. **Modules** are self-contained documents which expose some data definitions to external modules. **Submodules** contain reusable data definitions, accessible from external modules, but they cannot describe standalone objects. Each module is composed of a list of statements, which define domain entities (`container`, `list`), attributes (`leaf`, `leaf-list`), reusable schemas or data nodes definitions (`grouping`, `typedef`) to be imported across multiple documents.

YANG is more expressive and flexible than other schema-definition languages, such as XML Schema Definition, as it supports the definition of reusable modules, complex communication patterns and extensions of existing modules (through the `augment` keyword). Furthermore, YANG is widely adopted in the network control industry domain to define communication schemas between endpoints. In particular, the YANG model is adopted in several network standards, such as the European Telecommunications Standards Institute (ETSI) Network Functions Virtualisation Solutions (NFV-SOL) protocol [7] and the Open Network Foundation Transport API (TAPI) [11], as well as in technical documents issued by Cisco Systems, the Internet Engineering Task Force (IETF) and Internet Assigned Numbers Authority (IANA).

3.2   Layer Interaction: Automatic Model Generation and Update

The Web Ontology Language (OWL) [15] enables modeling complex and structured knowledge representation. An OWL Knowledge Base is divided into a Terminological Box (TBox, a.k.a. ontology), which contains classes (a.k.a. concepts) and properties (a.k.a. roles) in the knowledge domain, and an Assertion Box (ABox), which includes specific assertions (or facts) concerning individuals (a.k.a. instances) of a particular problem within the domain.

The proposed approach is based on converting the YANG information model into a corresponding OWL ontology representation. The translation is performed by *yang2OWL*, a specifically devised tool, whose architecture is depicted in Fig. 1. It comprises two main components: the **YANG Parser** reads input YANG modules, then it builds an intermediate Abstract Syntax Tree (AST) representing the syntactic structure of the input files; the **OWL Ontology Factory** consumes the intermediate data structures to generate the OWL ontology.

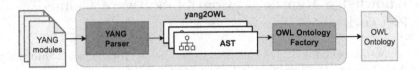

Fig. 1. yang2OWL architecture

Each AST node represents a YANG statement and contains the corresponding *keyword*, *argument* and optional metadata. The OWL Ontology Factory translates each node representing a schema entity to an OWL class, while the leaf attributes are converted to data properties. For instance, the following YANG schema tree [2] is converted to the classes and properties shown in Fig. 2.

```
module: tapi-common
  +--rw context!
    +--rw uuid?  uuid
    +--ro tapi-topology:topology* [uuid]
    |  +--ro tapi-topology:node* [uuid]
    |  |  |  +--ro tapi-topology:uuid     uuid
    |  +--ro tapi-topology:link* [uuid]
    |  |  |  +--ro tapi-topology:uuid     uuid
    |  +--ro tapi-topology:uuid     uuid
    ...
```

(a) Classes   (b) Data properties   (c) Object properties

Fig. 2. OWL ontology generated from YANG

The example defines a `context` container having a list of `topology` objects, each of which contains two lists of `node` and `link` objects respectively. All entities contain a `uuid` primitive attribute. Each YANG object (`context`, `topology`, `node` and `link`) is translated to the corresponding OWL class shown in Fig. 2a. The leaf properties are associated to the data properties in Fig. 2b. If a YANG element contains children objects, the OWL Ontology Factory creates corresponding object properties to link the parent container with each child class. In the previous example, since `topology` contains a list of `nodes`, the `topologyHasNode` property is added (Fig. 2c).

The proposed *yang2OWL* tool allows generating ontologies starting from different information models. For example, in the first implementation described in Sect. 4, the tool is used to generate the ontology corresponding to the ONF TAPI YANG models. The tool automatically generates the OWL ontology from the YANG schema definitions, enabling the ABox generation by annotating individuals generated from the domain configuration instances which are valid w.r.t. the initial YANG modules. They are usually encoded in a lightweight data interchange format like JavaScript Object Notation (JSON) [10]. For instance, a `SemanticAnnotator` has been implemented in the software prototype described in Sect. 4.2, which is able to enrich the KB with the individuals obtained from the JSON documents retrieved from the SDN controller interface. The following example of an object serialized in JSON format complies with the schema of the previous YANG example:

```
{
    "uuid": "Context_1",
    "topology": [{
        "uuid": "00000001-0000",
        "node": [
            {"uuid": "00000004-0001"},
            {"uuid": "00000004-0002"}
        ],
        "link": [{"uuid": "00000008-0000"}]
    }]
}
```

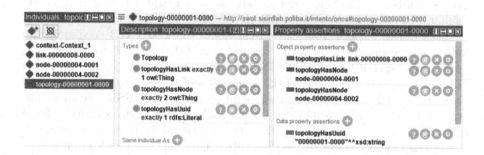

Fig. 3. Individuals generated from JSON document

The JSON document describes a network context, having a single topology composed of two nodes and a link. Each entry represents either an atomic attribute (*e.g.*, "uuid": "00000001-0000"), a JSON object or a list of those (*e.g.*, "link": [...]). Each object is translated as an OWL individual, with its key identifying the reference OWL class, and primitive properties are represented with data property assertions on the parent individual. The root JSON Object is assumed to be of the same type as the root object specified in the YANG module (`Context`). Following these guidelines, the translation of the previous JSON object results in five individuals: one of type `Context`, two `Nodes`, one `Link` and one `Topology`, as depicted in Fig. 3. The leaf `uuid` values are adapted as data properties, and object properties reflect the JSON structure, hence the `Topology` individual is related to the two `Node` individuals and the `Link` through the `topologyHasNode` and `topologyHasLink` properties, respectively.

4   Resource Orchestration: A Semantic-Based Approach

The proposed semantic-based DSS for network management and orchestration uses the classes and the roles extracted from the YANG information model, as described in Sect. 3. In what follows, the ontology introduced to model the contextual features of the network is discussed, as well as the overall framework architecture and capabilities.

4.1   Network Management: A Rule-Based Reasoning Approach

The proposed DSS is able to automatically detect network Quality of Service (QoS) violations and to suggest the appropriate corrective actions. As described in Sect. 3, the tool *yang2OWL* can obtain a detailed network description from the YANG information model and the contextual data provided by the SDN controller, which exposes a northbound TAPI RESTful connector. The generated ontology, however, lacks several logic relationships between the domain classes, since they cannot be modelled through YANG constructs, *e.g.*, both link `AvailableCapacity` and `CostCharacteristic` in TAPI definition can be modelled as subclasses of a generic Key Performance Indicator (KPI) superclass which is useful in this scenario, but this is not explicitly stated in YANG modules. To overcome this limitation, the proposed approach follows a two-level ontology design pattern [16]: relevant entities of the **TAPI KB** –containing all individuals generated through the `SemanticAnnotator` w.r.t. the ontology produced by *yang2OWL* (named **TAPI Ontology**)– are mapped to higher-level **DSS KB** entities, which embed the description of the contextual relationships between network components and are expressed w.r.t. a **DSS Ontology**. The latter is structured as shown in Fig. 4. `NetworkEntity` and Network Service Level (NSL) respectively represent a generic network entity and a network quantitative characteristic (*e.g.*, bandwidth, latency, jitter, hops count, energy consumption). Each network entity can be further classified as a `Topology`, a `Node`, a `Link` or connectivity service (`Service`). Nodes having connectivity service endpoints are classified as `Hosts`, otherwise they are treated as `Switches`. NSL has three key properties: `hasTarget`, indicating the network entity associated with the measurement or constraint; `hasValue`, containing the reference value; `hasType`, indicating the KPI measure. This class specializes into actual measurements (`NSLV` - Network Service Level Value class) and requirements inferred from the TAPI Ontology or enforced by the user (`NSLA` - Network Service Level Agreement class). Requirements are further classified either as `MaximumNSL` or `MinimumNSL` if they represent an upper or lower bound on the KPI, respectively. As an example, to represent the energy consumption of a `Node` individual, the system adds a `NSLV` individual to the KB, having `hasType` property set to "Energy", the `hasTarget` object property in relationship with the `Node` individual and the `hasValue` property set to the numeric value of energy consumption; `NSLA` individuals are defined in a similar way. If the DSS detects a violation between a `NSLA` and `NSLV`, the latter is reclassified as a `Violation`.

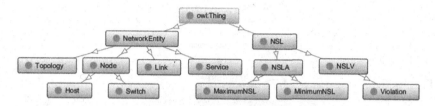

Fig. 4. Semantic network management system - DSS Ontology

Following this approach, individuals in the DSS KB can be collected at runtime by mapping each relevant entity in the TAPI KB representing a node, link, topology, connectivity service, network service level requirement, or resource consumption to a new individual described w.r.t. the new DSS Ontology.

Since OWL cannot easily represent "if-then-else" clauses, which are convenient in network orchestration scenarios, SWRL [5] is adopted to extend OWL capabilities by means of Horn clauses. Basically, SWRL is exploited to execute three tasks:

1. Infer additional DSS individual facts from TAPI ABox assertions. An example is reported hereafter in a Protégé-like syntax [13], in which SWRL is used to retrieve the maximum link capacity for a `MaximumNSL` individual from the `TotalPotentialCapacity` individual in the TAPI ontology:

```
Link(?link), MaximumNSL(?nsl
mappedFrom(?link, ?t_link), hasType(?nsl, "Capacity")
linkHasTotalPotentialCapacity(?t_link, ?t_capacity),
availableCapacityHasTotalSize(?t_capacity, ?t_size),
totalSizeHasValue(?t_size, ?value) => hasValue(?nsl, ?value)
```

2. Detect `NSLA` violations, like in the following example, which states that a `NSLV` greater than a corresponding agreement upper threshold implies a violation:

```
MaximumNSL(?nsla), NSLV(?nslv), NetworkEntity(?ne)
hasTarget(?nsla, ?ne), hasTarget(?nslv, ?ne),
hasType(?nsla, ?type), hasType(?nslv, ?type),
hasValue(?nsla, ?req), hasValue(?nslv, ?value)
greaterThan(?value, ?req) => Violation(?nslv)
```

3. Execute actions on individuals when specific conditions are verified, as shown in the following rule stating that, when an energy constraint violation occurs for a particular network topology, topology rearrangement must be executed:

```
Violation(?v), Topology(?t), hasType(?v, "Energy")
hasTarget(?v, ?t) => execute(recompute_nodes, ?t)
```

4.2   Framework Architecture

Figure 5 shows the overall architecture of the proposed DSS. It integrates reasoning capabilities by means of *Owlready2* [8], a Python module which allows mixing object-oriented and ontology-based programming patterns, as it maps OWL classes, instances and properties to the corresponding built-in Python language constructs.

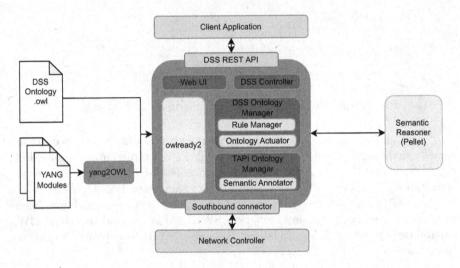

Fig. 5. Semantic network management architecture

An abstract `OntologyManager` class is defined to include several common methods. For example, the `update` method is used to generate the ABox individuals at runtime. In the proposed system, this abstract class is specialized as `TAPIOntologyManager`, to handle the ontology generated from YANG modules, and as `DSSOntologyManager`, to cope with the high level DSS ontology. Furthermore, the `OntologyManager` allows extending system functionalities by means of the plugin design pattern. The following plugins have been provided:

- **SemanticAnnotator**, previously introduced in Sect. 3, allows `TAPIOntologyManager` to translate the network descriptions in JSON format to OWL Individuals;
- **RuleManager** provides Create, Read, Update and Delete (CRUD) operations to edit SWRL rules at runtime;
- **OntologyActuator** automates the execution of tasks. The component exploits the `execute` object property, which can be specified as the tail of a SWRL rule, in the form of `execute(?f, ?t)` atom, where `?f` represents a Python function and `?t` is an individual, so that whenever the head of the rule is verified, OntologyActuator invokes the Python `?f` function passing `?t` as an argument.

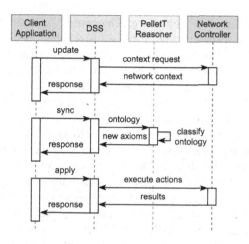

Fig. 6. Semantic network management system - Sequence diagram

When the system starts, it loads both the DSS ontology and the TAPI ontology, using Owlready2. The sequence diagram in Fig. 6 shows how the components interact when a specific operation is executed. The system can execute the following three basic operations:

- **Update**: invokes the `update` method for each `OntologyManager` to collect ABox individuals. In particular, the `TAPIOntologyManager` queries the SDN controller to retrieve the network context and exploits the `SemanticAnnotator` to generate the OWL individuals from the response, as described in Sect. 3.2. Subsequently, the `DSSOntologyManager` updates the high-level contextual individuals w.r.t. the newly collected TAPI individuals, as described in Sect. 4.1;
- **Sync**: it exploits the inference services of the *Pellet* [18] reasoner to classify the KB and apply the SWRL rules to execute the tasks described in 4.1;
- **Apply**: it exploits the functions exposed by the `OntologyActuator` to execute the suggested corrective actions.

The system is intended to be controlled by third-party client applications through the `DSS REST API`. A minimal Web User Interface (UI) –relying on the REST API– is also provided, which summarizes the DSS performance metrics and the semantic-based outcomes (like the active `NSLAs` and the suggested corrective actions) and interacts with the `DSSController` to define new `NSLAs` or `NSLVs`, or to execute one of the aforementioned `update`, `sync` and `apply` actions.

5 Early Validation

For a preliminary functional validation of the proposed framework, the system prototype has been assessed in a small testbed, consisting of a simple network with four nodes connected by four links, managed by a network controller exposing a northbound TAPI interface. The context specification contains NSL descriptions, such as capacity and hops. At first, the DSS Web UI shows only generic ontology data, since it has no knowledge about the network status. For this reason, update and sync have been executed to gather the factual knowledge on the underlying topology. Since the service allows third-party applications to specify NSLVs, both TAPI specific data (hops number and node capacity) and external measurements (*e.g.*, energy consumption) have been considered. After these operations, the Web UI correctly shows the new information.

Figure 7 reports two dashboard screenshots, showing different system states. Initially, Fig. 7a shows the NSLA and NSLV values, as well as the network topology with the connectivity services already enabled. Since no requirement violation has been detected, the system does not suggest any corrective action. Figure 7b shows the system status after the insertion of a new NSL constraint by the user, through the REST Connector API.

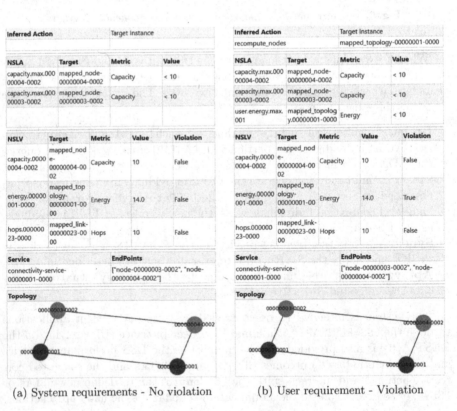

(a) System requirements - No violation   (b) User requirement - Violation

Fig. 7. DSS dashboard

This new requirement is identified with the name *user.energy.max.001* and has a value < 10 units. Measurement *energy.00000001-0000* violates the new constraint, since its value is 14. The system therefore suggests to execute path computation of the connectivity service. After applying the suggested corrective action, the system recomputes the path for each connectivity service, suggesting to turn off the nodes *00000003-0001* and *00000004-0001*, since they are not needed to keep the connectivity service alive.

6 Conclusion and Future Work

The paper has proposed a DSS for network management and orchestration, leveraging Semantic Web languages and technologies. The core idea of the proposed architecture is to automatically generate a low-level OWL ontology from the YANG information model describing the network configuration, by using the novel *yang2OWL* translator. However, this ontology may lack some information and relationships the YANG model cannot express. For this reason, a two-level ontology modeling is adopted, in order to enrich the contextual information with more complex semantic descriptions by using a higher-level ontology. SWRL rules have also been introduced for mapping facts between the two KBs as well as for triggering specific actions when a constraint violation is detected. The preliminary DSS prototype exploits an automated reasoning engine to evaluate the rules on the overall KB and generate suggestions for corrective actions if needed.

Future work will concern extending the ontology modeling and the proposed framework in order to implement more advanced functionalities. The investigated case study will be expanded accordingly. From a performance standpoint, attention will be devoted to ensure the adopted reasoning procedures comply with the strict latency requirements of solutions in the network management domain. Furthermore, the scalability of the proposed approach will be validated using network simulators. Several approaches will be investigated for managing large and complex networks, such as partitioning the topology in sections or using a hierarchical approach, aggregating groups of interconnected and close nodes into logical higher-level nodes; this could reduce the number of modeled individuals in the ABox and in turn the overall computational load.

Acknowledgments. This work has been supported by Italian PON project *NGS* (New Satellites Generation Components).

References

1. Bjorklund, M.: The YANG 1.1 data modeling language. RFC 7950, Internet Engineering Task Force (2016)
2. Bjorklund, M., Berger, L.: YANG Tree Diagrams. RFC 8340, Internet Engineering Task Force (2018)
3. Bonfim, M., Freitas, F., Fernandes, S.: A semantic-based policy analysis solution for the deployment of NFV services. IEEE Trans. Netw. Serv. Manage. **16**(3), 1005–1018 (2019)
4. Enns, R., Bjorklund, M., Schoenwaelder, J.: NETCONF configuration protocol. RFC 4741, Internet Engineering Task Force (2006)

5. Horrocks, I., Patel-Schneider, P.F., Boley, H., Tabet, S., Grosof, B., Dean, M.: SWRL: A Semantic Web Rule Language Combining OWL and RuleML. W3C Member Submission, W3C (2014), https://www.w3.org/Submission/SWRL/

6. Kim, S.I., Kim, H.S.: Semantic ontology-based NFV service modeling. In: 2018 Tenth International Conference on Ubiquitous and Future Networks (ICUFN), pp. 674–678. IEEE (2018)

7. Kojukhov, A., et al.: Network functions virtualisation (NFV) release 2; protocols and data models; VNF package specification. GS NFV-SOL 004 v2. 3.1. Group specification, ETSI (2017)

8. Lamy, J.B.: Owlready: ontology-oriented programming in python with automatic classification and high level constructs for biomedical ontologies. Artif. Intell. Med. 80, 11–28 (2017)

9. Latah, M., Toker, L.: Artificial intelligence enabled software-defined networking: a comprehensive overview. IET Netw. 8(2), 79–99 (2019)

10. Lhotka, L.: JSON Encoding of Data Modeled with YANG. Technical Report 7951 (2016). https://doi.org/10.17487/RFC7951, https://www.rfc-editor.org/info/rfc7951

11. Lopez, V., et al.: Transport API: a solution for SDN in carriers networks. In: ECOC 2016; 42nd European Conference on Optical Communication, pp. 1–3. VDE (2016)

12. Molina Zarca, A., Bagaa, M., Bernal Bernabe, J., Taleb, T., Skarmeta, A.F.: Semantic-aware security orchestration in SDN/NFV-enabled IoT systems. Sensors 20(13), 3622 (2020)

13. Musen, M.A.: The Protégé project: a look back and a look forward. AI Matters 1(4), 4–12 (2015)

14. Oliver, I., Panda, S., Wang, K., Kalliola, A.: Modelling NFV concepts with ontologies. In: 2018 21st Conference on Innovation in Clouds, Internet and Networks and Workshops (ICIN), pp. 1–7. IEEE (2018)

15. Parsia, B., Rudolph, S., Krötzsch, M., Patel-Schneider, P., Hitzler, P.: OWL 2 Web Ontology Language Primer (Second Edition). W3C Recommendation, W3C (2012). http://www.w3.org/TR/owl2-primer

16. Sacramento, E.R., Vidal, V.M., de Macêdo, J.A.F., Lóscio, B.F., Lopes, F.L.R., Casanova, M.A.: Towards automatic generation of application ontologies. J. Inf. Data Manage. 1(3), 535–535 (2010)

17. Sendra, S., Rego, A., Lloret, J., Jimenez, J.M., Romero, O.: Including artificial intelligence in a routing protocol using software defined networks. In: 2017 IEEE International Conference on Communications Workshops (ICC Workshops), pp. 670–674. IEEE (2017)

18. Sirin, E., Parsia, B., Cuenca Grau, B., Kalyanpur, A., Katz, Y.: Pellet: a practical OWL-DL reasoner. J. Web Semant. 5(2), 51–53 (2007)

19. Xiang, W., Wang, N., Zhou, Y.: An energy-efficient routing algorithm for software-defined wireless sensor networks. IEEE Sens. J. 16(20), 7393–7400 (2016)

Semantic Matchmaking
for Argumentative Intelligence
in Ubiquitous Computing

Corrado Fasciano[1,2], Michele Ruta[1], and Floriano Scioscia[1]

[1] Polytechnic University of Bari, via E. Orabona 4, 70125 Bari, Italy
{corrado.fasciano,michele.ruta,floriano.scioscia}@poliba.it
[2] Exprivia S.p.A., via A. Olivetti 11, 70056 Molfetta, Italy
corrado.fasciano@exprivia.com

Abstract. The Semantic Web of Things enables the exchange of knowledge fragments through machine-to-machine interactions, supporting collaborative decision-making among ubiquitous smart objects. Available methodologies, however, have often limited generality of applications and interpretability of results. This paper introduces early work on a novel structured argumentation approach, integrating Dung-style abstract argumentation with Description Logics reasoning. A semantic matchmaking scheme, exploiting non-standard, non-monotonic inferences, allows the appraisal of argument relations. This enables the automatic evaluation of an argumentative graph with a graded acceptability ranking of arguments and a formal explanation. The proposal is general-purpose, but oriented toward SWoT multi-agent systems, as illustrated in a vehicular network case study.

Keywords: Bipolar Weighted Argumentation · Description Logics · Semantic matchmaking · Web Ontology Language (OWL)

1 Introduction

The Semantic Web of Things (SWoT) [23] integrates Semantic Web technologies into Internet of Things contexts. In SWoT environments, individual knowledge fragments are disseminated by heterogeneous connected smart objects. Knowledge exchange occurs via machine-to-machine interactions, which can be considered as an ongoing *dialogue* among objects, which behave as autonomous agents. This vision fits classical *argumentation* paradigms [14]: *Abstract Argumentation* (AA) [9] is a simple but powerful formalism to reason over conflicting knowledge. It studies the acceptability of arguments based purely on their relationships and abstracted from their content. Basically, an argument is a set of assumptions, together with a conclusion that can be drawn by one or more reasoning steps.

Nevertheless, proper integration of principled argumentation frameworks in SWoT contexts is still an open problem. The majority of available approaches belongs to AA, thus they overlook the *structure* of arguments: this is, however, a fundamental aspect for the appraisal of relationships between arguments which are obtained from information generated by devices. Furthermore, AA frameworks can explain outcomes about the acceptability of arguments only in a shallow way, based on information about the direction and possibly type (attack or support) and/or numerical weight assigned to each relationship between a pair of arguments. This is a barrier for more meaningful interpretability of models and results, which would increase users' confidence in automatic argumentation facilities.

This paper introduces early work on a general-purpose but SWoT-oriented approach for integrating argumentation frameworks with Knowledge Representation and Reasoning (KRR). Information generated and shared by a device (or, generalizing, an agent) is represented as an annotation in standard Semantic Web languages, based on reference ontologies. Each annotation takes the role of an argument. Referring to the Bipolar Weighted Argumentation Framework (BWAF) family –which include both attack and support relationships, with an assigned weight to represent connection type and strength– type and weight are assessed exploiting non-standard, non-monotonic inference services for semantic matchmaking [8,20]. This enables (i) a more meaningful appraisal of individual relationships, (ii) assessment of the accuracy and reliability of collected information in SWoT device networks and (iii) interpretability of results, by virtue of logic-based explanation capabilities of the adopted inferences. The approach aims to deal with key open challenges for the realization of fully automatic argumentation, as discussed *e.g.*, in [2]: how arguments are constructed (*structural layer*), what are the relationships between arguments (*relational layer*), and how a constellation of interacting arguments can be evaluated and conclusions can be drawn (*assessment layer*).

The remainder of the paper is organized as follows. Section 2 recalls useful background on argumentation –and particularly BWAF– as well as on reasoning in the SWoT. Section 3 describes an early approach integrating KRR and argumentation, while Sect. 4 outlines an illustrative case study regarding a vehicular ad-hoc network (VANET) comprising vehicles and roadside units, with the goal of dynamic collaborative management of the traffic flow around a road interruption point. Related work discussion is in Sect. 5, before conclusion.

2   Background

In what follows, preliminary notions regarding the Bipolar Weighted Argumentation and the Semantic Web of Things are recalled to make the paper self-contained.

2.1   Bipolar Weighted Argumentation

The *Argumentation Framework* (AF), introduced by Dung [9], is a graph-based formalism to reason over conflicting knowledge without considering the internal structure of the arguments, but only their relationships of *attack* –denoting

Fig. 1. BWAF legend: S_1 attacks R_1, S_2 supports R_2

conflicts between pairs of arguments– and the *semantics* for evaluating them. *Extension semantics* divide all subsets of arguments according to some acceptability criteria, *e.g.*, *conflict-freeness, defense, admissibility* [4]. An argument is *accepted* if it belongs to an extension (*i.e.*, an acceptable subset of arguments), and *rejected* otherwise. Another family of semantics proposed in the literature, called *gradual semantics*, focuses on individual arguments, and assigns them a numerical weight –typically called *overall strength*– to explicitly rank them according to their degree of acceptability [1].

Dung's original formalism for abstract argumentation has been extended along many lines, giving rise to a large and thriving literature [5,24]. Bipolar Weighted AF (BWAF) [18] incorporates two of the most important generalizations of Dung-style AFs: the bipolar AF (BAF), and weighted AF (WAF). In a BAF [7] two kinds of interactions between arguments are possible: the *attack* and the *support* relationships. Differently, in a WAF [10], a numerical weight is associated with all attack relationships between arguments, representing the relative strength of the attack. The main novelty of the BWAF is to allow not only weighted attack, but also weighted support relationships between arguments. This is achieved by assigning a positive or negative weight to each relationship.

Definition 1. *A BWAF is a triple* $\mathcal{G} = \langle \mathcal{A}, \hat{\mathcal{R}}, w_{\hat{\mathcal{R}}} \rangle$, *where* $\mathcal{A}$ *is a finite set of arguments,* $\hat{\mathcal{R}} \subseteq \mathcal{A} \times \mathcal{A}$ *is a set of relationships and* $w_{\hat{\mathcal{R}}} \colon \hat{\mathcal{R}} \mapsto [-1, 0[\cup]0, 1]$ *a weighing function. Attack relationships are defined as* $\hat{\mathcal{R}}_{att} = \{\langle a, b \rangle \in \hat{\mathcal{R}} \mid w_{\hat{\mathcal{R}}}(\langle a, b \rangle) \in [-1, 0[\}$ *and support relationships as* $\hat{\mathcal{R}}_{sup} = \{\langle a, b \rangle \in \hat{\mathcal{R}} \mid w_{\hat{\mathcal{R}}}(\langle a, b \rangle) \in]0, 1] \}$. *Given two arguments* $a, b \in \mathcal{A}$ *and a path* $\langle a, x_1, x_2, \ldots, x_n, b \rangle$ *from a to b, then:*

- *a bw-attacks b if the product of weights* $w_{\hat{\mathcal{R}}}(\langle a, x_1 \rangle) \cdot w_{\hat{\mathcal{R}}}(\langle x_1, x_2 \rangle) \cdot \ldots \cdot w_{\hat{\mathcal{R}}}(\langle x_n, b \rangle)$ *is negative.*
- *a bw-defends b if the product of weights* $w_{\hat{\mathcal{R}}}(\langle a, x_1 \rangle) \cdot w_{\hat{\mathcal{R}}}(\langle x_1, x_2 \rangle) \cdot \ldots \cdot w_{\hat{\mathcal{R}}}(\langle x_n, b \rangle)$ *is positive.*

A BWAF can be depicted as a directed graph whose nodes represent arguments, relations represent attacks (with solid edges from the attacker to the attacked node) and supports (with dashed edges), and weights represent the relative strength of relationships, as exemplified in Fig. 1.

2.2 The Semantic Web of Things

The Semantic Web of Things (SWoT) [23] consolidates the Semantic Web and the Internet of Things (IoT). Its goal is to support user activities and provide general-purpose innovative services by improving intelligence of embedded objects and autonomic information management in pervasive contexts. In order to facilitate sharing and understanding of unambiguous knowledge across heterogeneous ubiquitous micro-devices, Semantic Web languages and technologies grounded on Description Logics (DLs) [3] are used, including the *Web Ontology Language* (OWL) 2 [17]. Specifically, this work adopts an OWL 2 subset corresponding to the *Attributive Language with unqualified Number restrictions* ($\mathcal{ALN}$) DL. It provides moderate expressiveness, while granting polynomial complexity to both standard and non-standard inference tasks.

Semantic matchmaking techniques [20] are useful in SWoT contexts, as they compare ontology-based annotations to retrieve the most relevant *resources* for a given *request*. Unfortunately, *Subsumption* and *Satisfiability* standard inference services on concept expressions only manage full matches, which are quite rare in practical scenarios. Furthermore, in both cases the output is Boolean, hence these services can only provide "yes/no" answers without an explanation of the outcome. The following non-standard, non-monotonic inference services [8,20], implemented in *Tiny-ME (the Tiny Matchmaking Engine)* [21], support gradual approximate matches and logic-based explanation:

- *Concept Contraction*: if a *request* R and a *resource* S are not compatible with each other, Contraction determines which part of R is conflicting with S. By retracting only conflicting requirements G (for *Give-up*) in R, an expression K (for *Keep*) remains, which is a contracted version of the original request. The solution G to Contraction explains "why" the conjunction of R and S is not satisfiable;
- *Concept Abduction*: if request and resource are compatible, but S does not subsume R, Abduction determines what should be hypothesized in S in order to obtain a full match, *i.e.*, to make the subsumption relation true. The solution H (for *Hypothesis*) to Abduction can be interpreted as what is requested in R and not specified in S, thus providing an explanation for missed Subsumption in an Open World Assumption;
- *Concept Bonus*: a resource S could contain features not requested in R, – possibly because the requester did not know or consider them– which could be useful in a query refinement process. For this purpose, this service extracts a Bonus concept B from S, which denotes what the resource provides even though the request did not ask for it.

Moreover, adopting a *normal form* for concept expressions allows defining a metric space with a *norm* operator $|| \cdot ||$. This work focuses on $\mathcal{ALN}$ concept expressions in Conjunctive Normal Form (CNF): the CNF norm of G and H can then represent a semantic distance *penalty* for Concept Contraction and Abduction, respectively; similarly, $||B||$ provides a measure of relevance for Bonus [20].

3   Knowledge Representation, Reasoning and Argumentation

This section describes how knowledge representation and automatic reasoning could be exploited for the evaluation and explanation of a bipolar weighted argumentative graph.

3.1   Interpretable BWAF

Starting from an argumentative graph obtained from semantically annotated messages exchanged in a network of smart devices in SWoT contexts, this work explores the argumentation process composed of: (i) argument relationship appraisal, (ii) argument acceptability assessment, (iii) explanation of outcomes. In this perspective, each device is associated with a semantic-based annotation representing its shared knowledge in the field. Annotations are expressed as (unfolded and CNF-normalized) concept descriptions w.r.t. a common domain ontology $\mathcal{T}$, and they are shared following the network topology. Given two generic smart devices D_R and D_S in a SWoT network, their annotations – denoted as R and S respectively– are treated as arguments, since they state knowledge owned by the devices. The set of exchanged annotations thus takes the role of $\mathcal{A}$ in the BWAF $\mathcal{G}$, and the set of pairwise device interactions coincides with the set of relations $\hat{\mathcal{R}}$ between the corresponding arguments. If D_S communicates with D_R ($D_S \rightsquigarrow D_R$), in order to evaluate the acceptability of R and S, according to a matchmaking-based perspective [8,21] R and S can be considered respectively as request and resource, since in SWoT scenarios S can be used to "respond to needs" expressed in R. This peculiarity shows a possible argumentative relationship can exist with edge orientation from S to R.

Once the relationship orientation is determined, a knowledge-driven process can be devised to appraise its type, discriminating whether S attacks or supports R. Particularly, a semantic consistency check could be suitable for this activity: if $R \sqcap S$ is consistent, the relationship that links S to R is a support, otherwise it is an attack. Following this preliminary check, a non-standard inference services-based strategy could be devised to appropriately weight an edge connecting two nodes. This process is iterated for each edge in the graph.

3.2   Weighting of Relations

In order to establish a strategy assigning the correct weight to each edge between two nodes of a BWAF, it is crucial to identify which informative contributions take part respectively in the attack and support relationships.

In an attack, as the one shown in Fig. 1, the following four informative contributions should be taken into account to compute its weight:

A. the amount of conflicting information between the two arguments;
B. the amount of information confirmed by both arguments;

C. the amount of information in the attacked argument which is not confirmed nor rebutted by the attacker;

D. any amount of additional information in the attacker which is not present in the attacked argument.

Term A is the cause of semantic inconsistency, and thus of the attack relationship. Since the weight of an attack is a real negative number, the maximum emphasis should be given to term A. At the same time, the remaining three contributions are useful to mitigate the strength of the attack, since they express either agreement (term B) or non-disagreement (terms C and D). Considering the non-standard inference services recalled in Sect. 2.2 on R (the attacked argument) and S (the attacker), term A will depend on $||G||$ as determined by Concept Contraction; then, taking the compatible part K obtained from Concept Contraction, term B can be computed via two nested Concept Bonus inferences, as the inner Bonus yields the additional information in S w.r.t. K and the outer Bonus identifies what is "not additional", $i.e.$, common to both K and S; term C corresponds to $||H||$ induced from Concept Abduction between K and S; finally, term D can be computed via a (single) Concept Bonus between R and S.

Conversely, in case an argument S supports another argument R, two informative contributions should be identified and quantified. They respectively are: (i) the amount of information S is lacking to reach a full match with R; (ii) the amount of information S has in addition w.r.t. R. The former is directly determined via Concept Abduction, while the latter via Concept Bonus [8,20], as per definitions recalled in Sect. 2.2.

4   When Smart Objects Argue in the Street: A Case Study

In order to clarify peculiarities of the proposal, a case study has been carried out taking as reference SWoT contexts based on VANETs.

One of the two lanes of a two-way road has an interruption due to maintenance work. On each lane there is a temporary traffic light, allowing incoming vehicles from both directions to cross the part of the lane adjacent to the interruption alternately. Figure 2 depicts the situation.

The purpose of this scenario is collaborative argumentation in a network of intelligent devices for an efficient management of the occupation of the single lane used for temporary transit, estimating the traffic density in the proximity of traffic lights and the characteristics of incoming vehicles. *Each vehicle is able to describe itself by means of a semantic-based annotation, which provides information about the type of vehicle, traveling speed, size, etc. Roadside units include: two cameras, monitoring the traffic density and vehicle position w.r.t. the interruption in both lanes; the two traffic lights, managing the traffic in the conflict area by acquiring information from incoming vehicles and from the cameras themselves.* Two *Controllers* work as actuators in the scenario, maintaining the information to be considered winning –*i.e.*, acceptable decisions– at the end of the argumentation process and setting the two traffic lights accordingly.

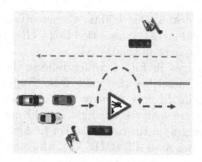

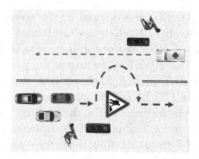

Fig. 2. Case study: first situation   ·   **Fig. 3.** Case study: second situation

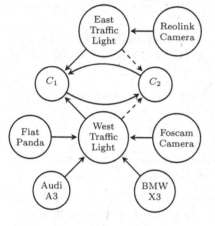

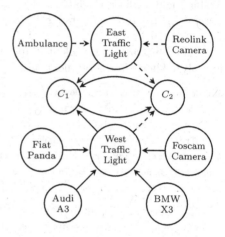

Fig. 4. $\mathcal{G}_1$: BWAF of first situation   **Fig. 5.** $\mathcal{G}_2$: BWAF of second situation

Two different situations are assessed in the case study. Figure 2 depicts the former, assuming an initial configuration with green East Traffic Light and red West Traffic Light for the next 30 s, no vehicle coming from the East and three cars coming from the West with low priority and expected time of arrival of 5, 10, and 15 s respectively. The roadside cameras detect no traffic on the East side and a presence of cars on the West side: it is reasonable to expect that, after collecting the information from the devices and executing the argumentation process, the configurations of the Traffic Lights will be promptly reversed to let the three cars pass. Figure 3, depicting the second situation, has the same starting configuration as the former, but in addition it sees the arrival of an ambulance in 5 s from the East. Due to the higher priority of the ambulance w.r.t. the three cars, Controllers should set the Traffic Lights to keep their current configuration, so as to allow the ambulance to quickly cross the road interruption point.

The case study uses a KB (not reported here due to lack of space) modeled in $\mathcal{ALN}$ DL. The Terminological Box ($TBox$) $\mathcal{T}$ contains all the classes used to describe the devices in the scenario: Vehicles, Traffic Lights, Cameras and Controllers. Each device is modeled as an individual of the Assertion Box (*ABox*) and its class expression is used as a single argument in the BWAF.

The BWAF $\mathcal{G}_1$–without weights on the edges–in Fig. 4, which reflects the situation in Fig. 2, shows how the node that describes the green *East Traffic Light* (*ETL*) suffers an attack by the roadside *Reolink Camera* (*RC*), which detects no vehicles in the vicinity and therefore believes the light should not stay green. Similarly, in the bottom half of the graph, the red *West Traffic Light* (*WTL*) is attacked by the three cars (*Fiat Panda, Audi A3, BMW X3*), which are approaching the traffic light and need to pass, and also by the *Foscam Camera*, which detects the presence of vehicles in the proximity. In addition, both the Traffic Light nodes are related to Controllers C_1 and C_2, which provide opposite arguments; $C1$ represents red *ETL* and green *WTL*, while $C2$ represents green ETL and red WTL.

As an illustrative example, the appraisal of the relationship of *RC* w.r.t. *ETL* is analyzed hereafter. Arguments are reported in OWL 2 *Manchester Syntax* [12].

```
RC: Camera and (hasTrafficDensity some owl:Thing) and
(hasTrafficDensity only NoTraffic) and (requiredTrafficLight some owl:Thing)
and (requiredTrafficLight only RedEastTrafficLight)
ETL: TrafficLight and (requiredTrafficLight some owl:Thing) and
(requiredTrafficLight only GreenEastTrafficLight) and
(hasTrafficDensity some owl:Thing) and (hasTrafficDensity only LowTraffic)
and (hasDurationSec min 30 owl:Thing) and (hasDurationSec max 30 owl:Thing)
```

The preliminary consistency check between *ETL* and *RC* fails, as the conjunction of the two expressions is unsatifiable due to the clash of mutually disjoint classes `RedEastTrafficLight` and `GreenEastTrafficLight`. The relationship is thus recognized as an attack and its weight must be computed by identifying the four information contributions as explained in Sect. 3.2. The strength of the attack, characterized essentially by the contrasting part between the two semantic annotations, is equal to the Give-up of Concept Contraction:

```
A := (requiredTrafficLight some owl:Thing) and
(requiredTrafficLight only GreenEastTrafficLight)
```

The remaining three terms mitigate the attack. The second term, quantifying the common elements between the two arguments, is:

```
B := (hasTrafficDensity some owl:Thing) and (hasTrafficDensity only LowTraffic)
```

This outcome is due to the semantic compatibility of classes `LowTraffic` and `NoTraffic` in the reference ontology. The third term of the formula quantifies the information in the attacked argument *ETL* that is absent from the attacking one *RC*:

```
C := TrafficLight and (hasDurationSec min 30 owl:Thing) and
(hasDurationSec max 30 owl:Thing)
```

Finally, the information that RC has in addition to ETL is:

```
D := Camera and (hasTrafficDensity only NoTraffic)
```

Class expressions in A, B, C and D provide the formal explanation which makes the relationship interpretable.

The situation depicted in Fig. 3 is instead represented by the BWAF $\mathcal{G}_2$ in Fig. 5. In this case, the green ETL receives a support from both the *Ambulance* and the RC: the former describes itself as a special high priority vehicle, ready to overcome the road interruption in a time of 5 s; the latter detects the presence of vehicles in proximity and states the ETL should stay green. The bottom half of the graph, on the other hand, remains completely unchanged w.r.t. the previous situation. Although seemingly small, the differences of $\mathcal{G}_2$ w.r.t. $\mathcal{G}_1$ have a significant impact on the overall acceptability of arguments. In fact, a preliminary acceptability assessment has been conducted by exploiting the *ARGUER (ARGuing Using Enhanced Reasoning)* argumentation reasoner [18]. It was used on the BWAFs in both scenarios, evaluating the extensions by means of the (a) preferred and (b) stable semantics.

The preferred semantics for $\mathcal{G}_1$ produces the following extensions:

{Reolink, Controller C_1, Foscam, Fiat Panda, Audi A3, BMW X3},
{Reolink, West Traffic Light},
{East Traffic Light, Controller C_2, West Traffic Light},
{East Traffic Light, Foscam, Fiat Panda, Audi A3, BMW X3}.

Conversely, the stable semantics for $\mathcal{G}_1$ produces a single extension:

{Reolink, Controller C_1, Foscam, Fiat Panda, Audi A3, BMW X3}.

This happens because the stable semantics is more "skeptical" as, by definition, it requires the satisfaction of stricter constraints. The solutions produced by stable semantics, if they exist, are therefore considered more reliable than those produced by the preferred semantics. The expected result from the argumentation process on $\mathcal{G}_1$ is confirmed by the stable extension, which includes the Controller C_1, whose semantic description specifies red East Traffic Light and green West Traffic Light. Consequently, the system must reverse the configuration of the two traffic lights.

The preferred semantics for $\mathcal{G}_2$ produces the following extensions:

{Reolink, Ambulance, East Traffic Light, Controller C_2, West Traffic Light},
{Reolink, Ambulance, East Traffic Light, Foscam, Fiat Panda, Audi A3, BMW X3},
{Controller C_1, Foscam, Fiat Panda, Audi A3, BMW X3}.

The stable semantics for $\mathcal{G}_2$ produces a single extension:

{Reolink, Ambulance, East Traffic Light, Foscam, Fiat Panda, Audi A3, BMW X3}.

In this case the stable semantics does not include the Controller C_2 as expected, but the presence of the ETL argument in the extension allows to consider that its current green state is the acceptable one. In both argumentative graphs, the adoption of extension-based semantics does not appear completely satisfactory since (i) the arguments expected as "winning" may be out of the resulting extensions (ii) in SWoT scenarios a more fine-grained evaluation of the decisions to be enacted is fundamental. A ranking semantics that fully exploits the weights of the relationships of a BWAF, calculated by arranging the informative contributions identified in this proposal, could solve these issues.

5   Related Work

In recent times, the argumentation theory originally promoted by Dung [9] is increasingly exploited in Internet of Things (IoT) contexts to model interactions among smart devices and to enable autonomous argumentation-based coordination. In [15], argumentation theory is employed to coordinate smart vehicles on a congested road. Arguments represent both data collected through vehicle sensors and possible actions. By processing the argumentative graph, each vehicle agent is able to solve conflicts, identify winning arguments (*i.e.*, suggested actions) and change lane appropriately according to the current road configuration. In [14], the argumentation graph models object interactions actualizing a sequence of dialogues in natural language. The main goal is to define an argumentation-based decision-making system, overcoming the limitations of traditional rule-based approaches. The vision is exemplified in two real-world scenarios regarding traffic management and ambient-assisted living.

Despite both works showing the feasibility and usefulness of argumentation in IoT, adoption of formal argument models and automatic relation appraisal is still an open challenge. Combining knowledge representation and non-monotonic reasoning with argumentation frameworks can lead to significant improvements, allowing to handle issues such as defeasibility and inconsistency in ways that traditional logics are not able to support [19]. Along this vision, early proposals exploited abstract argumentation for reasoning over inconsistent knowledge bases (KBs). The *Generalized Argumentation Framework (GenAF)* [16] has been defined to model an argumentative graph upon an underlying KB: each argumental atom represents a formula in the KB and every attack relation between two arguments models inconsistency or incoherence between conflicting sources of information. While it provides a general extension to AA, adaptable to different logics for representing knowledge inside arguments, conflict recognition is based only on consistency check. A deductive argumentation framework is presented also in [6] to reason with conflicting and uncertain ontologies. It models two different relations based on the argument structures. Differently from the previous work, each argument is also associated with a weight representing the information certainty degree. In both cases, the final argumentation graph is used to study the acceptability of arguments, but implementations in concrete scenarios have not been proposed and the reference logical formalisms are not related to standard Semantic Web languages.

As explained in [11,13], a knowledge-based approach can be exploited to: (i) annotate arguments w.r.t. a reference ontology providing the conceptualization and vocabulary for the particular knowledge domain; (ii) simplify graph sharing among different agents; (iii) autonomously identify support and attack relations among argument descriptions. A related approach for knowledge fusion was introduced in [22] for SWoT VANETs: although providing acceptability evaluation and reconciliation of inconsistencies, it lacks the larger flexibility of Dung-style abstract argumentation.

6   Conclusion and Perspective

This paper has introduced a novel approach for integrating DL-based semantic matchmaking into argumentation frameworks. Non-standard, non-monotonic inferences, endowed with formal justification of results, allow a structured appraisal of relationships between pairs of arguments. The approach also provides a direct mapping from structured to abstract argumentation evaluation, specifically in BWAF. The conclusions on the overall acceptability of arguments become not only more fine-grained, but also more interpretable through meaningful explanations. The proposal is theoretically general-purpose, but motivated by collaborative autonomous decision-making and information reliability evaluation in SWoT networks of smart objects.

Notwithstanding, this work should be considered only as an early effort. While non-standard inferences analyze relationships between pairs of arguments structurally, further investigation is needed on the usage of induced CNF penalties for weighing them. A *score combination function* (a.k.a. *utility function*) is a possible approach to combine logical and extra-logical considerations in the appraisal. Furthermore, semantic explanations of relationships could be embedded into the argumentative graph itself. This would further improve transparency of the approach, making it immediate to interpret the model and its results.

Acknowledgments. This work has been supported by project TEBAKA (TErritorial BAsic Knowledge Acquisition), funded by the Italian Ministry of University and Research.

References

1. Amgoud, L., Ben-Naim, J.: Ranking-based semantics for argumentation frameworks. In: Liu, W., Subrahmanian, V.S., Wijsen, J. (eds.) SUM 2013. LNCS (LNAI), vol. 8078, pp. 134–147. Springer, Heidelberg (2013). https://doi.org/10.1007/978-3-642-40381-1_11
2. Atkinson, K.: Towards artificial argumentation. AI Mag. **38**(3), 25–36 (2017)
3. Baader, F., Calvanese, D., McGuinness, D.L., Nardi, D., Patel-Schneider, P.: The Description Logic Handbook. Cambridge University Press, Cambridge (2002)
4. Baroni, P., Caminada, M., Giacomin, M.: An introduction to argumentation semantics. Knowl. Eng. Rev. **26**(4), 365–410 (2011)
5. Baroni, P., Gabbay, D., Giacomin, M., van der Torre, L.: Handbook of Formal Argumentation, vol. 1. College Publications, London (2018)
6. Bouzeghoub, A., Jabbour, S., Ma, Y., Raddaoui, B.: Handling conflicts in uncertain ontologies using deductive argumentation. In: International Conference on Web Intelligence, pp. 65–72. ACM (2017)
7. Cayrol, C., Lagasquie-Schiex, M.C.: On the acceptability of arguments in bipolar argumentation frameworks. In: Godo, L. (ed.) ECSQARU 2005. LNCS (LNAI), vol. 3571, pp. 378–389. Springer, Heidelberg (2005). https://doi.org/10.1007/11518655_33

8. Di Noia, T., Di Sciascio, E., Donini, F.: Semantic matchmaking as non-monotonic reasoning: a description logic approach. J. Artif. Intell. Res. (JAIR) **29**, 269–307 (2007)

9. Dung, P.M.: On the acceptability of arguments and its fundamental role in non-monotonic reasoning, logic programming and n-person games. Artif. Intell. **77**(2), 321–357 (1995)

10. Dunne, P.E., Hunter, A., McBurney, P., Parsons, S., Wooldridge, M.: Weighted argument systems: basic definitions, algorithms, and complexity results. Artif. Intell. **175**(2), 457–486 (2011)

11. Heras, S., Botti, V., Julián, V.: An ontological-based knowledge-representation formalism for case-based argumentation. Inf. Syst. Front. **17**(4), 779–798 (2014). https://doi.org/10.1007/s10796-014-9524-3

12. Horridge, M., Patel-Schneider, P.: OWL 2 web ontology language manchester syntax (Second Edition). Note, W3C (2012). http://www.w3.org/TR/owl2-manchester-syntax/

13. Kökciyan, N., Yaglikci, N., Yolum, P.: An argumentation approach for resolving privacy disputes in online social networks. ACM Trans. Internet Technol. (TOIT) **17**(3), 27 (2017)

14. Lippi, M., Mamei, M., Mariani, S., Zambonelli, F.: An argumentation-based perspective over the social IoT. IEEE Internet Things J. **5**(4), 2537–2547 (2018)

15. Lovellette, E., Hexmoor, H., Rodriguez, K.: Automated argumentation for collaboration among cyber-physical system actors at the edge of the Internet of Things. Internet of Things **5**, 84–96 (2019)

16. Moguillansky, M.O., Simari, G.R.: A generalized abstract argumentation framework for inconsistency-tolerant ontology reasoning. Expert Syst. Appl. **64**, 141–168 (2016)

17. Parsia, B., Rudolph, S., Krötzsch, M., Patel-Schneider, P., Hitzler, P.: OWL 2 Web Ontology Language Primer (Second Edition). Recommendation, W3C (2012). http://www.w3.org/TR/owl2-primer

18. Pazienza, A., Ferilli, S., Esposito, F.: Constructing and evaluating bipolar weighted argumentation frameworks for online debating systems. In: 1st Workshop on Advances In Argumentation In Artificial Intelligence, XVI International Conference of the Italian Association for Artificial Intelligence, pp. 111–125 (2017)

19. Reed, C., et al.: The argument web: an online ecosystem of tools, systems and services for argumentation. Philos. Technol. **30**(2), 137–160 (2017). https://doi.org/10.1007/s13347-017-0260-8

20. Ruta, M., Di Sciascio, E., Scioscia, F.: Concept abduction and contraction in semantic-based P2P environments. Web Intell. Agent Syst. **9**(3), 179–207 (2011)

21. Ruta, M., et al.: A multiplatform reasoning engine for the semantic web of everything. J. Web Semant. **73**, 100709 (2022)

22. Ruta, M., Scioscia, F., Gramegna, F., Ieva, S., Di Sciascio, E., De Vera, R.P.: A knowledge fusion approach for context awareness in vehicular networks. IEEE Internet Things J. **5**(4), 2407–2419 (2018)

23. Scioscia, F., Ruta, M.: Building a semantic web of things: issues and perspectives in information compression. In: Proceedings of the 3rd IEEE International Conference on Semantic Computing, pp. 589–594. IEEE Computer Society (2009)

24. Simari, G.R., Rahwan, I. (eds.): Argumentation in Artificial Intelligence. Springer, Heidelberg (2009)

Smart District 4.0 Project: Validation of Results and Exploitation Perspectives

Nicola Magaletti[2]([✉]) [iD], Alessandro Massaro[1,2] [iD], Gabriele Cosoli[2],
and Angelo Leogrande[1,2] [iD]

[1] LUM University Giuseppe Degennaro, Strada Statale 100 Km 18, 70010 Casamassima, BA,
Italy
[2] LUM Enterprise S.r.l., Strada Statale 100 Km 18, BA 70010 Casamassima, Italy
magaletti@lumenterprise.it

Abstract. The paper provides an overview of the approach used for the result validation of the Smart District 4.0 (SD 4.0) project. The experimental phase of this project considered six applications based on Artificial Intelligence techniques. In particular, the project addressed some typical use cases, such as predictive maintenance in the mechatronics sector, traceability of the agro-food chain, management of suppliers in textile sector, technical-commercial virtual assistant for the business of automated warehouses, continuous monitoring of diabetic drivers in public transport, Decision Support System (DSS) for the automation in fertigation. The validation approach considers four key evaluation elements, such as (i) prototype readiness, (ii) probability to use the prototype, (iii) business impact and (iv) knowledge gain. The paper then discusses the macro functionalities of each prototype development for the six case studies, providing a metric based on a four-value scale radar chart.

Keywords: Artificial intelligence · Machine learning · IoT · Industry 4.0 · Blockchain · RPA

1 Introduction: SD 4.0 Scenario and Validation Approach

Digital transformation is an unstoppable process, but also an opportunity for companies to remain competitive and allow them to revise business models and operational processes. Especially for Small and Medium Enterprises (SMEs), this innovation wave nowadays increasingly promote Industry 4.0 technologies, which start on addressing plant automation but also provide opportunities to improve the collaboration processes and the supply chain management. In this context, modern digital platforms provide tools for flexible production and for the identification of qualified suppliers. Such platforms are then fundamental tools, which allow the companies to define innovative strategies for businesses and reach new markets. To this purpose, the SD 4.0 project has been conceived, within a Research & Development Call launched by the Italian Ministry of Economic Development (MISE), with the aim of sustaining the digitization process of the Italian SMEs.

G. Agapito et al. (Eds.): ICWE 2022 Workshops, CCIS 1668, pp. 149–159, 2023.
https://doi.org/10.1007/978-3-031-25380-5_12

The project involved two companies such as LUM Enterprise Srl and Noovle Spa. LUM Enterprise, the main contractor, is a consulting company, founded as a spin-off of the LUM University Giuseppe Degennaro, aiming at the development of innovative products and services with high technological value for SMEs. To this end, the company employs a multidisciplinary team that includes engineering, Information Technology (IT), data science and business consulting skills. In the first phase of activity, LUM Enterprise was mainly involved in the start-up and management of SD 4.0. The project, which started in February of 2018 and recently concluded, was conceived for a target made up of manufacturing SMEs of specific industrial sectors, relevant to the Apulian economy (Agroindustry, Textile-Clothing and Footwear, Mechatronics), with the aim of creating digital applications enforcing supply chain processes through a cloud Platform as a Services (PaaS) platform using Google technology. The main objectives of SD 4.0 project aimed to:

- involve selected Apulian SMEs in the use of tools new technologies addressed on Industry 4.0;
- analyze and implement new organizational models for production;
- develop collaboration cloud platforms supporting cooperation processes of the whole supply chain
- validate the applications in relevant industrial use cases.

The overall model conceived to involve SMEs in SD 4.0 is represented in Fig. 1.

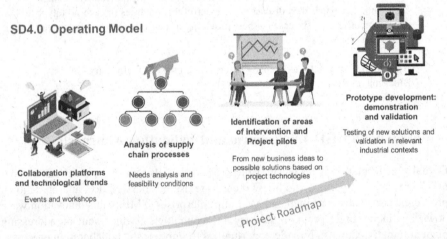

Fig. 1. The operating model of the SD 4.0 project driving SMEs in the Industry 4.0 scenario.

Along the project activities, we selected six experimental use cases (Pilot listed in the following Table 1) and then, during the final phase, we analyzed the related results achieved by implementing specific applications, which include a set of technologies, all of them provided by the SD 4.0 platform.

The used validation methodology considers the estimation of the following key parameters [1]:

Table 1. The company pilots for the experimentation phase.

Pilot	Production	Sector
Pilot 1	Polyurethane cutting machines	Mechatronics
Pilot 2	Automated logistics systems	Mechatronics
Pilot 3	Ice cream semi-product	Food agronomic
Pilot 4	Solutions for agriculture 4.0	Food agronomic
Pilot 5	Home textile products	Textile-clothing-footwear
Pilot 6	Solutions for safety and health 4.0	Medical devices

- *Prototype Readiness* (state of "immediate" use of a prototypal macro functionality): it is a "backward" parameter expressing the evaluation of the technology of the demonstrator prototype and its usability at the end of the experimentation;
- *Knowledge Gain*: it is a "backward" parameter useful to evaluate how the experimental phase itself is able to provide further knowledge, if compared with the "AS IS" condition;
- *Business Impact:* it is a forecast parameter about the technological impact for the "TO BE" business models;
- *Probability To Use*: the parameter is of a forecast type and is representative of the probability of use of the new technology implemented in the next few years.

The following discussion is addressed to describe four of these case studies (Pilot), the related macro functionality of the prototypal applications and the evaluation of four key parameters listed above, represented by radar charts.

2 Pilot 1: Main Functionalities and Results Assessment

Pilot 1 refers to a small manufacturer of automated cutting systems of polyurethane, used for the production of padded furniture like sofas and seats.

The prototype application developed within this pilot deals with monitoring the cutting blades, which is considered the most critical element of the whole machine [2]. In particular, the user interface of the platform, beside a set of dashboards for real-time monitoring of different parameters characterizing the status of the blade, provides a forecast of its duration over time through the analysis and processing of historical utilization data [2]. The prototype then consists of two macro functionalities: (a) the digital traceability of the maintenance process; (b) the predictive algorithms finalized to maintenance policies.

2.1 Macro function (a): Digital Traceability Inherent with the Use of the Entire Maintenance Process

Blockchain technology was used to ensure the traceability of the entire maintenance and assistance processes, as conceived after the analysis. Through the blockchain it is therefore possible to certify the usage history of the blade (notarization of the detections up to the breaking/replacement of the blade) as well as verify the correct process conditions up to the replacement operation, even as a guarantee of the assistance activities to be carried out. In addition, the possibility to trace the blade replacement by adopting a certified procedure becomes an important business advantage for the Company, as it allows to formalize the most relevant maintenance steps of the machinery, keeping a digital trace useful for any negotiation and provision of maintenance services. More generally, through the appropriate control panel, the company can better manage all the cutting machines sold, verifying their correct functioning at each customer. This technology then may enable a new operative model providing an important additional service for customers who rely on the company for the supply of cutting machines.

2.2 Macro Function (b): Predictive Maintenance Models

The main goal of the pilot is to enable the company to adopt predictive maintenance [3] policies for a particularly important category of their polyurethane cutting machines equipped by circular blades. The pilot case study starts with a cause-and-effect analysis of the components having a more significant impact on the availability, reliability, maintainability, safety, and integrity of cutting machines monitoring the blades as critical components. The continuous communication between the SD 4.0 platform and the cutting machines provides process data, which allows the activation of predictive models oriented to the optimization of products and services. In particular, the customer who buys a machine can use applications for receiving alerts on the state of the system and enable predictive maintenance policies in order to reduce possible breakdown costs. The blade monitoring system has been implemented in the SD 4.0 platform processing different parameters such as weight (of the piece to be cut), speed, temperature, elongation and size (of the piece to be cut). Predictive maintenance adopting clustering techniques is able to increase the efficiency of the production system. To this purpose, the application of neural network algorithms along with a combination of internet of things devices and cloud services have been used for collecting data and creating risk maps based on blade parameters.

2.3 Results Assessment

From the analysis of the two radar charts shown above, it emerges that the "*Predictive maintenance*" macro functionality has acquired the maximum score in all four parameters evaluated. The software platform, however, proved to be easily usable for the company, which was able to evaluate its potential, also about the recording of the historical data on the use of the blades and the notarization of the surveys up to the breaking / replacement of the same. Thanks to this experimental phase, the company has certainly acquired new knowledge, which will be useful for the activation of new services related to the assistance of its machinery. Finally, the impact on the business associated with the new technologies implemented is considered important for operations aimed at increasing bargaining power with the activation of new assistance and maintenance services, and in processes relating to the guarantee of machinery. The company turned to be very inclined to technology innovation and has participated in the development and tuning of the final prototype by expressing its needs which have been "*translated*" into software functionalities (display dashboard, parameterization of threshold values, methods of access to features such as blade selection, etc.). In Fig. 2 are illustrated the radar charts about the validation of the macro functions (a) and (b).

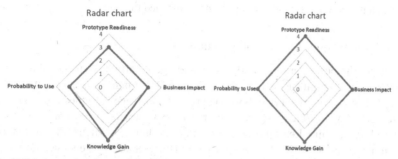

Fig. 2. Validation radar charts of the digital traceability (left) and predictive maintenance (right) functions.

3 Pilot 2: Main Functionalities and Results Assessment

This pilot involved a small hi-tech company, which develops automated solutions for the storage, distribution and sales of goods. The focus of this activity has been on the technical and commercial assistance processes [5]. In particular, objective of the developments has been a Virtual Assistant (VA) capable of understanding natural language expressions that allows the company to manage and deliver the first level of service for technical and commercial assistance, both through chabot and voice, reducing to a minimum the human intervention. Through the application as a whole, it is possible to collect data, allowing not only technical support to raise efficiency level of the assistance service, but also to the Sales Customer Service to elaborate and send personalized commercial offers to customers by retrieving e monitoring opportunities and contract renewals. The company, by means of the prototype application, has a customer care dashboard associated with the intelligent management of customers through a chatbot system. The prototype demonstrator of this pilot is concentrated on two macro functions: (a) process digitization; (b) Virtual Assistant. More details are provided hereinafter.

3.1 Macro function (a): Process Digitization

The technical and commercial assistance is empowered by the formulation of the Knowledge Base (KB) importing in the SD 4.0 platform digital data such as:

- Technical FAQs: a list of FAQs regarding technical assistance issues associated with the automatic SILO warehouse (company product), structured to associate a single assistance answer to a question, thus facilitating the learning of virtual assistance;
- Commercial FAQ: is structured a commercial question tree describing the commercial assistance paths based on the questions and answers given by the customer;

– SILO user manual: is provided an instruction manual for the use of the automatic vertical warehouse.

This smart component operates within a broader and integrated process, interconnected to a management platform providing assistance tickets.

3.2 Macro Function (b): Virtual Assistant

The focus of the new operating model is an intelligent Virtual Assistant, able to understand the natural language, which, through the SD 4.0 platform, allows the management of the first level of service, both via chatbot and voice call, thus reducing human resource activities. The chatbot service has been setup with the implementation of ontologies based on Machine Learning (ML) techniques (Ontology ML), built on state of the art documents and specific customer data set. This technology generates an interconnected knowledge graph with nodes containing ontology's data. As far as the question-answering methodology is concerned, the application adopted an ontological schema capable of mapping the content of arbitrarily structured documents as well as text mining techniques and a pre-trained deep learning model for natural language processing.

By using the application, it is possible to automatically collect further data and improve the quality of the service, up to the possibility of sending personalized commercial offers to customers.

3.3 Validation Results

The company has made important advances regarding the digitization of knowledge, and data information associated with its products, especially about the line of automatic warehouses. They currently have ready-to-use features with broad usage and business prospects. The expansion of knowledge in the field of intelligent chatbots, with the application of machine learning, was particularly useful for the company, knowledge that promoted its use because it was considered extremely efficient, both in terms of the answers provided to the customer, and for saving person-hours to be used for customer care. Chatbots can be trained using question-answers through the application of natural language for learning. The validation of the pilot experimentation by the company was carried out both for the formalization/digitization of the basic knowledge (Frequently Asked Questions, structure system in hierarchical tree modality of the commercial questions for chatbots, definition of the domain ontology), and the applicability and management of the chatbot system. The company has shown considerable interest in the macro functionalities developed by suggesting the fundamental requirements from time to time, then validating them, which led to the implementation of the final prototype. In Fig. 3 are illustrated the radar charts about the validation of the macro functions (a) and (b).

4   Pilot 5: Main Functionalities and Results Assessment

This Pilot involved a small manufacturer of textile household products. The demonstrator for this pilot is characterized by two macro functions: (a) digitization of the subcontractor

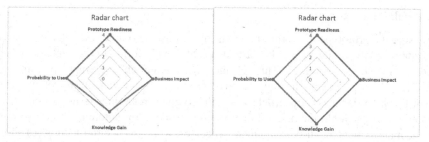

Fig. 3. Validation radar charts of the process digitization (left) and virtual assistant (right) functions.

management process; (b) sales forecast and recommendation models, hereinafter all described in more detail.

4.1 Macro Function (a): Digitization of the Subcontractor Management Process

The main objective of the experimentation was to introduce effective digital support tools able to reduce the manual activities, optimize the information flow between the actors, allow effective order management and create a community of subcontractors by a single user interface. The overall management of the production orders starts with a semi-automatic assignment of sub-orders to subcontractors. The overall business logic for this tool is addressed by combing the analysis of specific Key Performance Indicators (KPI), the real time monitoring of work in progress, the possibility of promptly detect, through automatic alerts and quickly react to unexpected events by allowing a synchronized management of logistics for the delivery and collection of the goods.

Through a web-based supervision platform, equipped with innovative support tools and integrated with the company legacy systems, the manager can control every single order in a simple and intuitive way.

In particular, AI based tools provide both an automatic detection of production tasks, directly achieved by the customer orders, as well as a "smart" proposal of their dispatching to the different sub-contractors. The platform then allows all the users involved to monitor, through a control checklist, the percentage of completion of the work in progress. The management of subcontractors like this structure guarantees an optimization of the times, the respect of the deadlines and the possibility of managing one or more orders in the same period.

4.2 Macro Function (b): Sales Forecast and Recommendation Models

The prototype platform integrates sales forecast and product recommendation models. Specifically, the Sales Forecast tool is important for monitoring sales trends, and the recommendation systems offer the possibility of suggesting the most suitable products for the specific customer, profiled based on his purchase choices.

4.3 Validation Results

By using the prototype platform, the company can use a complete set of functions for the control of the production orders. By means of this platform, it is possible to manage and control all the activities. Through the experimentation, the company gained its knowledge, matching with the digitization of business processes and the use of predictive algorithms. The business impact detected by the company regarding the use of both macro functions is very high: the macro function (a) is suitable for automating and speeding up the management and task assignment processes, while the macro function (b) allows the knowledge of products that will be more strategic. The pilot company will be able to use the platform tools for the next few years. In Fig. 4 are illustrated the radar charts about the validation of the macro functions (a) and (b).

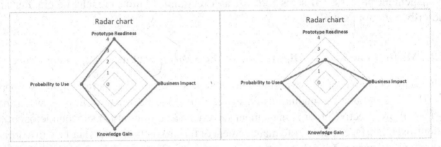

Fig. 4. Validation radar charts of the subcontractor management (left) and sales forecast – recommendation models (right) functions.

5 Pilot 6: Main Functionalities and Results Assessment

This experimental activity was carried out in collaboration with a small company, which provides products and services for telemedicine and e-health applications. Wearable technologies are now becoming available in everyday work life, enhancing existing safety functions and propelling novel applications that go beyond healthcare, wellness and workers safety. The real-time sensing and processing of data promise to improve and expand human life. Wearable technologies can collect real time and store individual body sensing data such as breathing, heart rate, blood pressure, Global Positioning System (GPS) location, heart rate acceleration, or environmental light level data. The project platform developed for this company then includes a "control room" just conceived for monitoring physiological parameters of drivers to provide assistance services to a public transport service company. In particular, we have addressed a use case on the monitoring of the health status of drivers exposed to diabetic risk. The driver is equipped with a Continuous Glucose Monitoring (CGM) device, capable of detecting and transmitting physiological parameters, such as blood sugar and others, indicative of their state of health [6]. The platform demonstrator is, therefore, mainly characterized by two macro functions: (a) process digitization, for efficient management of monitoring and intervention procedures through the control room; (b) predictive models improving safety risks. More details of both are provided below.

5.1 Macro Function (a): Supervision Process Digitization

A CGM sensor worn by driver during their working activities enables the remote control of diabetic status. The data acquired in quasi real time conditions (every 3–5 min), flows to the SD 4.0 platform feeding a Decision Support System (DSS) useful for supervisors monitoring through dashboards drivers' health conditions. The DSS generates alerts in cases of overcoming glucose thresholds (events of anomalous measured values). To ensure broad adoption of wearable technologies for workers safety, anyway, it should be recognized the importance of a new comprehensive incentive system as well as a clear legal framework to guarantee both social and economic benefits for all players involved, from workers to companies, to unions and insurance companies, to banks and legislators.

5.2 Macro Functionalities (b): Predictive Models

The prototype of control platform also integrates models for predicting various physiological parameters to generate early warnings and prevent risks during any working activities. This could happen, for instance, in cases of hypo- or hyper-glycaemia through the prediction of the glycemic index. To this purpose, different approaches have been developed and compared as traditional statistical methods (i.e. regression models) and Artificial Intelligence (AI) based models (neural networks). The use case addressed within the pilot considers the people transport situation, where the risk involves also the passengers. This approach anyway can be extended to many other working activities facing critical safety risk by specializing the software (risk detection and predictive models) as well as the hardware and, in particular, Personal Protective Equipment (PPE) such as eye protection, helmets and safety shoes equipped with built-in sensors and electronic devices.

5.3 Validation of Results

The company, through the development of the prototype platform, contributed to the development of a telemedicine platform focused on transport security field. This application represents a first exploration for the diversified use of technologies and skills typical of their native business (healthcare) with the aim of opening up new business fronts. Collaborative platforms integrating ML techniques offer prospects for the development of scalable solutions in different application contexts. Below are the radar charts concerning the macro functions (a) and (b).

For the macro function (a) the diagram refers to the management use of the control room, while for the macro function (b) the radar chart refers to the comparison of several predictive models in terms of the best service offered by "safe transport" with low risk of accidents (Fig. 5).

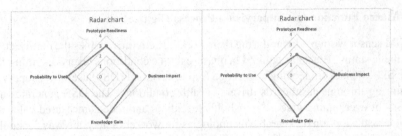

Fig. 5. Validation radar charts of the supervision (left) and predictive models (right) functions.

6   General Conclusions

All the six companies involved within the pilots increased their knowledge on the collaboration platforms and on the specific technologies and applications implemented for their case studies. The validation therefore primarily addressed the "TO BE" processes digitized and supported by the project prototype platform. In particular, most of the functionalities here discussed could have a significant impact on the future core business of each company, with a good probability of use. The adoption in the next few years of tools and AI applications like the ones tried within the experimental phase of the Project is highly probable for all pilots.

The business perspectives are clear and evident for all the companies involved in the final steps of project demonstrators. For all of them, artificial intelligence is an achievable goal for the immediate use of algorithms in production, process and service decision-making systems. The validation of project technologies, in general terms, is also inherent the scalability of the software framework. The use of platform testers such as managers and business executives of pilot cases provided important feedback on the usability and scalability of the entire SD 4.0 framework, which is declinable across multiple domains relating to the production processes of SMEs.

Finally, we are aware that the main goal achieved is to increase knowledge gain by practicing on innovative technologies and algorithms, rather than developing generic software prototypes. This is since each individual entrepreneur has shown considerable interest in understanding the potential of new approaches, such as the predictive algorithms and advanced classification techniques, in terms of the company's strategic business.

From this point of view, the topics of scientific research have also proved to be of considerable interest and curiosity, given that the SD40 project has led the managers and entrepreneurs of the companies involved to familiarize themselves with the use of all the innovative technologies implemented.

Acknowledgments. Smart District 4.0 Project has been supported thanks to the Italian *Fondo per la Crescita Sostenibile, Bando "Agenda Digitale", D.M. Oct. 15th, 2014.* This is an initiative promoted by Italian Ministry for the Economic Development aiming to sustain the digital transformation of the SMEs. Authors wish to express special thanks to the Noovle team for the fruitful collaboration all along provided during the development of the entire project.

References

1. Massaro, A., Magaletti, N., Cosoli, G.: Project management: radargram plot to validate stake-holder technology implemented in a research project. Zenodo (2022). https://doi.org/10.5281/zenodo.5872386
2. Magaletti, N., Cosoli, G., Leogrande, A. Massaro, A.: Predictive maintenance and engineered processes in mechatronic industry: an Italian case study. SSRN 4026193 (2022)
3. Massaro, A.: Electronic in advanced research industry: from Industry 4.0 to Industry 5.0 advances. Wiley/IEEE (2021). ISBN: 9781119716877. https://books.google.it/books?id=LP5FEAAAQBAJ
4. Magaletti, N., Cosoli, G., Leogrande, A. Massaro, A.: Process engineering and AI sales prediction: the case study of an Italian small textile company. SSRN 4026183 (2022)
5. Massaro, A., Magaletti, N., Cosoli, G., Giardinelli, V., Leogrande, A.: Text mining approaches oriented on customer care efficiency (2022). https://doi.org/10.21203/rs.3.rs-1339169/v1
6. Massaro, A., Magaletti, N., Cosoli, G., Leogrande, A., Cannone, F.: Use of machine learning to predict the glycemic status of patients with diabetes. In: The 2nd International Electronic Conference on Healthcare (2022)

1st International Workshop on Web Applications for Life Sciences (WALS 2022)

1st International Workshop on Web Applications for Life Sciences (WALS 2022)

Anna Bernasconi[1] ⓘ, Pietro Pinoli[1] ⓘ, Giuseppe Agapito[2] ⓘ,
and Luca Nanni[3] ⓘ

[1] Department of Electronics, Information, and Bioengineering – Politecnico
di Milano
{anna.bernasconi, ietro.pinoli}@polimi.it
[2] Department of Law, Economics and Social Sciences – "Magna Græcia"
University of Catanzaro
agapito@unicz.it
[3] Department of Computational Biology – University of Lausanne
luca.nanni@unil.ch

The recent advances in unraveling the secrets of human conditions and diseases have encouraged new paradigms for their diagnosis and treatment. In addition, the COVID-19 pandemic has attracted increasing attention toward the genetic mechanisms of viruses and infected hosts. The information related to these phenomena is increasing at unprecedented rates, directly impacting the design and development of data management pipelines and their applications. New ways of processing and exposing data and knowledge on the Web in healthcare and life sciences environments are thus strongly needed.

The International Workshop on Web Applications for Life Sciences (WALS) was held in 2022 for the first time.It aimed at being an initial meeting forum for Web Engineering, Data Management, and Bioinformatics researchers working on life sciences problems, offering the opportunity to share, discuss and find new approaches to support Search, Knowledge Extraction, and Data Science on the Web, thereby achieving important results for healthcare, precision medicine, biology, genomics, and virology.

The workshop has attracted high quality submissions; three papers (two full papers and one short paper) have been selected after a blind review process that involved two experts from the field for each submission. The full paper "CitrusGenome: A Bioinformatics Tool to Characterize, Visualize, and Explore Large Citrus Variant Datasets" was proposed by Alberto García, Ana León, Mireia Costa, Oscar Pastor, Daniel González-Ibea, Estela Pérez-Román, Carles Borredà, Javier Terol, Victoria Ibanez, Francisco R. Tadeo, and Manuel Talón. It discusses a web system to support research on genomic traits of agricultural interest. The full paper ``The Laniakea Dashboard and storage encryption components: a foundation for developing on-demand cloud services for Life Science`` was proposed by Marco Antonio Tangaro, Marica Antonacci, Pietro Mandreoli, Daniele Colombo, Nadina Foggetti, Giacinto Donvito, Graziano Pesole, and Federico Zambelli. It introduces the use of a web application and encryption mechanisms in the context of Life Science-oriented cloud services.

The short paper "Integration and Visual Analysis of Biomolecular Networks" was written by Paolo Perlasca, Marco Frasca, Cheick Tidiane Ba, Jessica Gliozzo, Marco Notaro, Mario Pennacchioni, Giorgio Valentini, and Marco Mesiti. It presents a web application that supports users in the integration and hierarchical navigation of several biomolecular networks.

All papers provided significant insights related to the problem under investigation; they also confirmed an interesting technical program that stimulated discussion.The program was complemented with an invited keynote by Raffaele Calogero (University of Torino) on the ability of current web applications to fulfil the needs of life science scientists.

Acknowledgements. We thank the Program Committee members for their hard work in reviewing papers, the authors for submitting and presenting their works, and the ICWE 2022 organizing committee for supporting our workshop.We also thank ICWE 2022 workshop chairs Cinzia Cappiello and Azzurra Ragone for their direction and guidance.

WALS 2022 Invited Talk

Are Web Applications Fulfilling the Needs of Life Science Scientists?

Raffaele A. Calogero

Department of Molecular Biotechnology and Health Sciences,
University of Torino

Abstract. Since biology and medicine are disciplines generating a massive amount of complex and hard-to-decipher data, bioinformatics is pervading the life science fields. Consequently, bioinformatics is a constantly growing field, producing a massive amount of computing tools. However, life science suffers from the lack of an adequate number of bioinformaticians. Furthermore, the number of life scientists understanding the need of building a background in basic programming is still very limited. The critical points highlighted above, taken together with the limited access to computing resources for many life scientists, have favored the development of a lot of web-based bioinformatics applications.In this presentation, I wish to focus on the state of the art of web applications for life science and discuss their strength and limits. Furthermore, I wish to propose the possibility to move to more advanced web applications, where users can interact with them in a more sophisticated way, but without the need of acquiring coding skills, e.g. using syntax-free programming or a no-code approach.

CitrusGenome: A Bioinformatics Tool to Characterize, Visualize, and Explore Large Citrus Variant Datasets

Alberto García Simón(✉)[iD], Ana León Palacio[iD], Mireia Costa[iD],
Oscar Pastor[iD], Daniel Gonzalez-Ibea, Estela Pérez-Román, Carles Borredà,
Javier Terol, Victoria Ibanez, Francisco R. Tadeo, and Manuel Talon

Universitat Politècnica de València, Valencia, Spain
algarsi3@pros.upv.es

Abstract. Citrus constitutes one of the most important and appreciated fruit crops, cultivated worldwide with an estimated annual production of 120 million tonnes. The amount of citrus genomic data currently available is considerable, and it is continually increasing at an unforeseen speed. Since the first citrus genome sequence was released in 2011, several genomes from relevant citrus species, varieties, and clones have been sequenced using next-generation sequencing technologies. This perspective opens significant opportunities for new and original discoveries based on SNP studies. However, the massive amount of publicly available data poses several challenges requiring further effort. In this work, we present CitrusGenome, a Genome Information System that overcomes these challenges and provides an efficient, user-friendly tool for performing SNP discovery analysis in citrus.

Keywords: Citrus · Genomics · Web application · Knowledge extraction · Big data

1 Introduction

Citrus is an important fruit crop that is cultivated worldwide with an estimated annual production of 120 million tonnes, with China, Brazil and the Mediterranean regions being the main producers. Citrus varieties include orange, mandarin, lemon, lime, grapefruit, citron and pummelo, and they are produced for fresh consumption and processed food. Genome resources in citrus have been increasing over the last decade and are currently rather abundant [21]. With the advent of next-generation sequencing technologies, several additional genomes have been *de novo* assembled [19,20,22].

All this amount of available citrus genomes is an excellent opportunity to perform comparative genomics, which focuses on analyzing variations of gene content, transposable elements, large genome rearrangements, structural variations, and small polymorphisms. Among the latter, single nucleotide polymorphisms

(SNPs) and small insertions and deletions (INDELS) are of great importance for plant breeding since they have proven to be major genetic determinants of relevant traits of agricultural interest [4,23]. SNPs have become the preferred choice as molecular markers for plant breeding programs due to their high level of polymorphism and reproducibility [13,17].

As the price of sequencing technologies drops, the number of available citrus genomes increases exponentially. To this day, thousands of genomes from several citrus varieties have been generated. This situation offers new opportunities for SNP discovery, but it poses several challenges. This work presents CitrusGenome; a Genome Information System developed in collaboration with the IVIA genomic center (*Insituto Valenciano de Investigaciones Agrarias*) to deal with these challenges and provide an efficient and user-friendly SNP discovery tool. CitrusGenome is a Model-Driven Development (MDD) [15] tool that is supported by the Conceptual Schema of The Citrus Genome (CSCG) [8], which precisely identifies and models the specific concepts and particularities of the working use-case. The CSCG allows us to characterize and integrate the data more rapidly, and it is the foundation of the database schema.

The remainder of the paper is structured as follows: Sect. 2 motivates the need for CitrusGenome. Section 3 presents the data model used to prepare the data and implement the platform. Section 4 illustrates the data preparation process. Section 5 details the architecture and functionality of CitrusGenome. Section 6 shows an example of use of CitrusGenome. Section 7 discusses the implications of CitrusGenome.

2   Motivation

The large amount of available genomics data poses several challenges related to computational efficiency, data management expertise, user interaction, and the inherent limitations of the several existing data types. Our collaboration with the IVIA allowed us to clarify these challenges and identify their implications in the IVIA's genomic big data analytics.

1. Computational efficiency: programming knowledge between the IVIA's bioinformatics is limited to Python scripting, a feasible procedure for a limited number of use cases. SNP query at the whole-genome level involving several samples is time-consuming, and this scripting is limited to people with specific knowledge and computing skills. Therefore, there is a need for a more efficient solution that does not require computing skills.
2. Data management expertise: These analyses often require *ad hoc* strategies to deal with the peculiarities of the data. For instance, clonal propagation and the occurrence of somatic mutation produce high rates of tissue chimerism, increasing the amount of noise background in SNP detection. Another example is that introgression events in domesticated varieties and genome rearrangements (deletions or translocations) create an unevenly distributed heterozygosity pattern across the genome, complicating a correct interpretation of the data. Therefore, there is a need to address such domain particularities.

3. User Interaction: IVIA's bioinformaticians declared that the user interfaces of most of the current genomics tools are unintuitive and hard to use. Such a statement is in line with the work of Pavelin et al., which reports that bioinformatics tools have frequently ignored the design of their user interfaces [16]. Therefore, there is a need for an intuitive and easy-to-use solution.
4. Data types: SNP analysis require integrating several types of genomic information, including gene topology and functionality characterization, functional annotation, biochemical pathway information, and protein domain composition, among others. Therefore, there is a need to integrate effectively the diverse and heterogeneous amount of data used.

3   Data Model

The CSCG is the ontological basis that correctly provides all the necessary information to manage citrus genomic data. IVIA experts provided their biological knowledge to understand and interpret the data, which allowed us to transform an immense amount of heterogeneous data into a well-defined conceptual schema to extract value using data analysis. Throughout these sessions, we analyzed the data to identify which elements were of higher importance, which allowed us to create and expand the CSCG through an iterative process until a stable version was achieved. Next, we introduce the resulting schema, a precise representation of the genomic domain tailored to the specific needs of the IVIA (see Fig. 1). This schema can be grouped into three main views:

The Structural View: This view describes the different regions that can be identified in the DNA sequence of citrus, providing a hierarchical dependency between the regions (i.e., CDSs are located in mRNA, and an mRNA is located in a gene).

The Functional View: This view groups entities with a given function inside our body. These entities include gene products (i.e., proteins and their structure), biological pathways, and ortholog groups. This view aims to effectively provide information about how gene products interact with the organism.

The Variations View: The last view models the variations that can occur with respect to the reference sequence, the appearance of such changes in specific citrus individuals, and their predicted effect using software annotation tools (i.e., SnpEff) [6].

4   Data Preparation

We prepared the data through three activities: data obtainment, data enrichment, and data transformation:

Data Obtainment: Five different data sources have been used to perform the Data Obtainment activity. The first source is the data that the IVIA has generated over the years by sequencing whole-genome sequences of citrus (i.e., variations in VCF format). The first version of CitrusGenome contains an initial set

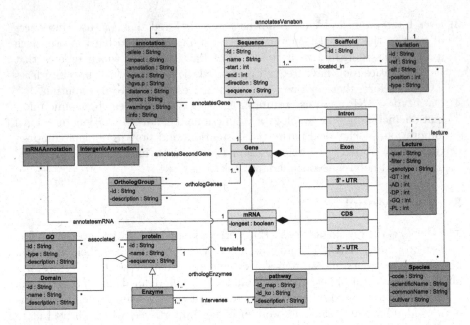

Fig. 1. The Conceptual Schema of the Citrus Genome. The structural view is depicted in green, the functional view is depicted in orange, and the variations view is depicted in blue (Color figure online).

of 57 full genome sequences from the most representative citrus varieties. The second source is the Citrus Genome Database (CGDB), from which sequences of reference and sequence features (e.g., genes, coding sequences, or untranslated regions, etc.) have been obtained. The third source is Gene Ontology [2,14], from which data to enrich genes with functional information has been obtained. The fourth source is InterPro [12], from which protein characterization data has been obtained. The fifth source is the Kyoto encyclopedia of genes and genomes (KEGG) [1], from which pathway and enzyme data have been obtained. The result of this activity is the set of data used to create the CitrusGenome database.

Data Enrichment: A functional effect prediction software, SnpEff [6], has been used to predict the putative effect of the variations gathered from the 1,000 genomes obtained by the IVIA in the Data Obtainment activity. The result of this activity is the DNA variation files annotated with additional information such as functional consequences.

Data Harmonization: the CSCG guided the data harmonization process, which was executed by a set of Python scripts. The PyVCF library [5] was used to parse VCF data, and the PySAM library [7] was used to parse SAM/BAM format files. Besides the Python scripts, three additional tools have been used to reduce the execution time of the scripts. First, we used Cython [3], a Python language extension, to compile to C code. Second, we used bgzip, a Samtools utility, to compress and decompress genome sequence data. Third, we used Tabix [11], a Samtools library, to index tab-delimited genomic data. The result of this activity is a set of CSV files with harmonized, technology-agnostic data that was prepared to populate the database system. For each class and each relationship of the CSCG, a CSV file was generated.

Database Construction: We constructed the database using Oracle as the database management system because it allows us to use native bitmap indexing [28], which is a feature that is used to increase query efficiency when filtering by low-cardinality data (i.e., data with few different values). Additional elements have been defined to improve query construction and efficiency: i) a non-materialized view (a virtual table that does not physically store data) to simplify query construction; ii) a materialized view (a virtual table that physically stores data) to simplify query construction and increase its query efficiency; iii) two temporary tables (two virtual tables that are created and destroyed during query execution) to increase query efficiency. The result of Database Construction was an instantiated and populated database with the harmonized data (i.e., 551 million elements, 1.26 billion relationships, and 6.87 billion attributes) (Fig. 2).

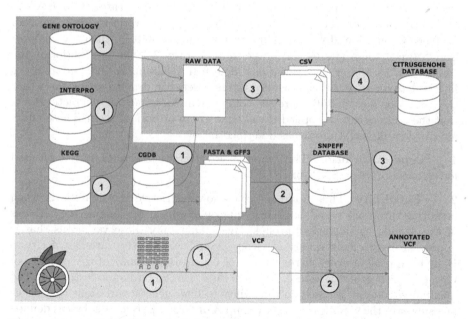

Fig. 2. Schematization of the data preparation. External data sources are depicted with a green background. IVIA data is depicted with a lilac background and includes the DNA variations identified in their crop studies. The data generated during the data preparation step is depicted with a yellow background. Numbers represent the data transformations carried out during each activity: 1 represents the data obtainment activity, 2 represents the data enrichment activity, 3 represents the data harmonization activity, and 4 represents the database construction activity (Color figure online).

5   CitrusGenome Platform

Architecture

Our CitrusGenome tool has a three-tier architecture (see Fig. 1). The first tier is the frontend, which was developed in javascript using the Angular framework and multiple open-source visualization libraries. The second tier is the backend. It was developed in javascript using node.js, which is a javascript runtime built on the V8 JavaScript engine. The communication between the frontend and the backend is twofold: tha backend has an Application Programming Interface (API) that uses the GraphQL query language; and there is a bi-directional, real-time communication channel through WebSockets that uses the socket.io framework. The third tier is the database, which was developed using the Oracle database management system. The communication between the backend and the database uses Knex.js, which is an SQL query builder library for javascript.

Functionality

CitrusGenome allows advanced SNP discovery to be performed through a two-step workflow. In Step 1, two groups of citrus varieties are created (Group A and Group B). In Step 2, the variations of the selected citrus varieties are compared.

Once Group A and Group B have been defined (Step 1), then the comparison between these groups can be performed (Step 2). The tool performs the comparison as follows: the variations identified in Group A and Group B are filtered based on a set of user-defined filters. Users can define a set of filters that the variations must fulfill before the comparison. An important characteristic is that these filters can be applied to only one group or both of them. These filters are divided into eight groups as described below.

1 — **Type of variation**: This group allows the type of variation to be selected for comparison (e.g., SNPs or INDELs).

2 — **Flexibility**: This group refers to how restrictive the analysis is when accepting variations based on their frequency of appearance among the varieties of the defined citrus variety groups. By default, only those variations that i) appear in every citrus variety of Group A and none of the varieties of Group B, or ii) appear in every citrus variety of Group B and none of the varieties of Group A are accepted. However, in some cases, this might be too restrictive. The 'flexibility' concept is based on the ability to filter genetic variations that occur in a subset of the varieties of either Group A or Group B. Such a subset is defined by indicating a minimum and maximum threshold of varieties to be considered. There are multiple reasons for including this option: working with large groups of varieties, genetic variations that are wrongly identified or mapped in the sequencing process, or varieties that exhibit a phenotype caused by different genes, etc.

The filter allows setting two constraints per group to be set. The first constraint indicates the minimum number of times that variations should be reported in one group (e.g., if this group contains four citrus varieties, we can discard variations that are not reported in all of them, or we can accept variations that are reported in at least three varieties, for instance). The second constraint indicates the maximum number of times that variations can be reported in the other group (e.g., if the other group contains four citrus varieties, we can discard variations that are reported in any variety, or we can accept variations that are reported in at most one variety) (e.g., having two groups of four citrus varieties (Group A and Group B), we can search for variations that appear in at least in 4 varieties of Group A and in at most in 0 varieties of Group B, or in at least in 3 varieties of Group A and in at most in 1 variety of Group B).

3 — Quality: This group allows a minimum threshold to be set for the total depth and genotype quality values of the variations (e.g., variations with a genotype quality higher than 70).

4 — Annotated impact: This group allows variations to be filtered based on their predicted putative impact. It is specific to SnpEff prediction software (e.g., variations with a moderate putative effect).

5 — Allele balance: This group allows multiple independent ranges of allele balance values to be indicated for Group A and Group B. (e.g., heterozygous variations in Group A and homozygous alternative variations in Group B).

6 — Sequence feature: This group allows searching for variations in a specific sequence feature (e.g., search for variations located in UTR).

7 — Sequence region: This group allows searching for variations in specific genomic regions (e.g., a gene or a larger chromosome region).

8 — Protein-related element: This group allows searching for variations that affect protein-related elements. This includes filtering variations that affect a specific protein, pathway, domain, or gene functionality (e.g., variations that modify biological entities that participate in a specific pathway).

Once the filters of the analysis have been established, the symmetric difference of the resulting groups of variations is performed. This comparison is performed at a genotype level. This means that if two varieties have the same variation with different genotypes, they are considered to be different variations. Finally, the user receives a unique identifier that can be used to determine if the analysis is in the queue, ongoing, or finished. The result of the analysis is presented to the user through different visualizations. The visualization is divided into three parts. In the first part, there is a visual representation of the obtained variations distributed over the chromosomes.

The second part is composed of a set of charts that provide a general, high-level visualization of the obtained variations that are grouped based on multiple criteria: the number of obtained variations per citrus variety, per chromosome, per predicted putative impact, per gene functionality based on Gene Ontology annotations, and per affected enzymes based on KEGG annotations.

The third part contains an advanced grid that allows for a more specific, low-level analysis of the data. This grid provides researchers with a tool to do the following: perform advanced filtering of variations based on multiple criteria, show/hide columns, group the variations by any column any number of times, and perform pivoting and matrix operations.

Apart from the analysis page, the user can see the number of identified variations, genotype quality, and read depth for each sequenced variety in the database. This information is shown at a general level, where the information is shown aggregated, and genotype level, where the information is shown on a per genotype basis.

6   Using CitrusGenome

We now show how CitrusGenome can quickly generate knowledge from data. In this example, we identify differences between Citrus clementine (clementine) and the Citrus sinensis (sweet orange) that affect DNA repair and DNA replication processes. First, we create the required groups: Group A contains sequences of Citrus clementine from three cultivars (i.e., its origin) and Group B contains sequences of Citrus Sinensis from four cultivars. Second, we establish the desired filters:

1. **Type** of variation: SNP
2. **Flexibility**: At least in 3 varieties of group B and at most in 0 varieties of group A **or** at least in 2 varieties of group A and at most in 0 varieties of group B.
3. **Quality**: $DP >= 10$ and $GQ >= 90$.
4. **Annotated Impact**: High, moderate, low, and modifier.
5. **Allele Balance**: No filter applied.
6. **Sequence Feature**: No filter applied.
7. **Sequence Region**: No filter applied.
8. **Protein-related element**: genes annotated with the GO:0006281 or the GO:0006260 codes, which correspond to DNA repair and DNA replication respectively.

CitrusGenome identifies 5,108 variations (see Fig. 3). As Fig 4 shows, Citrus sinensis varieties contain almost four times more variations than Citrus clementine varieties, and half of the variations are located in the chromosomes 2, 5, and 8. Besides, only 18 annotations have a high impact and almost 75% of the variations alter transferases enzymes[1].

Using the grid's capabilities, we can identify the most relevant variations (i.e., those whose effect is HIGH and the altered protein has a relevant role in biological pathways of interest). As a result, only four variations have been identified (see Table 1) whose effect is that three premature stop codons appeared, four start codons were lost, and one exon was lost. These changes affect one enzyme (the DNA-directed DNA polymerase) and two metabolic pathways (the purine and pyrimidine metabolisms). These results are consistent since we are looking for

---

[1] Any enzyme that catalyze the transfer of specific group of atoms from one molecule to another.

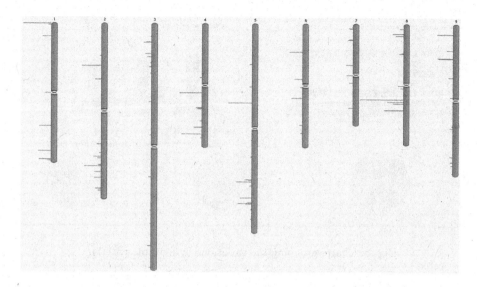

Fig. 3. Distribution of the variations over the citrus chromosomes.

variations that alter DNA repair and replication, purines and pyrimidines make up nucleotide bases (the building block for DNA), and the DNA-directed DNA polymerase catalyzes DNA-template-directed extension of the DNA strand.

Table 1. Relevant variations identified using the grid's capabilities.

DNA Position	Gene	Gene Description	DNA Change	Protein	AA Position	AA Change	Effect
Chr2-29,774,121	14398	Y-Family DNA polymerase H	A > T	14398	730	Leu > Stop	Stop gained
				14408	724	Leu > Stop	Stop gained
Chr5-16,510,959	86	DNA binding	T > A	86	1	Met > -	Start lost
				124	1	Met > -	Start lost
Chr5-16,510,960	86	DNA binding	G > T	86	1	Met > -	Start lost
				124	1	Met > -	Start lost
Chr8-18,024,731	27762	Replicator Factor C1	G > T	27762	911	Ser > Stop	Stop gained, splice region

7   Discussion

CitrusGenome is a repository of citrus genomic data and a genomic tool that provides a highly efficient, flexible, and in-depth SNP discovery analysis with advanced data visualization and user interaction. The unique characteristics of this tool, which are detailed throughout the rest of the article (i.e., the boost of computational efficiency, automation of tasks, and the improvement of data management), make it a relevant bioinformatics platform for citrus-related studies. Although there are other tools available to work with citrus genomic data, none of them offers the particularities of the CitrusGenome platform regarding comparative analysis of specific citrus DNA sequences.

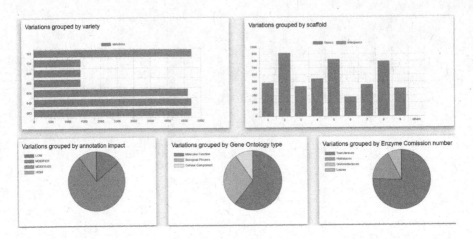

Fig. 4. Charts grouping the variations by multiple criteria.

Citrus is composed of about 160 genera and includes more than 1600 species, and the taxonomy, origin, and dispersal of citrus have been a long-standing matter of controversy [18]. In this context, comparing tens of grouped citrus DNA sequences is of great importance because it allows creating more rapid phylogenetic relationships. Current citrus cultivars are primarily hybrids of three fundamental pivotal species: pure wild mandarin, citron, and pummelo. For instance, most edible mandarins contain varying amounts of pummelo introgression that may account for up to 20% of the genome sequence, revealing that introgression has played a fundamental role in citrus domestication, as in other crops [9]. This situation has technical implications for the computational analysis of genetic diversity since introgressions tend to generate high heterozygosity rates. CitrusGenome considers this characteristic and offers users solutions to deal with such heterozygosity.

CitrusGenome provides a high degree of flexibility and freedom to bioinformaticians when performing the SNP discovery process, which is accomplished by implementing several features such as genotype-based characterization, complex attribute filtering, variation search based putative effect, etc. Far beyond their use in plants, SNPs are broadly utilized in other model organisms and humans [10], highlighting the interest in generating a computational framework for such analysis. One of the advantages of CitrusGenome is that, since it is model-based, the cost to modify the tool to process human data effectively is minimum because the only required change is to update the conceptual schema used to develop the tool. Thus, their benefits could be used in other domains such as health and precision medicine. Citrus SNP discovery analyses are a relevant topic in genomic studies. CitrusGenome provides a comprehensive set of SNP and INDEL variations, and it supports performing complex, in-depth analyses through an easy and intuitive user interface. Several challenges related to computational efficiency, automation, data management expertise, and the inherent limitations of data types have been enumerated in the Introduction. CitrusGenome has been developed to overcome these challenges by performing SNP queries involving several individuals at a whole-genome level in minutes, thus providing an efficient solution. Since computer skills are not necessary to use CitrusGenome, efficient access to the data and knowledge generation is available to anyone. User experience has also been a relevant consideration when we developed it. We integrated a huge amount of genomic information, including gene topology and functionality characterization, functional annotation, biochemical pathway information, and protein domain composition with the variation information, all of which allow for efficient SNP analyses. The extensive set of implemented filters and the high degree of flexibility of the tool provides the necessary mechanisms to deal with the particularities of citrus genomic data, such as the high rates of heterozygosity. Finally, CitrusGenome offfers plenty of visualization components of variation distribution for proper interpretation. In summary, CitrusGenome is an advanced bioinformatics platform to perform complex SNP discovery analysis.

Acknowledgments. This work has been developed with the financial support of the Spanish State Research Agency and the Generalitat Valenciana under the projects PROMETEO/2018/176, INBIO 2021/AP2021-05, MICIN/AEI/ 10.13039/501100011033, and INNEST/2021/57 and co-financed with ERDF and the European Union NextGenerationEU/PRTR.

References

1. Aoki-Kinoshita, K.F., et al.: Gene annotation and pathway mapping in KEGG. In: Bergman, N.H. (ed.) Comparative Genomics. Methods in Molecular Biology, vol. 396, pp. 71–91. Springer, Cham (2007). https://doi.org/10.1007/978-1-59745-515-2_6 iSSN: 10643745

2. Ashburner, M., et al.: Gene ontology: tool for the unification of biology. Nat. Genet. **25**(1), 25–29 (2000). https://doi.org/10.1038/75556

3. Behnel, S., et al.: Cython: The best of both worlds. Comput. Sci. Eng. **13**(2), 31–39 (2011). https://doi.org/10.1109/MCSE.2010.118, http://ieeexplore.ieee.org/document/5582062/

4. Butelli, E., et al.: Changes in anthocyanin production during domestication of Citrus. Plant Physiol. **173**(4), 2225–2242 (2017). https://doi.org/10.1104/pp.16.01701

5. Casbon, J.: PyVCF-A Variant Call Format Parser for Python (2012). https://pyvcf.readthedocs.io

6. Cingolani, P., et al.: A program for annotating and predicting the effects of single nucleotide polymorphisms, SnpEff: SNPs in the genome of Drosophila melanogaster strain w1118; iso-2; iso-3. Fly **6**(2), 80–92 (2012)

7. Developers, P.: Pysam: a Python module for reading and manipulating SAM/BAM/VCF/BCF files (2018). https://github.com/pysam-developers/pysam

8. García S, A., et al.: Towards an effective and efficient management of genome data: an information systems engineering perspective. In: Cappiello, C., Ruiz, M. (eds.) CAiSE 2019. LNBIP, vol. 350, pp. 99–110. Springer, Cham (2019). https://doi.org/10.1007/978-3-030-21297-1_9

9. Janzen, G.M., et al.: The extent of adaptive wild introgression in crops. New Phytol. **221**, 1279–1288 (2019). https://doi.org/10.1111/nph.15457. iSSN: 14698137

10. Kumar, S., et al.: SNP discovery through next-generation sequencing and its applications. Int. J. Plant Genomics **2012**, 1–15 (2012). https://doi.org/10.1155/2012/831460

11. Li, H.: Tabix: fast retrieval of sequence features from generic TAB-delimited files. Bioinformatics **27**(5), 718–719 (2011). https://doi.org/10.1093/bioinformatics/btq671

12. Mitchell, A.L., et al.: InterPro in 2019: improving coverage, classification and access to protein sequence annotations. Nucleic Acids Res. **47**(D1), D351–D360 (2019). https://doi.org/10.1093/nar/gky1100

13. Nadeem, M.A., et al.: DNA molecular markers in plant breeding: current status and recent advancements in genomic selection and genome editing. Biotechnol. Biotechnol. Equip. **32**, 261–285 (2018). https://doi.org/10.1080/13102818.2017.1400401. iSSN: 13102818

14. Ontology, T.G.: The gene ontology resource: 20 years and still GOing strong. Nucleic Acids Res. **47**(D1), D330–D338 (2019). https://doi.org/10.17863/CAM.36439

15. Pastor, O., et al.: Model-Driven Architecture in Practice: A Software Production Environment Based on Conceptual Modeling. Springer (2007). https://doi.org/10.1007/978-3-540-71868-0, google-Books-ID: eKfKNEQs6XMC

16. Pavelin, K., et al.: Bioinformatics meets user-centred design: a perspective. PLoS Comput. Biol. **8**(7), e1002554 (2012). https://doi.org/10.1371/journal.pcbi.1002554

17. Rafalski, A.: Applications of single nucleotide polymorphisms in crop genetics. Curr. Opin. Plant Biol. **5**, 94–100 (2002). https://doi.org/10.1016/S1369-5266(02)00240-6. iSSN: 13695266

18. Talon, M., et al.: The Genus Citrus. Elsevier, Amsterdam (2020). https://doi.org/10.1016/c2016-0-02375-6, https://www.elsevier.com/books/the-genus-citrus/talon/978-0-12-812163-4

19. Wang, L., et al.: Genome of wild mandarin and domestication history of mandarin. Mol. Plant **11**(8), 1024–1037 (2018). https://doi.org/10.1016/j.molp.2018.06.001

20. Wang, X., et al.: Genomic analyses of primitive, wild and cultivated citrus provide insights into asexual reproduction. Nat. Genet. **49**(5), 765–772 (2017). https://doi.org/10.1038/ng.3839

21. Wu, G.A., et al.: Sequencing of diverse mandarin, pummelo and orange genomes reveals complex history of admixture during citrus domestication. Nat. Biotechnol. **32**(7), 656–662 (2014). https://doi.org/10.1038/nbt.2906

22. Xu, Q., et al.: The draft genome of sweet orange (Citrus sinensis). Nat. Genet. **45**(1), 59–66 (2013). https://doi.org/10.1038/ng.2472

23. Zheng, X., et al.: Natural variation in CCD4 promoter underpins species-specific evolution of red coloration in citrus peel. Mol. Plant **12**(9), 1294–1307 (2019). https://doi.org/10.1016/j.molp.2019.04.014

The Laniakea Dashboard and Storage Encryption Components: A Foundation for Developing On-Demand Cloud Services for Life Science

Marco Antonio Tangaro[1,2] , Marica Antonacci[2] , Pietro Mandreoli[1,3] ,
Daniele Colombo[3] , Nadina Foggetti[2] , Giacinto Donvito[2] ,
Graziano Pesole[1,4] , and Federico Zambelli[1,3(✉)]

[1] Institute of Biomembranes, Bioenergetics and Molecular Biotechnologies, National Research Council (CNR), Via Giovanni Amendola 122/O, 70126 Bari, Italy
[2] National Institute for Nuclear Physics (INFN), Section of Bari, Via Orabona 4, 70126 Bari, Italy
[3] Department of Biosciences, University of Milan, Via Celoria 26, 20133 Milano, Italy
federico.zambelli@unimi.it
[4] Department of Biosciences, Biotechnologies and Biopharmaceutics, University of Bari, Via Orabona 4, 70126 Bari, Italy

Abstract. Laniakea makes easy the provisioning of on-demand Galaxy and other applications on scientific e-infrastructures. We describe its user dashboard and storage encryption modules as a versatile foundation for other Life Science oriented Cloud services.

Keywords: Laniakea · Galaxy · Cloud computing

1 Background

The Life Science community faces the peculiar situation of producing and needing to access, process, and share an enormous amount of data from a multiplicity of sources thanks to high-throughput technologies becoming increasingly available to research laboratories [1]. A common bottleneck for fully exploiting those data is often represented by inadequate access to computing infrastructures. This inadequacy can take many forms, e.g., an actual lack of local computing resources, but more often, it is due to usability barriers that prevent taking advantage of existing infrastructures.

Many initiatives have recently aimed to improve access to scientific computing infrastructures and develop HPC [2, 3] and Cloud [4–6] solutions targeted at several research communities. If, on the one hand, those solutions can democratize access to cutting-edge computational and storage resources also to individual scientists and small

---

M. A. Tangaro and M. Antonacci—contributed equally to this work.

G. Agapito et al. (Eds.): ICWE 2022 Workshops, CCIS 1668, pp. 179–191, 2023.
https://doi.org/10.1007/978-3-031-25380-5_14

research groups, on the other hand, they often rely on heterogeneous technologies, and generally accepted standards have yet to emerge [1, 7].

Initiatives like ELIXIR [8] and EOSC-Life [9] work towards facilitating and promoting access to public Cloud and HPC resources at the European level for life science, coordinating and stimulating the adoption of shared solutions, hiding the complexity of the underlying distributed infrastructure to provide unhindered access to data and analytical tools.

The useGalaxy [10] public servers and the on-demand platform Laniakea@ReCaS [11], for example, exploit the Galaxy workflow manager [12] to provide computational and storage resources for the analysis of reasonably large datasets from various life science research domains such as genomics, proteomics, metabolomics, and imaging.

In particular, Cloud-based platforms for the provisioning of on-demand services are now beginning to emerge, enabling academic users to launch, use, and manage private instances of popular applications, covering advanced user requirements such as customisability, intensive use of IT resources, and data privacy and protection.

For instance, services based on Laniakea [13] can provide a straightforward solution for users needing complete control over their Galaxy production environment, such as training, development, or priority access to computational resources [11]. The platform also allows users to store the data undergoing analysis on encrypted volumes, significantly increasing their security. This feature can be helpful, for example, to meet General Data Protection Regulation (GDPR) compliance requirements for online services processing special categories of personal data, like clinical and human genomics ones. Indeed, the European data protection Board (EdpB) Recommendation on measures that supplement transfer tools to ensure compliance with the EU level of protection of personal data, suggests the use of encryption algorithm and its parametrization as one of the possible risk-mitigating countermeasures, along with data (pseudo)anonymization [14]. In the context of Task 6.6 of the EOSC-Pillar Project we have produced a study concerning the ethical and legal requirement needed to guarantee an effective balance between the FAIR, Open Science and Open Access Principles and the GDPR obligations [15].

However, accessible gateways to those on-demand services are needed to promote their uptake by the users' community.

The PaaS Orchestrator Dashboard has been developed in the context of the DEEP-HybridDataCloud project [4] for the selection and configuration of on-demand services. The Laniakea Dashboard further extends the Orchestrator Dashboard to include the storage encryption module and introduce several other Galaxy-specific features. However, in principle, they are general enough to be used for generating web interfaces for any on-demand service based on the same PaaS technology. For example, Fig. 1 shows the interface of Laniakea for the deployment of Galaxy-based virtual environments for bioinformatics and the same dashboard with applications to serve the Institute for Nuclear Physics Cloud.

We think that facilitating, both from the user and the service provider perspective, the deployment of on-demand software over cloud infrastructures, attaching it to encrypted storage if needed, can provide a boost to the adoption of cloud applications to serve the Life Science domain. Therefore, we released the Laniakea Dashboard and encryption components to ease the development of other on-demand services based on the INDIGO PaaS layer [16], and we detail herein their implementation to facilitate and encourage their adoption.

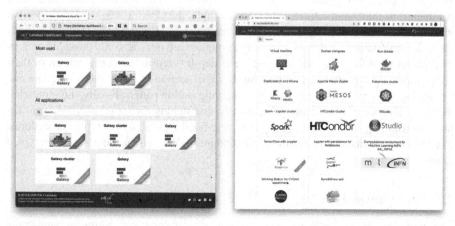

Fig. 1. The application selection page generated by the Dashboard for Laniakea (left) and INFN Cloud (right).

2   Implementation

2.1   Laniakea

The Laniakea architecture is founded on three main components: the Authentication and Authorization Infrastructure (AAI), the PaaS Orchestrator and the Dashboard that provides the web frontend.

The AAI layer, based on INDIGO IAM [17], enables single sign-on access to the Dashboard, the PaaS and IaaS services and resources, thus allowing users to deploy virtual resources (e.g., virtual machines and storage volumes) using the dashboard interface.

The PaaS Orchestrator [18] deploys the virtual resources over the cloud infrastructure and installs the required application(s), as with the Galaxy environment in the case of Laniakea, returning their endpoint to the user at the end of the procedure. Requests to the PaaS Orchestrator are described using TOSCA templates [19], which are YAML [20] documents usually encompassing three main sections: (1) the input parameters needed to configure the application, (2) the virtual hardware to be instantiated and the software to be installed and configured through dedicated Ansible roles [21], (3) the output to be returned, e.g., the instance IP-address, which will be made available to the user after the application deployment.

2.2 The Laniakea Dashboard

The PaaS Orchestrator allows the deployment of any application described by a suitable TOSCA document exploiting its RestFul API [22] or its CLI utility *orchent* [23]. However, to be used, it requires knowledge of the TOSCA language and some operational parameters of the Cloud infrastructure, for example, the Operative System of the virtual images, networking details, and available virtual hardware flavours. The Dashboard hides all those implementation details, exposing through a web interface only those parameters that are relevant for users and guiding them step-by-step in the configuration of their applications. This is achieved by parsing the input section of the TOSCA template and translating and rendering it into web-based configuration panels. Finally, the remaining TOSCA input are automatically filled prior to dispatching them to the Orchestrator for the deployment process, allowing the under-the-hood execution of complex procedures, like SSH keys management and their injection into VMs, and the handling of encrypted storage volumes.

2.3 Implementation Details

The main goal of the Dashboard is to generate user-friendly web forms by parsing the TOSCA document that formally defines the options and settings available to the user. To render the TOSCA input into easily manageable fields, each template is associated to an additional YAML parameters file, allowing to connect each input to an HTML element, e.g., dropdown menus, text fields, switch toggles, etc., specifying the available options when needed.

The Dashboard has been developed using Flask [24], a micro-framework for web development in Python. Flask is used for implementing the application routing system and for generating the web frontend starting from Jinja2 templates [25]. The Dashboard populates the application catalogue page adding one tile for every TOSCA template available to the service (Fig. 1). For each application, the Dashboard parses the input section of the corresponding TOSCA template and the additional information provided in the YAML parameter file and passes them as variables to the Jinja2 template engine, which creates dynamically the HTML configuration form corresponding to each application.

Figure 2 shows an example of an input type available in the TOSCA document used to select the hardware flavour of a virtual machine and the corresponding dropdown menu generated by the Dashboard.

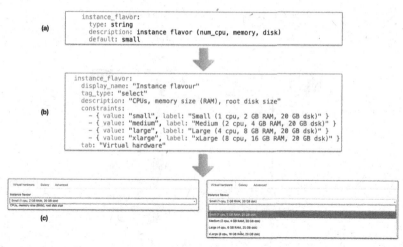

Fig. 2. (a) The input type available in the TOSCA document used to select the hardware flavour of a virtual machine. (b) The corresponding input in the YAML parameter file describing the available hardware presets. (c) The input field in the dashboard rendered as a dropdown menu.

2.4 Storage Volumes Encryption Procedure

For encrypting the storage volumes attached to the Virtual Machines (VMs), Laniakea relies on the LUKS (Linux Unified Key Setup) [26] disk encryption specification, the standard for storage encryption on Linux systems, implemented by the *dm-crypt* kernel module.

LUKS provides strong resistance to brute force attacks against low entropy user passphrases, i.e., short and based on dictionaries words, exploiting the PBKDF2 passphrase hashing. The storage volume is encrypted using a master key, in turn, encrypted using the hashed user passphrase combined with an additional input, commonly referred to as *salt*. Moreover, to protect against forensic-like attacks aimed at recovering deleted data, LUKS includes an anti-forensic splitter to split the master key before its storing. Finally, LUKS stores the setup information in the partition header at the beginning of the virtual block device, thus allowing to use multiple passphrases that can be changed or revoked anytime.

Only three parameters are needed to set up a new encrypted virtual block: the encryption mode, the cipher, and the passphrase. The resulting encrypted volume is then formatted with an *ext4* file system and finally attached to and mounted on the target VM as persistent storage. Therefore, any software installed on the target VM can perform read and write operations transparently on top of the encrypted storage layer (Fig. 3) as data is encoded and decoded on the fly by the kernel module.

The whole volume encryption procedure has been automated and integrated into the Laniakea Dashboard, leveraging the HashiCorp Vault [27] secrets management system to improve the service's usability.

HashiCorp Vault is a tool for securely storing and accessing "secrets", which can be defined as anything a user needs to control the access to, such as encryption passphrases.

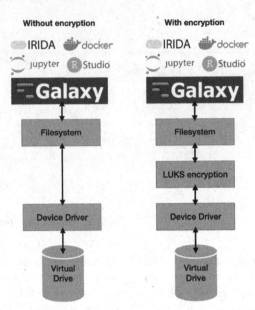

Fig. 3. Storage encryption scheme. When the file system is mounted, all the files it contains are available to the applications layer since data are transparently encrypted when writing and decrypted when reading.

Data on Vault are encrypted and stored on specific paths that, in the Laniakea configuration, depend on the user identity, defined as follows. When a user accesses Laniakea for the first time, it is associated with the AAI service's Universally Unique IDentifier (UUID). Moreover, the PaaS orchestrator assigns a UUID to each deployment. Laniakea saves the storage encryption passphrase in a unique path generated by combining these two UUIDs, which can, in turn, be read and written only by the owner of the deployment (Fig. 4).

Fig. 4. The IAM dashboard showing the user unique UUID (left). The HashiCorp Vault user interface (right) showing the unique path where the encryption passphrases are stored.

The authentication on Vault is token-based: after authentication, Vault tokens are dynamically generated based on the user identity. Vault policies grant or forbid access to specific paths and operations, controlling what the token holder can do within Vault. Therefore, a token generated with a specific policy allows writing, reading, updating, and deleting a secret only on the corresponding path. In the case of Laniakea, Vault has been configured with three policies for writing, reading, and deleting secrets, respectively (Table 1).

Table 1. Laniakea Vault policies.

Policy	Used by	Description
Write passphrase policy	Laniakea LUKS script (on the VM)	The passphrase on Vault in a path where only the owner can access to
Read passphrase policy	Laniakea Dashboard	The user can read owned passphrases through the Dashboard after authentication
Delete passphrase policy	Laniakea Dashboard	The passphrases are automatically deleted from Vault once the VM associated to the encrypted volume is deleted

The Laniakea volume encryption workflow is described in Fig. 5. When an authenticated user requests a new encrypted volume, a short-lived token is retrieved from Vault and delivered to the VM for the encryption procedure. This token is usable only once to write on Vault the encryption passphrase generated by the Laniakea encryption script. There is no update policy on Laniakea; therefore, this token is prevented from overwriting another passphrase. The storage volume is finally encrypted using the passphrase by the Laniakea LUKS script and attached to the target VM, while the passphrase is saved on Vault.

From the user's point of view, creating an encrypted volume is as simple as toggling the corresponding switch in the Dashboard.

Once the VM with the attached encrypted volume has been successfully deployed, the user can retrieve the encryption passphrase using the Dashboard (Fig. 6). The Dashboard also allows the user to re-mount the encrypted volume and restart the corresponding Galaxy instance directly from the web interface in case of VM failures, such as an unscheduled restart or switch-off.

Finally, the corresponding passphrase is removed from Vault once the VM associated with an encrypted volume is deleted by the owner.

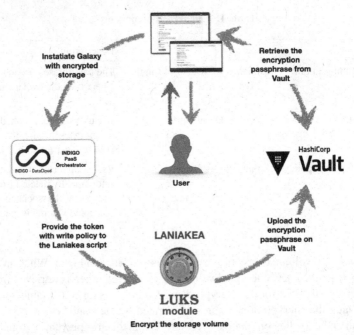

Fig. 5. The Laniakea storage encryption workflow. After authentication, the user requests a new Galaxy instance through the Dashboard, requesting storage encryption. Next, the Laniakea Dashboard contacts HashiCorp Vault to retrieve a one-time-only token, able to write the passphrase on Vault. The token, alongside all the other user-defined preferences, is sent to the PaaS Orchestrator to be used to deploy the Galaxy instance. Next, the Laniakea LUKS script encrypts the storage volume associated with the VM and, using the token, writes the passphrase on Vault. Finally, the user can retrieve the passphrase from the Dashboard.

3   Results

Figure 7 shows the TOSCA input required to configure the Virtual Hardware of a Galaxy instance on the left, rendered as a dropdown menu, allowing users to select the preferred virtual hardware configuration on the right. Similarly, Fig. 8 shows the Galaxy TOSCA input and the corresponding user interface generated by the Dashboard, allowing the customisation of the instance in terms of user credentials, Galaxy version and tools-set

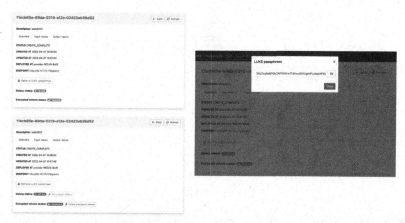

Fig. 6. The Laniakea Dashboard instance management section allows to check the status of Galaxy and of the encrypted storage (top left). If Galaxy and/or the storage volume are offline it is possible to restore them (bottom-left). This section allows also to retrieve the encryption passphrase (right).

to be installed (i.e., flavour). Not all the input required by the PaaS Orchestrator are rendered in the interface, since the Dashboard automatically manages some of them, e.g., the input parameters related to the storage encryption (Fig. 7).

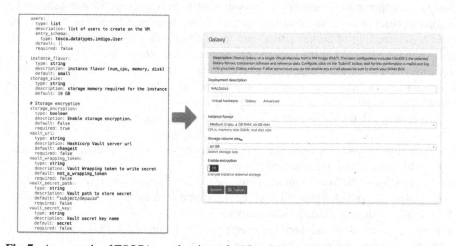

Fig. 7. An example of TOSCA template input for Virtual Hardware (left) and the corresponding web interface (right) generated by the Dashboard. Input related to the encryption procedure are automatically managed by the Dashboard if the encryption switch is turned on.

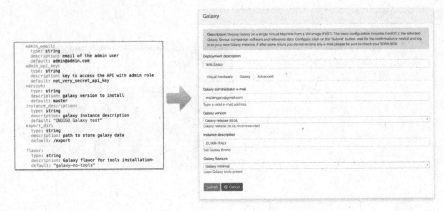

Fig. 8. TOSCA template input for the Galaxy application (left) and the corresponding web interface generated by the Dashboard (right).

To evaluate the impact of the storage encryption layer on the performance of the supported application, i.e., Galaxy, we measured jobs runtime and read/write speed on Virtual Machines with and without storage encryption turned on. The test consisted of a standard NGS mapping workflow that uploads Illumina reads on Galaxy and maps them on the human reference genome (GRCh38) using Bowtie2 [28]. The rationale is that, since mapping tools perform continuous read/write operations, Bowtie2 should be a good representative of tools most affected by the encryption layer. For the test, we used a subsampling of human paired-end reads downloaded from ArrayExpress [29] (ENA sample SRS4395742) so that the run would take about one hundred minutes on a non-encrypted Galaxy instance using twelve threads. The workflow was run fifty times consecutively, both on encrypted and non-encrypted Galaxy instances, at the ReCaS Bari Datacenter [30].

More in detail, the test is composed of the following steps:

- All Galaxy histories are deleted and purged, a new history is created, and the reads *fastq* files are uploaded to the new history.
- The mapping workflow is imported into the Galaxy instance and run. The workflow takes the two uploaded fastq files as input and performs mapping on GRCh38 using Bowtie2, producing a BAM file as output.
- During the files upload and the workflow execution *dstat* [31] monitors disk input/output speed. Sampling is made at 1 s intervals.
- Once the workflow is successfully finished, BioBlend [32] is used to retrieve the Bowtie2 job runtime, and the dstat output for both the upload and workflow execution phases is collected.

As shown in Fig. 9, the impact on the performance of using the encryption layer, as measured by our test, is limited to ~5% across the three measured parameters.

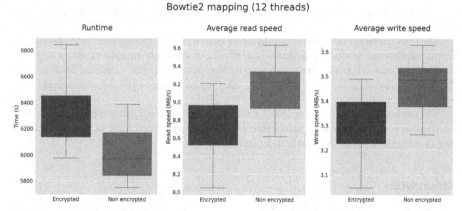

Fig. 9. Bowtie2 job runtime (left), average read speed (center) and average write speed (right). The test was performed on VMs with 16 virtual CPUs, 32 GBs of RAM and 200 GBs of storage. Bowtie2 was run using 12 threads.

4   Conclusions and Future Outlook

Exposing the configuration options of an on-demand applications service through a web interface, as made possible by the Laniakea Dashboard, allows for a better user experience. At the same time, the provider can quickly adapt its service to the specificities of the local Cloud platform and the provided applications by editing the TOSCA template while the user interface adjusts dynamically.

This approach, together with the encryption-made-easy feature introduced by the Laniakea Dashboard, can promote the adoption of the on-demand model for Life Science applications, making complex compute infrastructures with advanced features for data protection more readily available to potential users.

In the next iteration of Laniakea, the development strategy will be further generalized to better support and offer new applications beyond Galaxy and extend the support for users' secrets management, e.g., for application-specific credentials. Finally, while our data encryption approach protects users' data from malicious attackers obtaining unauthorized access to the encrypted volume from outside the VM to which it is attached to (i.e., attacks to the cloud facility), data are still potentially exposed to attacks against the VM itself, where Galaxy or other applications need to consume them. For this reason, Laniakea will soon provide the possibility to hide deployed applications beyond a Virtual Private Network, achieving more robust isolation of the research environment.

Acknowledgement. This work has been supported by the European Commission H2020 research and innovation program under grant agreements with ID 653549, 777435 and 857650.

The authors thank ELIXIR-Italy and ReCaS-Bari for providing the computing and bioinformatics facilities.

Availability of Supporting Source Code. The Laniakea web portal is available at https://lan iakea-elixir-it.github.io.

Source code and service configuration files are hosted on Laniakea GitHub at https://github.com/Laniakea-elixir-it.

The PaaS Orchestrator Dashboard source code is available at https://github.com/indigo-dc/orchestrator-dashboard, while the production version of Laniakea Dashboard is available at https://github.com/Laniakea-elixir-it/orchestrator-dashboard/tree/laniakea-stable. Laniakea TOSCA Templates and parameters files are here: https://github.com/Laniakea-elixir-it/laniakea-dashboard-config.

The Laniakea encryption script source code: https://github.com/Laniakea-elixir-it/fast-luks.

Complete documentation for Laniakea, comprising a step-by-step guide of Laniakea installation, is available at https://laniakea.readthedocs.io.

References

1. Cremin, C.J., Dash, S., Huang, X.: Big data: historic advances and emerging trends in biomedical research. Curr. Res. Biotechnol. **4**, 138–151 (2022)
2. Castrignanò, T., et al.: ELIXIR-IT HPC@CINECA: high performance computing resources for the bioinformatics community. BMC Bioinform. **21**(10), 352 (2020)
3. European high performance computer joint undertaking. https://eurohpc-ju.europa.eu/. Accessed 23 Apr 2022
4. López García, Á., et al.: A cloud-based framework for machine learning workloads and applications. IEEE Access **8**, 18681–18692 (2020)
5. EOSC Portal: https://eosc-portal.eu/. Accessed 23 Apr 2022
6. Digital life sciences open call. https://www.eosc-life.eu/opencall/. Accessed 23 Apr 2022
7. Tomarchio, O., Calcaterra, D., Modica, G.D.: Cloud resource orchestration in the multi-cloud landscape: a systematic review of existing frameworks. J. Cloud Comput. **9**(1), 1–24 (2020). https://doi.org/10.1186/s13677-020-00194-7
8. Crosswell, L.C., Thornton, J.M.: ELIXIR: a distributed infrastructure for European biological data. Trends Biotechnol. **30**(5), 241–242 (2012)
9. EOSC Life: https://www.eosc-life.eu. Accessed 23 Apr 2022
10. UseGalaxy.org: https://usegalaxy.org/. Accessed 23 Apr 2022
11. Tangaro, M.A., et al.: Laniakea@ReCaS: exploring the potential of customisable Galaxy on-demand instances as a cloud-based service. BMC Bioinform. **22**(15), 544 (2021)
12. The Galaxy platform for accessible, reproducible and collaborative biomedical analyses: 2022 update. Nucleic Acids Res. **48**(W1), W345–W351 (2022). https://doi.org/10.1093/nar/gkac247
13. Tangaro, M.A., et al.: Laniakea: an open solution to provide Galaxy "on-demand" instances over heterogeneous cloud infrastructures. GigaScience **9**(4), giaa033 (2020)
14. https://edpb.europa.eu/system/files/2021-06/edpb_recommendations_202001vo.2.0_supplementarymeasurestransferstools_en.pdf. Accessed 23 Apr 2022
15. Foggetti, N., Donvito, G., Tangaro, M.A.: Legal framework for the use and re-use of health data for scientific purposes. https://zenodo.org/record/6334878Zenodo (2022). Accessed 23 Apr 2022
16. Salomoni, D., et al.: INDIGO-DataCloud: a Platform to Facilitate Seamless Access to E-Infrastructures. Journal of Grid Computing **16**(3), 381–408 (2018). https://doi.org/10.1007/s10723-018-9453-3
17. Ceccanti, A., et al.: The INDIGO-Datacloud authentication and authorization infrastructure. J. Phys. Conf. Ser. **898**, 102016 (2017)
18. INDIGO PaaS Orchestrator: https://indigo-paas.cloud.ba.infn.it. Accessed 23 Apr 2022

19. Topology and orchestration specification for cloud applications version 1.0. http://docs.oasis-open.org/tosca/TOSCA/v1.0/os/TOSCA-v1.0-os.html. Accessed 23 Apr 2022
20. The Official YAML Web Site: https://yaml.org/. Accessed 23 Apr 2022
21. Ansible: https://www.ansible.com. Accessed 23 Apr 2022
22. RESTful orchestrator API guide. https://indigo-dc.github.io/orchestrator/restdocs/. Accessed 23 Apr 2022
23. Orchent: https://github.com/indigo-dc/orchent. Accessed 23 Apr 2022
24. Flask: https://flask.palletsprojects.com/en/2.1.x/. Accessed 23 Apr 2022
25. Jinja: https://jinja.palletsprojects.com/en/3.1.x. Accessed 23 Apr 2022
26. Fruhwirth, C.: New methods in hard disk encryption (2005)
27. Vault by HashiCorp: https://www.vaultproject.io/. Accessed 23 Apr 2022
28. Langmead, B., Salzberg, S.L.: Fast gapped-read alignment with Bowtie 2. Nat. Methods **9**(4), 357–359 (2012)
29. Sarkans, U., et al.: From arrayexpress to BioStudies. Nucleic Acids Res. **49**(D1), D1502–D1506 (2021)
30. Antonacci, M., et al.: The ReCaS project: the Bari infrastructure. In: High Performance Scientific Computing Using Distributed Infrastructures. World Scientific, pp. 17–33 (2015)
31. Dstat: https://linux.die.net/man/1/dstat. Accessed 23 Apr 2022
32. BioBlend: https://bioblend.readthedocs.io. Accessed 23 Apr 2022

Integration and Visual Analysis of Biomolecular Networks Through UNIPred-Web

Paolo Perlasca(ID), Marco Frasca(ID), Cheick Tidiane Ba, Jessica Gliozzo(ID),
Marco Notaro(ID), Mario Pennacchioni, Giorgio Valentini(ID),
and Marco Mesiti(✉)(ID)

Anacleto Lab. - Department of Computer Science, University of Milan, Milan, Italy
{perlasca,frasca,valentini,mesiti}@di.unimi.it

Abstract. The integration of heterogeneous biological data into a common network representation is of paramount importance in different areas of biology and medicine. The size of the generated network in many cases prevents the possibility of its graphical visualization, inspection, and identification of characteristics. In this paper, we present the main features of UNIPred-Web (UNIPred-Web is available at https://unipred.di.unimi.it/), a web application realized to support the user in the integration of several biomolecular networks and for their visualization and navigation at different resolution levels. In particular, the identification and effective visualization of hierarchical communities allow an easy exploration of the entire network, while protein function prediction functionalities support the user in the interpretation process.

Keywords: Visualization of biomolecular networks · Web services for protein function · Network integration · Community hierarchy detection

1 Introduction

Nowadays a huge amount of heterogeneous biomolecular data can be integrated in a single network, whose nodes and edges are the biological entities and their pairwise relationships, respectively. The network can be exploited to conduct different kinds of analysis in various areas of biology and medicine. In this context the visual exploration and navigation of the integrated network is fundamental for supporting the user in the interpretation and understanding of the network properties. Even if many systems have been proposed for such purpose (e.g. GeneMANIA [1], STRING [7], and IMP 2.0 [8]), many of them do not provide functionalities for supporting customized network integration, predicting the function of non-annotated bio-molecules and navigating the network at different resolution levels. Recently we have proposed UNIPred-Web [5,6], a web application that represents biological networks through property graphs and supports the user in their integration and visualization according to different perspectives, and in the prediction of protein functions. Moreover, communities of bio-molecules that are tightly connected can be identified and organized in a

G. Agapito et al. (Eds.): ICWE 2022 Workshops, CCIS 1668, pp. 192–197, 2023.
https://doi.org/10.1007/978-3-031-25380-5_15

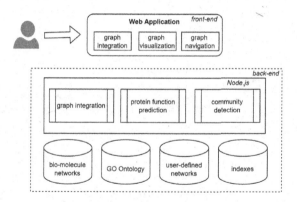

Fig. 1. UNIPred-Web architecture

hierarchy. This hierarchy is then exploited for a visualization of the network at different resolution levels where both bio-molecules and communities are drawn with their relationships. The user can choose the communities to zoom in, thus showing further details, and the parts of the network that need to be aggregated.

In this demo-paper we wish to show the developed software with all the provided modules in action. Specifically, prediction of a specific GO term for each protein of a network integrating multiple and heterogeneous protein interactions; aiding drug repositioning or novel insights about unknown disease mechanisms by identifying new candidate targets. Moreover, we will show how a network can be visualized at different resolution levels and exploit this visualization for some considerations on the relationships existing among the network components. We will also show the kinds of predictions that can be carried out and their representation on the network visualization. In the remainder we describe the UNIPred-Web architecture and some use-cases realized through our system.

2 UNIPred-Web Architecture

UNIPred-Web presents a client-server architecture (see Fig. 1) based on different technologies (MySQL, R, Node.js, JavaScript, Cytoscape.js, Angular.js) which has been designed with the specific aim of making the client-side experience as smooth as possible by moving the more expensive operations to the server-side.

The front-end application exploits JavaScript, Angular.js and Cytoscape.js for: *i*) creating the interfaces for the specification of the network integration; *ii*) the prediction of the protein functions; *iii*) supporting the interaction with the user (buttons, pop-up menus, selection of colors/sizes/shapes of visualized graphs); and *iv*) creating an interactive visualization of the network. Moreover, modules have been included for supporting the exploration and navigation of a network by using a community hierarchy built on top of it. The graphical primitives rely on APIs made available by the server.

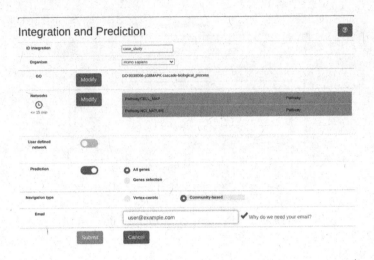

Fig. 2. Integration and prediction panel

The Node.js server is used as glue between the requests sent by the front-end and the results returned by the back-end modules. The graph integration and protein function prediction modules rely on the COSNet and UNIPred methods [2,3]. The community hierarchy has been realized by means of a variant of the Louvain algorithm described in [5]. Moreover, the Node.js server takes care of managing the user requests queue by defining and applying a management policy that prevents a user from blocking the system with his own experiments.

UNIPred-Web has a database of more than 2000 biomolecular networks that cover 9 different organisms (Escherichia coli, Arabidopsis thaliana, Saccharomyces cerevisiae, Caenorhabditis elegans, Drosophila melanogaster, Danio rerio, Homo sapiens, Mus musculus, and Rattus norvegicus) and includes a novel Human-virus protein interactions network, named *CoV-human*, recently proposed in [4] and retrieved from the BioGRID database. Moreover, users can include their own networks and manage their own experiments.

The integrated network is coupled with different indexing structures (details in [5]) that are exploited to simplify the passage from one representation to another. By means of them, the time required for the computation of the network visualization at each resolution level is strongly reduced. Also in networks with thousand of nodes, a smooth navigation among the communities and an easier identification and retrieval of the target proteins is allowed.

3   Integration and Visualization Functionalities

Suppose a biologist is interested in the exploration of tumor pathways and wishes to integrate the following two human networks made available in our database: `Pathway.NCI_NATURE` (about signaling, regulatory events and cellular processes with 2126 vertices and 10122 edges) and `Pathway.CELL_MAP` (about signaling pathways underlying cancer with 408 vertices and 598 edges).

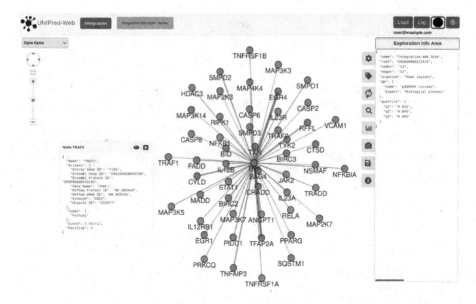

Fig. 3. Main interface with vertex-centric visualization

By means of the panel in Fig. 2, the user can select these networks from our database, the GO term according to which the integration should be carried out, and whether the predictions have to be inferred for the entire set of genes or just for a specific subset. The user can choose between *i*) "vertex-centric visualization" targeted on the neighborhood of a user-defined protein or a *ii*) "community-based navigation". The system evaluates the time required for such integration and enqueues the integration request. In the vertex-ventric visualization, the integrated network (2 255 nodes and 10 673 edges) is visualized centered on the selected protein TNF as shown in Fig. 3.

The user can exploit the GUI functionalities for changing the color of the network nodes, and also inspect the details contained in the network nodes and edges. Moreover, the force-based visualization currently shown in Fig. 3 can be changed and other perspectives adopted. The integrated network can be exported or a PNG image generated and downloaded. The user can expand the current visualization by including nearby proteins to those already visualized.

4   Navigation and Aggregation Functionalities

In a different context, a researcher could be interested in finding proteins involved in the adhesion of SARS-CoV-2 virus to the surface of human cells, which are novel candidate targets for drug development/repurposing to prevent cell infection. To this end, the CoV-human network can be exploited to: *i*) visualize the interactions between human and three different coronavirus strains of interest (see [5] for further details about this network); and *ii*) to predict annotations e.g. for the GO BP term "adhesion of symbiont to host cell" (GO:0044650).

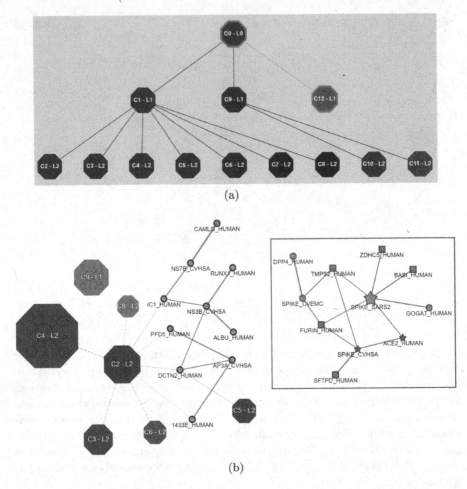

Fig. 4. (a) CoV-human hierarchical community, and (b) community-based exploration

The hierarchy of communities identified through our module is reported in Fig. 4(a). In the community-based visualization (left part of Fig. 4(b)), two kinds of nodes are used, one for representing proteins and one for representing communities. Moreover, the relationships among molecules and communities are shown with different edges (solid lines for relationships among proteins, dashed lines for relationships among communities, and dotted lines for those between communities and proteins). Moreover, the border of biomolecules is highlighted with the color of the parent community. The researcher can further explore the reported graph through the zoom-in and zoom-out functions. The zoom-in command expands the content of a community, which can be composed by child communities or proteins (if the user decided to expand a leaf community in the hierarchy). On the contrary, the zoom-out command permits to undo the expansion and move towards upper levels in the hierarchy. The researcher can also search for a specific protein (e.g. the `SPIKE_SARS2`) and the system will point out the community containing it (by highlighting its border with the yellow color). Then, by expanding the communities in the path from the root to the leaf community, the subnetwork in the right-hand side of Fig. 4(b) can be shown, containing the novel candidate proteins for the functional term `GO:0044650` centered on the viral Spike glycoprotein. The nodes are colored with a red shade whose intensity reflects the prediction score, whereas the thickness of the links is proportional to the edges' weights. The shape of the nodes is "prediction-aware": a star for proteins known to be annotated with the considered GO term, a square for the proteins predicted to be annotated for the GO term with a high score. It is worth noting that only two viral proteins (`SPIKE_SARS2` and `ACE2_HUMAN`) were already annotated with the functional term (`GO:0044650`), whereas all the other human proteins were predicted to be annotated with the functional term `GO:0044650` by UNIPred-Web. This means that they are strong putative candidate proteins for this GO term and the associated scores are also confirmed by recent literature [5].

5   Concluding Remarks

In this paper we have reported the main characteristics of UNIPred-Web by exploiting two use cases. The interested user can play on his own with the software and see the many functionalities that have been realized. As future work we plan to further expand the visualization capabilities of our tool for handling more complex networks containing different kinds of nodes and edges.

References

1. Franz, M., et al.: GeneMANIA update 2018. Nucleic Acids Res. **46**(W1), W06–W64 (2018)
2. Frasca, M., et al.: UNIPred: unbalance-aware network integration and prediction of protein functions. J. Comput. Biol. **22**(12), 1057–1074 (2015)
3. Frasca, M., Valentini, G.: COSNet: an R package for label prediction in unbalanced biological networks. Neurocomputing **237**, 397–400 (2017)
4. Gordon, D.E., et al.: A SARS-CoV-2 protein interaction map reveals targets for drug repurposing. Nature **583**(7816), 459–468 (2020)
5. Perlasca, P., et al.: Multi-resolution visualization and analysis of biomolecular networks through hierarchical community detection and web-based graphical tools. PLoS ONE **15**(12), e0244241 (2020)
6. Perlasca, P., et al.: UNIPred-Web: a web tool for the integration and visualization of biomolecular networks for protein function prediction. BMC Bioinform. **20**(1), 1–19 (2019). https://doi.org/10.1186/s12859-019-2959-2
7. Szklarczyk, D., et al.: STRING v11: protein-protein association networks with increased coverage, supporting functional discovery in genome-wide experimental datasets. Nucleic Acids Res. **47**(D1), D607–D613 (2018)
8. Wong, A.K., et al.: IMP 2.0: a multi-species functional genomics portal for integration, visualization and prediction of protein functions and networks. Nucleic Acids Res. **43**, W128–W133 (2015)

Author Index

Printed in the United States
by Baker & Taylor Publisher Services